Geoffrey R. Sharpe is a Fellow of t[illegible] Surveyors, a Fellow of the Chartered I[illegible] of the CIOB Building Conservation [illegible] a member of a Diocesan Advisory Committee for the Care of Churches and a past chairman of a building conservation trust. He is author of *Traditional Buildings of the English Countryside: An Illustrated Guide*.

Geoffrey R. Sharpe

Historic English Churches

A Guide to their Construction, Design and Features

I.B. TAURIS
LONDON · NEW YORK

Published in 2011 by I.B.Tauris & Co Ltd
6 Salem Road, London W2 4BU
175 Fifth Avenue, New York NY 10010
www.ibtauris.com

Distributed in the United States and Canada Exclusively by Palgrave Macmillan,
175 Fifth Avenue, New York NY 10010

ISBN: 978 1 84885 807 7 (HB)
ISBN: 978 1 84885 189 4 (PB)

A full CIP record for this book is available from the British Library
A full CIP record is available from the Library of Congress

Library of Congress Catalog Card Number: available

Typeset by JCS Publishing Services Ltd, www.jcs-publishing.co.uk
Printed and bound in Great Britain by TJ International Ltd, Padstow, Cornwall

Contents

Illustrations

Preface

The historic churches and cathedrals of England's towns and countryside are among the many old buildings that never fail to be a continuing source of fascination and curiosity to those interested in the past. The primary aim of this book is to provide a clear insight into how the medieval craftsmen achieved such remarkably high standards without the benefit of modern technology and equipment, and to supply information that can assist in the care and protection of historic churches. Using a limited range of tools the early craftsmen were able to create lasting edifices by way of techniques and skills passed from one generation to the next. I begin with the way the building process was initiated and how the medieval masons planned and managed a project. This is followed by an explanation of how the main features, such as the foundations, walls and other structural elements were constructed. Coupled to this is a description of the methods used by the different craftsmen, including the masons, blacksmiths and carpenters. The references to church design include features which can give clues to the date and origin of a structure. Coverage begins at the time of the Anglo-Saxons and continues through the subsequent phases up to the period of the Victorians.

I am hugely indebted to the librarians at a number of cathedral libraries, the RIBA, the RICS and the Victoria and Albert Museum for their help and the excellent service they provided. Without their interest, cooperation and painstaking methods the project would have been much more problematical and difficult. I am also grateful for the help I received from the clergy in many parishes and to my fellow professionals Ian Yule, Trevor Francis, Tony Pass and John Edwards, who checked the manuscript with such meticulous care. My thanks also go to Peter Bishop and to my daughter and son-in-law, Sally and Ben Jones, for the help they gave with the photographs.

Geoffrey R. Sharpe

Introduction

Church Sites and Classification

Site Origins

The places used by the pagans for ceremonies and worship gradually became the focal points for preaching by the early Christian missionaries, which resulted in many of the original churches being built on pagan sites. Most parish churches are located in or near established communities but occasionally they can be discovered in mystifying isolation.

A number of explanations may be possible; most often it is the outcome of the devastation caused by the fourteenth-century pandemic known as the Black Death. Entire communities were wiped out, leaving the settlements to decay and eventually disappear except for the more robustly built church. Some ancient parish churches began as private chapels (*capella*) and were built by the large landowners and the manorial lords, positioned at the choice and convenience of the provider. Others resulted from an ancient form of tenure known as frankalmoign, in which a lay person donated land for a church subject to a deed of chantry. In times of turmoil and uncertainty villages and hamlets might also be destroyed by conflict or economic decline, and this can explain the present-day remoteness of churches in some locations. A few also stand in unlikely positions as the result of a remodelling of the local landscape by a large landowner which necessitated the resettlement of an entire community, leaving only the parish church. In areas prone to flooding every effort was made to ensure the parish church was built well clear of the flood plain, so the church may have been some distance from the main settlement. Through the exigencies of the old feudal system the Church could also acquire land by mortmain, a process which sometimes influenced its eventual siting. Any lay person who had no heirs could provide for his/her land to be transferred immediately to the Church at the time of his/her death. This avoided escheating – that is, reverting to the feudal lord – which would otherwise happen if a tenant died without heirs. The use of mortmain not only meant a loss of tenure but also deprived the lord of revenues which would otherwise have been received. Over time the benefits the Church received in this way were gradually diluted through amendments to the law, and eventually became non-existent.

Following the Dissolution of the Monasteries under the Act of 1539 a number of abbey and priory chapels were taken over by local communities and then used as parish churches. Some were exceptionally large and many parishes found it necessary to demolish parts to reduce the ongoing burden of upkeep. Ancient crosses positioned near but outside the boundaries of a churchyard invariably pre-date the church and were erected to mark the assembly point for open-air services. If a church was subsequently built nearby it was usual for it to be placed in a way that ensured the shadow did not fall on the original cross. This was done as an expression of reverence and dedication. A few of these crosses have a niche in the shaft made to take the pyx, the receptacle containing the host. In many churchyards large stone crosses of medieval origin can be found in a prominent point, more usually in a southerly location. These were provided as a collective memorial to the dead as few graves were marked with stone tablets, crosses or headstones until the late seventeenth century.

Well-worn signs, initials or names cut into the boundary walls of old churchyards are a reminder of how all boundaries were at one time maintained by parishioners. Known as church marks, they indicated who was responsible for keeping the boundaries in a state of good repair.

Another historical feature of interest is an original lychgate. The term is derived from the Old English word *lich*, meaning a corpse. The funeral service of the 1549 prayer book required that the priest meet the corpse at the churchyard entrance, and so lychgates were constructed to provide shelter for that purpose. In more recent times there has been a tendency to reintroduce lychgates as an architectural feature. Apart from showing heavier weathering, those of medieval origin can often also be identified by the presence of a resting slab for the coffin. At the Church of St Leonards in Heston, Middlesex, there is a lychgate of particular interest as it has a rare example of a tapsel gate which dates from 1450. Originally designed to be self-closing, it was operated by a counterbalance housed in the roof. As the gate was opened, a central pivot rotated, drawing a chain which wound around a wheel at the top of the pivot. This in turn connected to two more wooden pulley wheels and then down to a weight. The weight rose as the gate was opened and descended to return the gate to the shut position

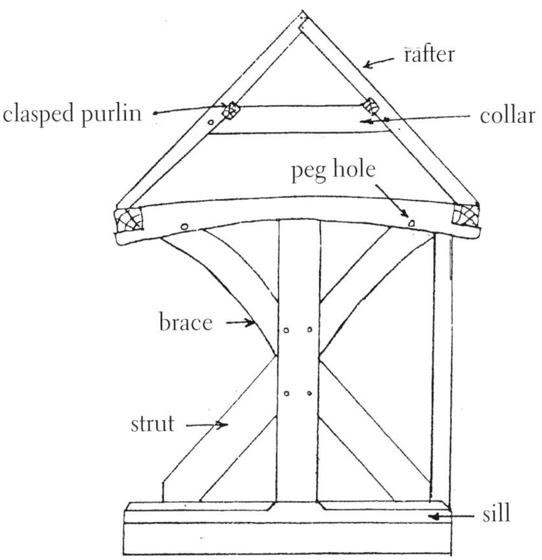

1. Lychgate, Heston, Middlesex – using original methods and techniques, the structure has been fully restored by McCurdy & Co. Detailed information available at www.mccurdyco.com *(photo by kind permission of McCurdy & Co, Historic Timber Restorers, Standford Dingley, Berkshire)*.

when released. The counterbalance is now missing but other parts of the mechanism have survived (Fig. 1).

Different Types of Church

Just as there is a huge variety in the type of church building, so too were there different origins to what we might generally describe as a 'church' today. Essentially, a church is a building consecrated for religious worship. A cathedral is a church that contains the cathedra or throne of the bishop of the diocese, and chapels have a different status and are buildings licensed for worship but have not been consecrated as a church. Much can be gleaned about the history of a church from the original records, with the early purpose and function often having changed over time. Oratories, for example, were places of worship licensed under canon law for public, semi-public or private use, but the term is now generally applied to a small private chapel built within the walls or confines of a larger property. The term originally had a different meaning and came from the Congregation of the Oratory founded in Rome in 1575 by St Philip Neri. It provided for communities of secular priests who worked under strict rules of obedience but did not take vows. A chapel of ease is one which provides a more convenient facility to worship for those living at some distance from the parish church. Mention is also occasionally made of a slipper chapel, which is the place where pilgrims went to remove their shoes before entering a shrine barefoot.

A pro-cathedral is not a cathedral as such, but a church within a diocese that is regularly used by the bishop when circumstances, such as distance, prevent him from conducting certain duties at the diocesan cathedral. An abbey was once the site of a major monastic establishment in which the abbot was also a bishop. A priory is a religious establishment presided over by a prior or prioress, and while of junior status to an abbey (which was headed by an abbot or abbess) several attained religious eminence and a level of prosperity which far exceeded that of many abbeys. Minsters (*monasterium*) were churches attached to a religious community led by a high-ranking priest under a monastic order, but the term has come to be acquired by some cathedrals that never enjoyed formal connections with a monastic establishment. The term chapelry is sometimes given to the daughter church of a minster. Free chapels are an anomaly from much earlier times; most originated as chapels for either the military, the Knights Hospitaller of the Order of St John of Jerusalem or the Knights Templar. Sometimes known as chapels peculiar they were outside the jurisdiction of a bishop of the diocese. Chapels royal are private chapels attached to the royal court. In the past, religious houses sometimes built a chapel at or near the gate entrance for use by lay visitors, employees and others. Known as a *capella ante portas*, many became parish churches after the Reformation. A proprietary chapel is one which has been built and maintained by a private individual. Historical references occasionally mention a church as having been a thane church, which signifies that it has Anglo-Saxon origins and it could have served royalty or a person of high military rank or a member of the nobility.

In earlier times the consecration of a church involved an elaborate ceremony, which was then celebrated annually with a public holiday and a feast. The practice of dedication to a saint, or a group of saints or a religious event dates from the fourth century. One benefit was the individual identity this gave to different churches in close proximity to each other. An example is St Mary-le-Bow in London, which clearly differentiates it from any other church dedicated to St Mary in the London area. During the middle ages many dedications were added to or changed, often as a matter of expediency concerning patronage or the result of a political motive. Changes also occurred when smaller churches became separate parishes. An effigy of the patron saint or a small tablet commemorating the dedication can sometimes be found in a small niche over the south or west door of the nave.

Unlike in the past, there is now no difference between the rank of rector and vicar. The title vicar is derived from the Latin *vicarius*, meaning deputy. Originally the appointment was made by the appropriate monastery, who engaged a secular parish priest as deputy to the monks nominated to oversee the parish. The title rector went to a parish priest who received the benefit of tithes and, although tithes were abolished in 1936, the title has perpetuated. In the present day a priest who is the leader of a team ministry is sometimes referred to as a team rector. A prebendary was originally the holder of a cathedral benefice termed a prebend and again such endowments no longer exist but the title has remained.

Before the Dissolution most of the abbeys in England were major monastic centres and enjoyed a higher standing and superior status to priories. Where a bishop was also an abbot the community would be administered by a prior and its church designated a cathedral priory.

Cathedrals are occasionally described as being in either the Old or New Foundation. Cathedrals in the Old Foundation are those which began with secular canons. When Henry VIII dissolved the monastic establishments and their chapters, those with secular clergy remained undisturbed, while the cathedrals served by monks were refounded with secular canons to become the New Foundation. In more recent times a third category has emerged, covering churches which have been raised to cathedral rank; these are sometimes mentioned as being in the Modern Foundation.

The Role of the Archaeologist in the Investigation of Churches

Archaeology has made a valuable contribution in revealing how the early churches were planned and developed. Now a scientific discipline, archaeology has gone beyond the stereotype of simple excavation and has advanced into the investigation of buildings, artefacts and other items – both below and above ground. The role of the archaeologist in the investigation of old churches, monuments and sites now brings together many different skills in a way that has considerably enhanced our knowledge of the past.

At various stages in our history, turmoil, unrest, poverty, economic stagnation and overall decline have all contributed to the loss of important parts of our church heritage. Probably no era saw more of this than the time of the Reformation in the sixteenth century, when there was almost total destruction of the monasteries, resulting in the ruination of large amounts of valuable medieval art. A considerable number of churches also suffered from vandalism and despoliation at this time. In addition, extensive damage was inflicted on churches during the Civil War, when extreme Puritanism caused the loss of much stained glass, statuary and other features. Depressed economic times also caused periods of neglect and apathy towards the proper care of churches and permanent damage has often been the result.

A church, like any other building, can quickly fall into disrepair and will eventually become a ruin if it is not protected from the elements. During periods of economic depression, many fell into such a state of ruin that they had to be abandoned and were quickly plundered for materials. After this it was only a matter of time before the effects of soil accumulation or erosion, and unrelenting saturation from rain made the fabric an ideal host for invading plant life. Some buildings were totally obliterated – the outcome often being aided by ground movements, animal burrowing, insect infestation and similar causes of destruction.

Archaeology has done much to unravel the important features and the unknown parts of these sites. It has also opened up a new understanding of how a number of existing churches have developed. Many originally regarded as being Victorian or a little earlier have been found to have origins going back as far as the Saxons or Normans. Archaeological investigations have been particularly valuable in identifying the various phases of development in the early churches, which in some cases have been extensive and frequent. Sometimes subtle differences between materials can be highly revealing and of special significance. It is information such as this which can play such an important part in the making of better-informed judgements in restoration and repair work and in assisting more accurate recording.

Church Building

Preliminaries

The gargantuan task of organising, managing and overseeing the building of a cathedral, priory or great church fell to the master mason (*magister operis*), who was also responsible for the preparation of the drawings. The plans and illustrations were drafted on parchment, and it was often the practice for them to be supplemented with a model, the final result often having been the subject of much discussion and negotiation. Once a scheme had been approved, the master mason then undertook a firm obligation to build strictly in accordance with the agreed submission. It invariably took time and patience, however, before he could bring together a suitable team of craftsmen. The entire workforce could amount to 300 to 400 or more, including a team of masons (*cementarii* or *lapicidi*) who worked as banker or fixer masons. The banker masons had the important function of carving the various stones into the required shapes. The fixer masons worked on the actual placing of the stones, with any particularly fine decorative work more often requiring the services of a sculptor (*caesores lapidum*).

Highly skilled carpenters (*carpentarii*) were also very necessary, as were blacksmiths (*fabri*), who forged the tools and maintained them in good working condition. All the trades had the support of labourers (*operatii*) and some semi-skilled workers (*artificas*). In the early medieval period it was usual for the Church to select and provide all materials, but this changed later on and the function fell on the master mason, who occasionally had the difficult task of selecting and supervising the winning of stone from the quarry face, although a specially appointed quarry mason was more often employed for this role to ensure quality and standards were fully safeguarded. It has been estimated that around 70,000 to 80,000 tons of stone were needed to build a cathedral and between 1,200 to 1,500 trees had to be felled for the provision of sufficient timber.

Spades (*besha*) and picks (*picoys*) were both used for digging out the foundations. In addition to the standard rectangular type a triangular-shaped spade (*didal*), and a small hand spade (*spyddell*) also formed part of the equipment for ground works. In the middle ages, iron was scarce and a costly material – steel was even more so. Consequently implements such as spades and shovels (*batilla*) were often made from wood fitted with iron shoes. Most cutting tools were forged from iron with a piece of steel welded onto the edge. Water had to be transported from the source of supply to the point of operation in wooden casks or barrels fitted with poles (*stangs*), which enabled them to be carried by two or more men.

The preliminary work also involved the setting up of onsite workshops, organising the regular supply and transport of sand, stone and other materials, providing lime kilns and ensuring a constant supply of clean water. There was also a need to consider in advance how certain areas could be accessed as the work proceeded. The handling and placement of stone needed much forethought because dressed stone blocks were usually too large to be laid by hand. In order to avoid damage to the faces a device known as a lewis (*lowys*) was used in the mechanical lifting and placement of stone (Fig. 2). Either the three-legged or chain types were used, with dovetailed mortices cut into the top of each block before lifting could begin. The three-legged device consisted of a parallel piece of iron between two dovetailed iron legs which held firm to the sides of the dovetail as the load was taken up (Fig. 2c), whereas to secure the load the chain lewis relied on two curved legs which had an outward gripping action (see Fig. 2a). This technique goes back to at least Roman times and is still in use today, the main alteration being the replacement of iron fitments with steel. A simple pincer gripping method known as the chain dog was also used for lifting irregularly shaped rough stone and other materials (Fig. 2b). The range of extra duties over and above those more normally undertaken by the mason eventually led to the use of the term architect for those who designed, planned and managed a project. Some original documents refer to an 'architectus', which later seems to have changed to 'architector'.

At parish level the work was more often undertaken in an entirely different way. It has generally been assumed most local churches were built with voluntary labour. While undoubtedly there are many situations where this has occurred there is evidence to indicate that a number of parish churches were built by craftsmen either under contract or by direct labour, with the local clergy having a major influence over the layout and design.

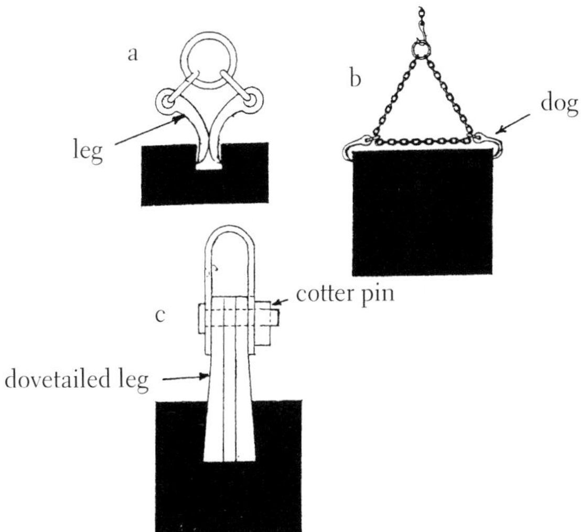

2. Stone-lifting devices – (a) a chain lewis. A slightly dovetailed hole is formed on top of the stone to prevent the legs from slipping when they grip the sides on lifting. (b) a chain dog. A steel chain is passed through the ring of each dog; when the tension is taken up on lifting, the dogs bite into the surface and hold secure. (c) three-legged lewis. A rectangular piece of metal is sandwiched between two dovetailed legs. The recess cut into the stone has to be the exact size of the lewis. The two dovetailed legs are first inserted, followed by the centre piece. The whole is then secured by a cotter pin and is ready for lifting. The lewis is dismantled on completion of the operation.

Scaffolding (*scaphalda*) was formed from a framing of wood poles lashed together by strong rope, the vertical ones being called standards (*signa*), the horizontal pieces set at right angles to the standards being known as ledgers (*dorsa*), with diagonal members (*diagonales*) being used to brace and strengthened the structure. Hurdles (*herdells*) laid flat were regularly used instead of planks. Access to the various levels of scaffolding was mostly by movable ladder, but old illustrations seem to indicate that wherever possible there was a preference for the use of ramps. In order to avoid scaffolding having to be continually taken down to ground level for reassembly, the outrigger technique was devised, this being a temporary framework suspended around the point of operation which could be used without the need for additional support from below (Fig. 3). Not only could this be done at any height, it also enabled the structure to be dismantled and re-erected as the work progressed, thereby making substantial savings in cost. Permanent access to various parts was provided through the installation of spiral stairways within the body of the wall. Narrow horizontal walkways were also formed in this way and, apart from giving improved access during building operations, also afforded good accessibility for future maintenance work. Evidence suggests that some materials such as timber lengths were moved to the point of operation with a sling chain, but cradles (*credills*) which could be raised and lowered as necessary were also installed for access and supplying lighter materials. If difficulties arose over taking heavy stone blocks to the exact fixing point, iron rods known as kevells enabled them to be rolled and slid into position.

Much ingenuity and endeavour had to be used in lifting heavy weights to high levels. The common pulley and rope fixed to a gantry and shear-legs was in regular use, but heavier weights often presented difficulties. The problem was solved by the windlass (*wyndhuse*), which had a large wooden cylinder mounted on a frame attached to a heavy rope. This had at least two turning handles so that extra muscle power could be provided by two or more operatives. Later adaptations also had brakes and a ratchet, which made the appliance more effective and less tiring to operate. One version was worked by a treadmill that provided considerably enhanced lifting power (Fig. 4). Throughout the middle ages the crane was gradually developed and improved using a system of counterweights and double pulleys. Some were pivoted and were able to cover a wide circumference

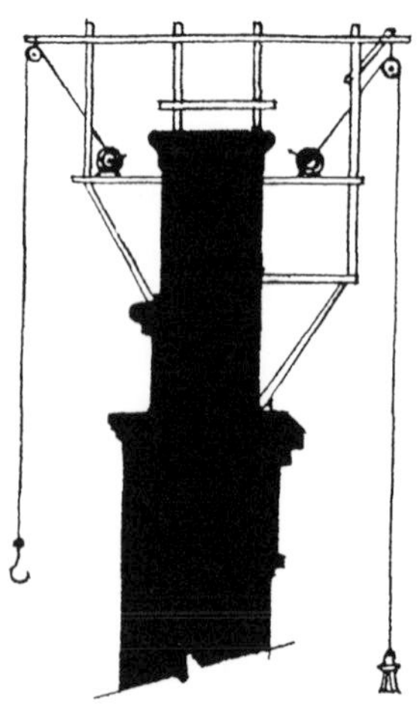

3. Outrigger scaffolding

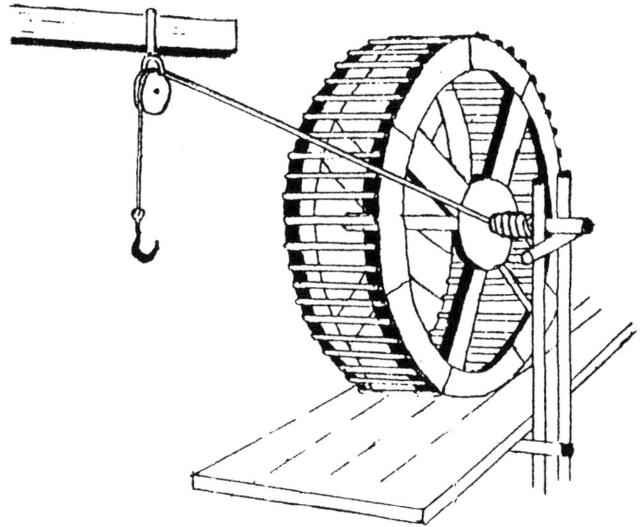

4. Treadmill

and most could be readily dismantled and reassembled as the work advanced. As industrialisation developed, an iron winch was perfected with geared wheels, a brake and a sophisticated form of ratcheting. At this stage the use of ropes for heavy loads started to be phased out in favour of chains, which made the entire operation safer and more reliable.

With a large cathedral, building operations could extend over a long period of time, a hundred years not being uncommon. The process often progressed in stages, with extended time lags occurring between each phase. When this happened exposed parts were given temporary protection, usually in the form of a capping containing a mixture of earth, straw and slaked lime or similar.

1 The Construction of Churches

Cements and Concrete

Lime and Cements

The use of mortar enables bricks and stones to be bonded solidly together so that stresses from superimposed loads can be distributed. It also reduces to a minimum voids or paths through which air or moisture might penetrate the structure. Many people do not realise that, in addition to taking compressive forces, mortar also has a function in the transmission of shear and tensile forces. A loss of strength will occur if the bond between the blocks and the mortar fails. The lime or cement in the mortar is termed the matrix and the sand the aggregate. These are mixed to the proper consistency with clean water in different proportions, depending upon the type and character of the work. The mineral content and natural pigments in the sand can affect colour, and the quality of the lime or cement determines the strength. Although they are rare in church walling, black mortars can be seen from time to time. Accounts at Westminster dated 1532 refer to the use of black mortar in flintwork. Lamp-black or burnt moulding sand from the blacksmith seem to have been the most preferred ingredients, but ground ashes and ground clinker are also mentioned in old accounts.

The mortars used in early church building were always a mixture of lime and sand, and it has long been assumed the ratio was generally one part of lime to three equal proportions of sand. However, a large number of analysed examples, especially those from the earlier medieval churches, have been found to be 1:1½ or 1:2, and further research has revealed the proportions can sometimes vary within the same structure. It seems that where there was a need for extra strength or better weather protection it was often the practice to increase the ratio of lime to sand.

The lime was originally produced by calcinating in a wood kiln (*calciformium*) either limestone or chalk to a high temperature, which had the effect of removing the calcium dioxide content. Coal-fired kilns did not come into normal use until the Industrial Revolution. After kilning, the resultant quicklime had to be slaked with water until it was hydrated, and the mixture was then turned over with a shovel on a boarded platform with, if necessary, more water being added until the correct consistency was achieved. The lime could then be mixed with sand and used as mortar, although for certain works lime putty was needed. Lime putty mortar is a soft plastic paste made by mixing one part fat lime and three parts by weight of water. The term 'fat' was given to the rich lime derived from the more pure white chalk deposits which are non-hydraulic (they can only set by reacting with carbon dioxide in the atmosphere) and are slow to set. After mixing, the lime putty mortar was left until it stiffened into a pliable and workable condition, when it is ready for use. With especially fine jointing some masons preferred to use a mix of one part lime putty to three parts of crushed stone dust.

In the British Isles most of the limes produced in this way were non-hydraulic, giving a setting process which slowly converted the slaked lime back into calcium carbonate. A limited number of formations, such as the blue lias deposits, however, contain contaminants of silica, clay, alumina and iron, which gives them hydraulic properties that enable them to set in the presence of water without the total reliance on carbonation. These limes were originally known as 'water limes', and the various constituents can continue to harden when under water to form calcium silicates and calcium aluminates. They are usually identifiable through their colour, in various ranges of grey, buff or reddish brown. In the presence of moisture all natural hydraulic limes have varying levels of hydraulicity because of differences in composition and in the integrity of the kilning. These variations were originally classified as: 'eminently hydraulic', which gave a setting time of one to four days; followed by 'moderately hydraulic', which takes between five to fifteen days; the slowest was the 'feebly hydraulic', which takes around fifteen to twenty-one days. This has now been amended under British and European Standards to include strength after twenty-eight days.

Non-hydraulic limes can be given some hydraulic properties through the addition of a pozzolanic additive such as crushed brick, tile or earthenware. The term pozzolan comes from the Roman practice of using volcanic ash from the region of Pozzuoli near Naples for the same purpose. From around the beginning of the seventeenth century onwards much experimentation went on in the manufacture of various hydraulic cements. In 1796 James Parker patented a new cement he called Roman cement produced from argillaceous clay (septaria), found in the seabed around Harwich and the Isle of Sheppey. Kilned at a low temperature, it was not only hydraulic but also proved to be most durable and could withstand persistent damp. Unless it was retarded it had a quick setting time of between twenty and forty minutes, making it an ideal material for working in locations affected by tidal waters or under heavily saturated conditions. As a mortar it was generally used in the proportions of 1:1½ or 1:2 with evidence indicating that stone masons preferred it for fixing cement joggles (see below, Fig. 32). Its high level of iron oxide makes it identifiable by giving it a distinctive dark pinkish-brown colour. Similar cements followed, such as Medina cement, which was made from clay taken from the beds of the river Medina on the Isle of Wight and is much lighter in colour. All these cements attained greater strength than hydraulic lime but less than Portland cement.

In 1824 Joseph Aspdin patented Portland cement, which eventually brought about many changes to the building process. The original product had some deficiencies, but in 1845 Isaac Johnson improved the quality by kilning to a higher temperature, giving considerably enhanced properties. In masonry this gradually led to the widespread use of 'compo' – the name often given to cement–lime–sand mortars – a practice which continued up to the end of the Second World War, the usual proportions being one part cement, two of lime and nine of sand. Records going back to the mid-eleventh century indicate that in conditions of excessive damp it was often the practice to use a special cement compounded from either wax and pitch or wax and resin, which was applied in a molten state. The research for this book did not reveal any direct evidence of this having been specified in church work, but there can be little doubt that it would have been used where there was a pressing need to guard against damp.

Concrete

The use of concrete is often perceived as being a relatively new development, but in reality its origins go back to the early civilisations, at least as far as the Ancient Egyptians and the Chinese. Moreover, archaeological evidence indicates that both the Greeks and the Romans had a full understanding of how to adapt and apply concrete to best effect. The word concrete comes from the Latin *concretus*, which means 'combined as one'. The concrete produced in Britain up to Norman times has been found to have a close similarity to that made by the Romans, with the constituent materials being in much the same proportions. It was frequently used as a core material in walling, a perfect example being the abbey ruins in Reading, where the wall facing has either been pillaged or has fallen away to expose the concrete hearting. In addition to the chemical set, all untempered natural hydraulic limes in the British Isles require a certain amount of carbonation from the atmosphere to achieve full strength. This is a reaction which cannot occur underground, which is the main reason why concrete was not generally used in foundation work during the medieval period. It is likely that other problems would have arisen over the strength and setting of the concrete as a result of possible damage from iron pyrites, salts, shale and mica in the ground. Some mineral salts in the ground water also had the capacity to reduce the quality of concrete. Nevertheless, the medieval masons were aware that by introducing an artificial pozzolanic material such as trass, crushed brick, tile or even broken-down earthenware the strength and hydraulic properties of the lime could be considerably increased. By the late seventeenth century pozzolanic rock was being imported from Holland to make hydraulic concretes and mortars. It came from a natural formation at Andernach in Germany where it was quarried and shipped in lumps to Holland, and then pulverised and exported as 'Dutch terras'. As the constituent materials improved and developed, lime concrete continued to be used until well into the nineteenth century.

Foundations (*Fundamentum*)

The skilled masons of the medieval period had a good understanding of the basics of constructional stability and they built to proven and well-tried methods. The conclusive evidence is in the large number of cathedrals and churches which have stood on the original foundations to the present day. The lack of any need for major intervention has resulted in much foundation work remaining concealed, and as a result there is still much to be learnt. For a better overview it has been necessary to search old specifications and contract documents. Investigations have revealed much clear and precise information: in some cases the dimensions and statements relating to trench depth and width indicate that the builders had a full appreciation on how downward and lateral pressures needed to be resisted. While they lacked any knowledge of structural engineering in the form we use today, they were nevertheless able to produce a satisfactory outcome through a combination of accumulated knowledge from the past, accurate onsite observations and intuitive judgements. The intricacy, volume and height of the churches they built were considerable achievements; without any scientific awareness they were able to deal with the complexity of the different stresses caused by compression, tension and shear in materials and components, using practices handed down from one generation to the next. This is very much in contrast to the methods now used, by which stress and strain can be accurately calculated by means of mathematical formulae.

Stress can be briefly defined as the cohesive force by which the particles of a body resist an external force. It acts in a number of different ways, such as compressive, tensile, vertical, horizontal and transverse stresses. Compressive stress occurs when forces compress a material or push the particles closer together. The opposite force is tensile stress, in which external forces cause either the stretching or pulling apart of particles away from one another. Vertical stress arises from a tendency of a beam to shear under load, whereas horizontal stress occurs if two opposite forces acting on a material are not quite in line; this results in a tendency for the fibres to fail through a sliding action. Forces which cause bending stress result in the top fibres in a beam becoming shortened and those at the bottom being lengthened. A more complicated form of stress is transverse stress, which can arise from a combination of tensile, compressive and shearing stress. Strain is a term that is frequently misunderstood and misapplied and is the effect stresses have on a material to cause either an alteration in form or deformation. When a member or structure is said to be in equilibrium it refers to a point where there is no tendency for movement under the simultaneous application of forces.

The determination of these forces by means of the laws of physics was unknown to medieval builders – one of the factors which mark a wide divergence between the methods of the past and the present. The safety of an entire structure can now be predetermined through structural mechanics in which the various elements of design and all load-bearing components are calculated from formulae, starting from the foundations upwards. This has enabled considerable savings to be made in the quantity of materials used, whereas medieval builders deliberately selected oversized components to ensure structural integrity. In the British Isles the first evidence of the use of load-bearing building components which had been determined through calculation appears towards the end of the Renaissance. General acceptance of the advantages this offered was slow to start, and structural engineering did not become properly integrated into the construction process until the early part of the nineteenth century.

With small churches old foundation methods varied considerably and on occasion have been found to be almost non-existent. It was usual practice to lay large stones as a base upon which the walling could be built

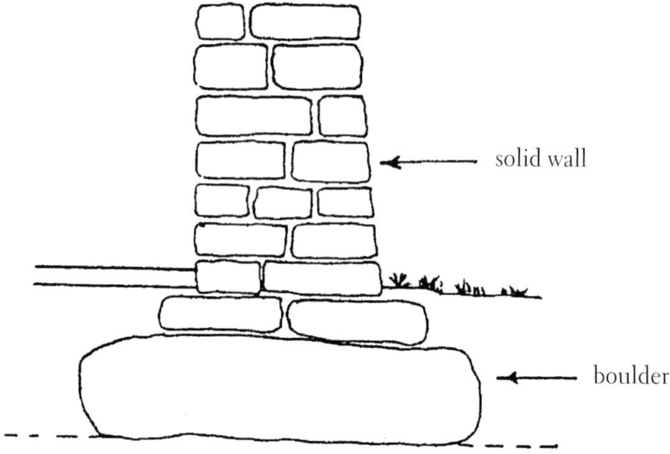

5. Boulder and stone foundation

(Fig. 5). Many churches rest on shallow foundations; a number have been taken to a depth little more than the top of the subsoil. The base was then rammed and beaten, and after the foundation stones had been laid, the spaces between were filled and consolidated with sand, gravel and small stones.

From the earliest phase of the medieval period timber piles (*pylyng*) were sometimes driven into the bed of foundations if the bearing capacity of the ground was suspect and a firm base could not be found by excavation. The support provided by this solution was largely dependent on the friction between the surfaces of the piles and the adjacent soil. The piles were sunk into the ground by suspending a rope and pulley from sheer legs, and a heavy block of wood or iron was hoisted to the maximum height and then allowed to fall on the head of the pile, using horses or oxen to take the weight. There were limitations on the depth of penetration this could achieve, and there can be no doubt that under certain circumstances it would not have been possible to go down to a good load-bearing stratum.

Unless foundations could be carried on a shallow rock bed, all trenching for the larger churches had to be hand dug down to a point which gave a stable and adequate base. Working in layers, it was the practice to fill the trenches with broken stone and block the voids with sand and gravel (described as *gravellam*). Each layer was then firmly consolidated by ramming with a beetle (a large wooden block, often fitted with multiple handles, which enabled several operatives to ply it simultaneously) before proceeding with the next layer. Some specifications placed much stress on the need for thorough compaction (Fig. 6). Load distribution carried in this way can have remarkable strength and longevity: an everyday example is the way railway sleepers rest securely on carefully sized and well-firmed stones which are able to withstand the heavy moving and static weight of trains.

In his book *Building in England Down to 1540* (published 1952) L.F. Saltzman refers to the foundations of the tower to St Stephen's Church, Bristol, going down to a depth of 31 feet (9.4 m) and he also describes the work of the rebuilding of Eton College Chapel at around 1453. The specification required the foundation trench to be carefully laid with a course of flat Yorkshire stone. This was followed by a course of mixed Yorkshire and Tenyton stone, with a final layer of blocks at the top set in a lime/gravel mortar. The footings had to extend beyond the wall by 2 feet (0.6 m) on the south, and presumably around the remainder too. Another technique used alternating layers of consolidated gravel and squared-dimension stone.

In situations where ground conditions were suspect for the building of larger churches different solutions had to be found. If the usual practice of widening trench-work to spread the load was inadequate builders had to

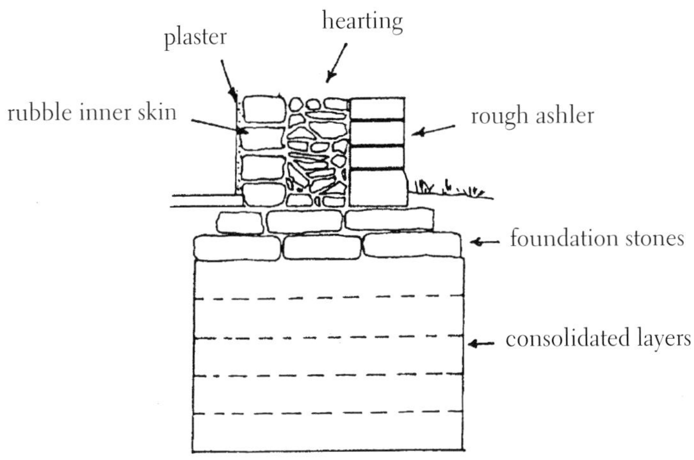

6. Layered and consolidated foundations

find different methods through innovation, with archaeological evidence indicating that it was usually achieved by using timbers as strengtheners, which encouraged settlement to be more uniform and reduced the risk of cracking. The use of timber in this way varied: one method involved filling and consolidating stones in the manner already described until close to ground level, and then placing longitudinal timbers known as crossunders (*crossaundre*) on top. Small broken stones or crushed chalk was then spread and rammed down between them and up to the top face of the timbers. In Chapter V of his book, Saltzman also refers to a similar method discovered by Biddle in the Old Minster at Winchester. A different technique involved longitudinal timbers being placed in parallel with the line of the trench and on top of the first layer of consolidated stones. Sometimes cross-pieces fixed at right angles connected the main foundation timbers (Fig. 7). In the same chapter, Saltzman mentions that this form was discovered by Peers under the choir at York Minster. The longitudinal stability of a structure was always the main problem, with transverse stability being much easier to achieve through the use of buttressing.

Point loading, where concentrated loading is applied to a selected spot or component – such as a column – created different considerations. The laying of large, flat, heavy and roughly squared foundation stones on a firm base was one answer, subject to their being of sufficient width, thickness

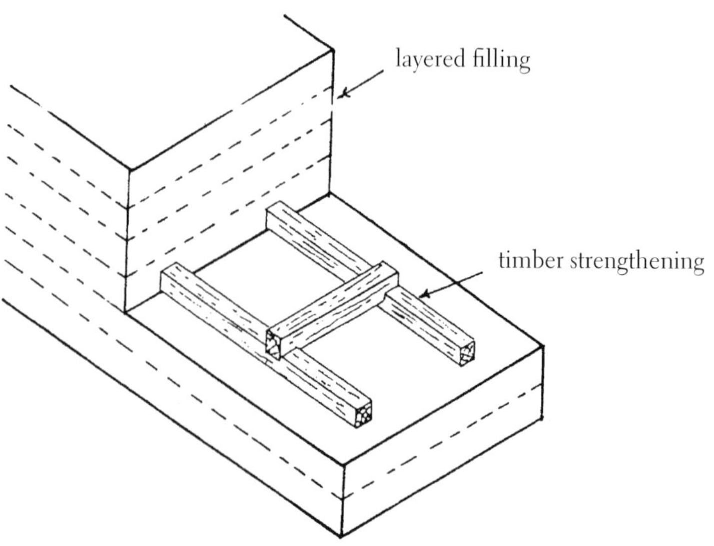

7. Timber strengthening to foundations

and strength. Foundation stones of this type are often incorrectly termed stylobates, which is the description used in Classical architecture for an above-ground substructure on which rest the columns of a colonnade. In the parts where the bearing capacity of the soil could be unreliable, builders usually resorted to the use of iron-tipped wooden piles under the foundations, often supplemented with grid timbers placed over the pile heads. Unseasoned elm and alder were the preferred species because of their higher tolerance to conditions of persistent dampness. Placed over this was either a series of stones compacted in gravel or layers of small well-consolidated stones mixed with sand. In more difficult parts a further option was to drive piles in closely arranged clusters (Fig. 8); earlier documents often refer to these as staddles or needles, the whole being capped with well-rammed layers of broken stone and gravel. To prevent any tendency of spread in more vulnerable ground it was sometimes the practice to encase the staddles in an upright ring of timbers known as starlings (Fig. 9). The tips of these were cut to a wedge for easier driving, and they performed a restraining role similar in function to the poling boards used in present-day trenching.

The eventual use of brick in church building resulted in the foundation trenches normally being taken down to a suitable load-bearing stratum. From this, footings were constructed entirely of brick; each course was gradually offset (Fig. 10), the earlier use of consolidated gravel having been discarded. It is a practice which continued until the 1890s, when builders began to lay a bed of concrete upon which brick footings were

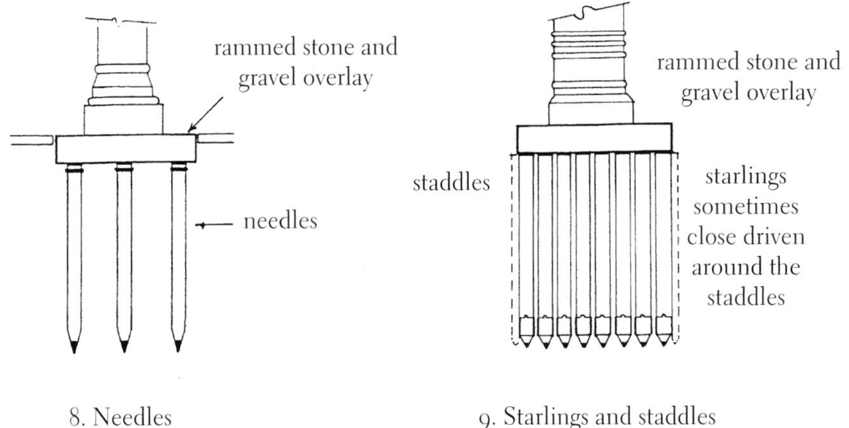

8. Needles

9. Starlings and staddles

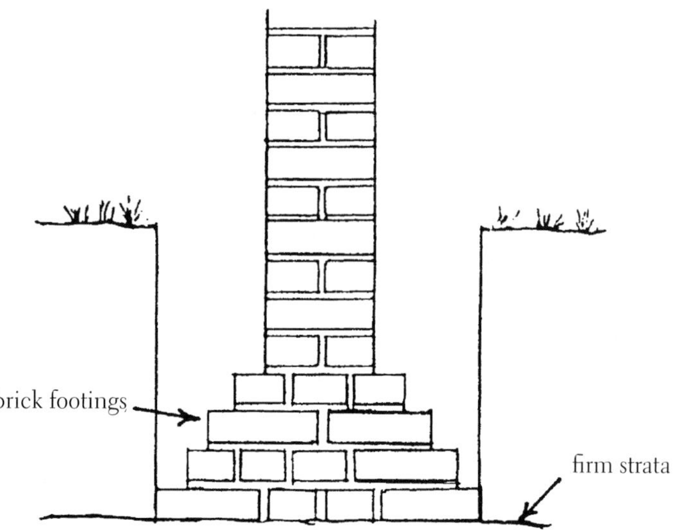

10. Brick footings

superimposed. This contrasts with the modern method of placing masonry walling directly onto concrete strip foundations.

The builders of the time were unaware that, when properly executed, these techniques would be in accordance with Newton's Third Law of Motion. It is now one of the basic structural engineering rules, which states that when forces act between two bodies and A exerts a force on B, then B exerts an equal and opposite force on A. This is vital in the building of a structure as the weight always exerts a downward force into the ground. If this is not resisted by an equal and opposite upward reaction a structure will settle and distort or fail structurally.

Wall Construction

Brickwork

Most of the original Saxon churches were built of timber, with the only remaining known example being at the Church of St Andrew, Greensted, Essex, where part of the wall to the nave was built in the traditional Scandinavian split-log or stave technique. A dendrochronological analysis has dated this to around AD 850. A number of masonry-built churches from Saxon times and some from the Norman period have been part constructed in materials described as *spoila* – stone, bricks and tiles reclaimed from Roman works. A good example can be seen in the Roman bricks used in the walls of the Saxon Church of St Botolph, Hardham, West Sussex, which have been taken from a nearby Roman settlement.

After the departure of the Romans in the early part of the fifth century, brick making was abandoned and did not re-emerge until the second half of the twelfth century. Brick was used infrequently in church construction, even when reduced costs made brick a more popular material. The exception was the East Anglian region, where brick (*breke*) was used for church building because of a shortage of local stone. Dressed stone was usually used for windows, door openings and similar features, but in a few East Anglian churches the tracery and other items are also in moulded brick. Still, the reluctance to use brick in church work continued elsewhere. Good examples of pre-Reformation churches which are in brick can be found at Layer Marney and Chignal Smealy in Essex, and at Shelton in Norfolk. Notable brick-built churches outside the East Anglian region are at Small Hythe in Kent and Lutton and East Hordon in Lincolnshire. The illustration in Figure 11 is the tower at St Mary's Church, Shinfield, Berkshire, which is brick built and dates from 1630. It is in English bond (see Fig. 11) and was later severely damaged by cannon fire during the Civil War when the tower was used by Royalist troops as a lookout.

The early bricks were burnt in clamps or wood-fired kilns. When produced in this way the best quality always came from the centre of the firing, with many of those in the outer layers being left soft and underburnt. Known as samel bricks, these were picked out and used for filling and rough work and are readily identifiable by their distinctive salmon-pink colouring. A change began in the late seventeenth century when brick started to be used for the building or rebuilding of church towers, and by the late eighteenth and early nineteenth centuries it rapidly replaced stone for many forms of building work, and was much used as a backing material and sometimes as facing in churches. By the end of the nineteenth century, brick had become a regular material for the construction of smaller churches. Where bricks appear in the earlier churches they are smaller in size and are in English bond, with the stretchers and headers being placed in alternate layers. This contrasts with the Flemish bond used in the late seventeenth and eighteenth centuries, where the headers and stretchers appear alternately in the same course (Fig. 12). A stretcher is a brick with the long side facing outwards; a header is a brick with the end laid outwards. Bonding is the

11. Brick church tower

interlacement of bricks whereby the vertical joints in one course are covered by bricks in the adjoining courses (Fig. 12).

The durability and strength of a wall is dependent on good bonding, particularly to avoid continuous or near-continuous vertical jointing. In the early stages of the medieval period bonding was somewhat haphazard, although by Tudor times it had become more consistent and uniform, and had been forged into the English bond style. In some original work, elongated 'through' bricks known as cogging bricks were sometimes used to provide additional strength. Flemish bond is the weaker style although it is generally considered to be aesthetically superior. It is also more economical as a greater number of broken bricks can be cut and used as bats (half bricks). Variations do occur to both bonding techniques, although they are seldom found in church work. Below is a chronological summary of the variations between brick sizes.

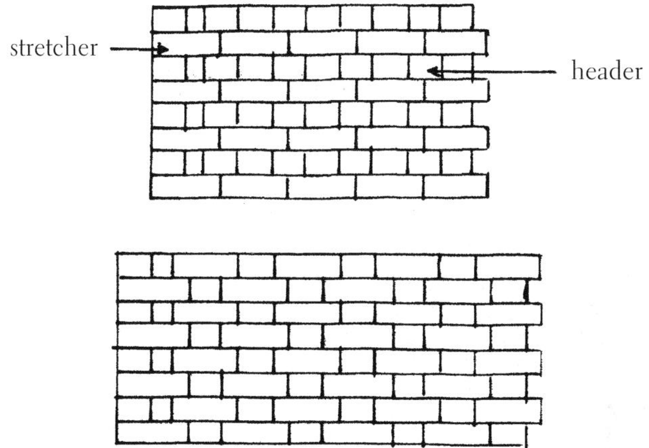

12. Brick bondings – *top:* English bond; *bottom:* Flemish bond

~

Chronological Summary of Variations in Brick Sizes

1200 About this time the first English bricks (then known as waltyles) were made. No set size established. Dimensions usually varied from 12”–11” x 6” x 1¾”–2¾” (306 mm x 279 mm x 70 mm). Brick lengths of up to 15”–20” (381–508 mm) have been discovered. All these sizes are now described as ‘great bricks’.

During the thirteenth century Flemish craftsmen settled in East Anglia and introduced smaller brick sizes. The dimensions varied from 9¾”–8” x 4¾”–3¼” x 1¾”–2½” (230–203 mm x 103–77 mm x 44–52 mm).

1490 About this time a notable era in English brickwork began. Bricks moulded to various shapes including the replication of stone ornamentation. ‘Tudor bricks’ mainly sized 9” x 4¾” x 2” (228 mm x 102 mm x 50 mm).

1571 Bricks sizes were determined by decree and were required to be 9” x 4½” x 1¼” (228 mm x 103 mm x 57 mm). The ruling was not effectively enforced and some bricks from this period are likely to have different dimensions.

1700 From about this time, brick sizes tended to diminish to 8½” x 4⅛” x 2⅜” (204 mm x 101 mm x 51 mm). The trend towards reduced brick sizes resulted in the introduction of the frog.

1729 Size regulated by statute to 8¾” x 4⅛” x 2½” (205 mm x 101 mm x 52 mm). These bricks became known as ‘statute bricks’.

1784 Brick tax introduced.

1840 Imperial brick size introduced: 8¾” x 4⅛” x 2½” (205 mm x 101 mm x 52 mm). In parts of the Midlands and the North of England the thickness was increased to 3” (75 mm).

1850 Brick tax abolished.

1965 A British Standard came into being under BS 3921: 1965, which stipulated dimensions as 8⅝” x 4⅛” x 2⅝”.

1969 The British Standard size was metricated to 215 mm x 102.5 mm x 65 mm under BS 3921: Part 2.

~

In his book *Mechanick Exercises* published in 1703, Joseph Moxon refers to the tools used by bricklayers. An item of particular interest is the original brick-axe, which looked more like a chisel. He also mentions a small tinsaw for cutting and a circular rub stone of around 14 inches (35 cm) in diameter used to rub bricks down to a required shape. A small hand-held float stone provided an alternative technique, with the bricks being rubbed to shape against a template (*platt*). Later, a tool known as a scutch appeared for dressing cut surfaces and a more conventional type of brick-axe evolved, although the original type remained in circulation until around 1840. Decorative and ornamental brick designs could be produced with specially moulded bricks or by rubbing bricks to a required outline. An alternative method was the cutting and sculpting of fired bricks in situ. After some initial shaping with either a brick-axe or a scutch, much of the finer working was carried out using strips of copper, to incise and score in the detail. The final finishing was mostly worked by gentle abrasion with a small stone. A few churches display carved-brick ornamentation: some good examples are the trefoils in the early sixteenth-century porch at the Church of St John the Baptist, Pebmarsh, Essex, and the carvings on the north porch at Hardwick parish church in Norfolk.

In around 1520 the use of fired clay advanced to the production of terracotta. It did not come into general use for church work at this stage, but again exceptions are to be found, the more notable examples being the tombs at Layer Marney Church, Oxburgh, Essex and the sedilia (stone seats for use by the clergy) at Wymondham Church, Norfolk. Terracotta did, however, feature in many of the brick churches built in the Victorian and Edwardian periods, with terracotta blocks often being used in the door and window jambs (*jamwys*) and in various features and ornament. In essence, terracotta is made from fine clay mixed with other materials such as crushed sand which is then moulded and fired at a high temperature. This produces hard compacted units of high-quality material which have a particular sharpness of detail in a form not attainable with ordinary brick clays. Faience is the term given to the same material with a glazed finish.

Stonework

The hardness and durability of stone is highly dependent on its mineral constituents and on the state and density of the aggregation. While the particle parts might be hard, the stone itself will be soft if the binding material is of poor quality. The medieval masons understood this and operated with an accumulation of knowledge from the past and an intimate understanding of the qualities and faults of the stones on which they worked. They also knew how to utilise stones of different compositions and how to identify good and bad stone within the quarry stratifications. In each architectural period the masons had a preference for a particular size of block but in general terms the blocks tended to become larger as time went on.

Building stones need to be laid in accordance with their natural bedding plane and be placed in the wall horizontally. In other words, good practice requires them to be used as found in the quarry (Fig. 13). Exceptions to this are those circumstances where projections should be parallel to the perpends (vertical joints) and in arches where the bed needs to be at right angles to the thrust. Nevertheless, in medieval masonry this rule was not always fully observed and occasionally blocks can be found set with the grain the wrong way. This is often the reason why some stones have weathered badly in relation to the others; if the bedding surface is set vertically it makes the stone more vulnerable to decay and the laminations prone to become detached and to break off.

In parish churches deficiencies in the application of the stonework can often be the result of inadequate bonding, uneven bedding or too frugal use of mortar. The faulty selection of stone from the same quarry can be a further contributory factor. In many quarries stone is not of the same quality throughout and it can sometimes be difficult to distinguish between the poor and good formations except for the trained eye. When different types are used together, excessive decay can also occur through the incompatibility of certain stones. The mixing of limestone with sandstone has frequently resulted in the rapid decay of the sandstone. Similarly soft,

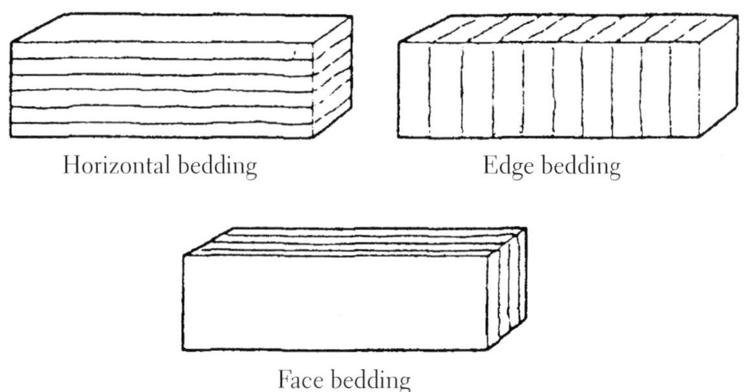

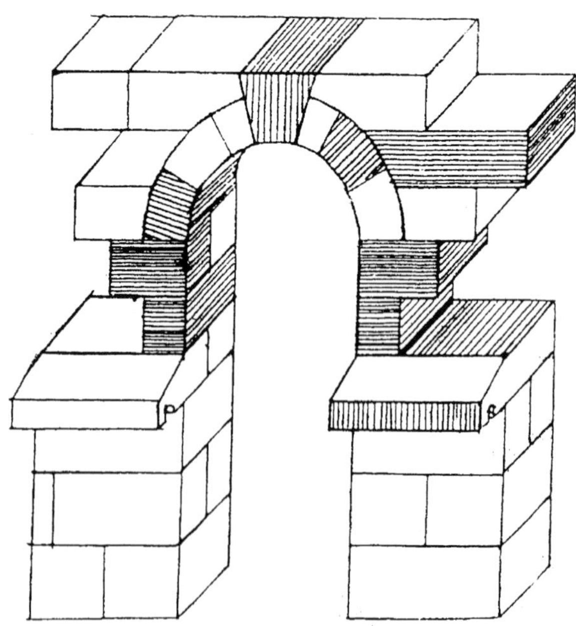

13. Stone bedding; the hatching indicates the correct bedding planes for an arch and sills

limestone is likely to be found suffering from deterioration where it has been used in combination with hard magnesian limestone.

A poor-quality mortar can be another reason for a substandard outcome, especially if small stones or large pieces of grit of various sizes have been allowed to contaminate the mix. This can take some stones out of level and cause uneven bearing. This should not be confused with the insertion of uniform and equal-sized pea gravel or similar, which was sometimes used in mortar jointing to help resist lateral movement or drag. The size of the quoins (corner stones – *coynes*) can be an additional indicator of the quality of the masonry. They bond the walling where it meets at the corners and need to be equal or larger in size than the main building blocks. Some strength and stability is lost if they are smaller.

Most stones taken from a quarry contain a mixture of water and minerals known as 'quarry sap'. Stone should not be used in this condition and needs to be left to season until it has dried out and hardened. In some of the smaller churches the quality of the masonry was not always up to standard, and there are pointers suggesting that unseasoned stones were perhaps used at the time of construction. If exposed prematurely to the ravages of the weather the stone is likely to be permanently weaker and more vulnerable to erosion and decay. Apart from a few exceptions, Saxon stonework tends to be much rougher and to a poorer finish compared to the following periods.

Masonry Classifications

Masonry styles can be broadly grouped into ashlar (*acheley* or *assheler*), rubble (*ramell*) and block-in-course work (Fig. 14). Fine ashlar stone is accurately tooled to sharp right-angled corners and laid truly level, with thin mortar joints. As stone dressing improved and became more precise, masons were able to progressively reduce mortar jointing to a thickness which seldom exceeded ⅛ inch (3 mm), although work to this standard was rarely achieved before the fifteenth century. The best ashlar is laid with lime putty mortar (see page 14). In church building the facework is more usually plain but in some much later work parts can be found rusticated. Rustication is a method of working the face of individual blocks or courses in ways which make them more conspicuous and was a style much associated with Classical architecture (Fig. 15). The joints are deeply recessed in various ways in this style, and the surfaces may also be plain, worked or roughened; although the technique originated from the Romans it was rarely used in Britain in medieval times. In the early medieval

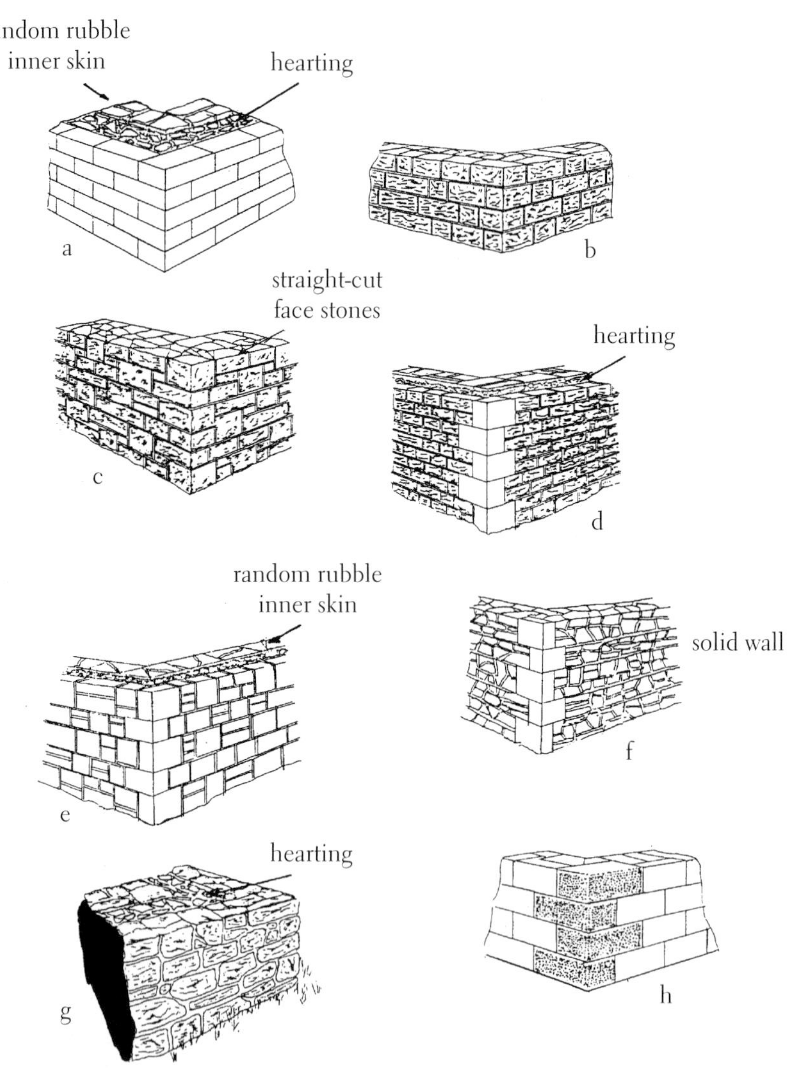

14. Forms of stone walling – (a) plain ashlar; (b) block in course (the stones are of equal height but have differing lengths); (c) squared and snecked rubble; (d) regular-course rubble (the stones are of various lengths but all the courses are of uniform height); (e) squared rubble built to courses (the bonding stones in each course are equal to the full height of the course in which they occur); (f) random rubble built in course; (g) random rubble; (h) ashlar with punched and chamfered quoins

period most walling then described as ashlar was 'straight cut' (Fig. 14c) – only the face was properly squared to a finish, leaving the rest of the stone that would not be seen in irregular form. It is a practice which was sometimes continued into more recent times. Dressing is the term applied to mouldings, finely worked surfaces and sculptured decoration (*talliat*) when used on a building for the purposes of refinement or ornament apart from tracery. The backs of some dressed stones were left rough with the express objective of providing a better bonding surface for the mortar.

The term rough ashlar now applies where stone has been cut and squared to a proper finish and is reasonably true and square on all sides.

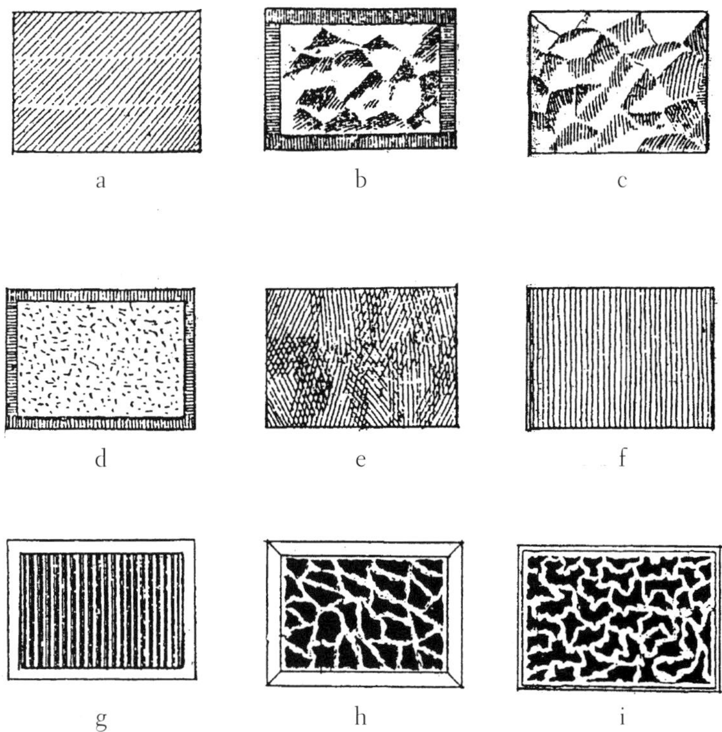

15. Dressed-stone finishes – (a) boasted or droved; (b) hammer dressed with draughted margins; (c) hammer dressed; (d) pointed; (e) combed or dragged; (f) tooled; (g) furrowed; (h) vermiculated; (i) reticulated

In order to reduce costs, most ashlar work was confined to the wall facing, with the remainder being in rubble work. This was bonded into the ashlar or worked with two skins with a hearting between (Fig. 14a). The hearting was a rubble fill consolidated with lime mortar. During the post-medieval periods old records sometimes describe rubble-filled walling as 'impletion walling'. For thinner walls such as parapets, solid ashlar or squared stone blocks were used with extra 'through' stones (*theughe*) provided to give firmer bonding and added stability (through stones – *thrughe stanes* – extend from one face to the other). In cases where parts of the original church walling have survived to become a section of a later structure, mortars of earth or a mixture of earth and lime have sometimes been discovered. References to this have also been found in old accounts and the practice is known to have endured until well into the fourteenth century. In some of the early Saxon churches, walling from the foundations up to ground level has been found to have been assembled without mortar, the application of a dry-stone technique probably being an attempt to combat rising damp.

Rubble is the general term for masonry where the stones are either of various sizes or irregular shapes, the different applications being coursed or uncoursed (the original term used for coursed walling was *tabulatis*). In church work a number of variations are likely to be found. An illustration in Figure 14 is an example of random rubble walling where the quoins have been hammer dressed to give a clear profile at the corners. Figure 14 also shows an example of random rubble built in courses, which is where the stones have been so placed to give true horizontal joints along the top and bottom lines of the quoins. A variation of this is also shown where the stones have been roughly squared, with some blocks equal to the full height of each course being featured intermittently. Another example is regular-coursed rubble where stones of a fairly uniform size have been used and, although of various lengths, are the same in height. Also shown is squared rubble which has been snecked. This is where stones of various sizes have been arranged in a particularly irregular or non-uniform way. When this is done, special consideration has to be given to the strength of the bonding, and to achieve a satisfactory result the insertion of specially prepared stones is necessary. This involves the use of through stones known as risers, flat stones called levellers and small gap-filling stones termed snecks. This avoids the need for excessive vertical jointing and makes for a stronger and more appealing wall.

Block-in-course work does not alter materially from coursed rubble, the essential difference is that the courses are deeper and have added strength from the inclusion of extra through stones (Fig. 14, see coursed rubble).

The style is more associated with engineering works and is less likely to be found in church building. Flintwork and polygonal walling are always categorised as rubble walling.

Plinths which project beyond the face of the wall can sometimes provide an indication of the wall's age. Few are seen in walls surviving from Saxon and early Norman times and the few that do exist are plain and simple in style with a chamfered top edge. This changed little in the Early English period, but during the Decorated phase they became a regular feature and are much taller and more prominent than before, and many have bold projections. In the Perpendicular period plinth heights increased further and many often feature intricately worked decoration. In the middle and later Gothic periods plinths were occasionally worked in two lifts, the upper part sometimes being termed a ledgment table (*tablamentis*) and the lower level an earth table (*solum tablamentis*).

Building Stone

In the past, churches have been constructed from a range of different materials, which may include a selection of various stones within the same walling. Whereas the great cathedrals and larger churches had the means to build in specially selected stone from elsewhere, costs dictated the use of locally available materials in the building of most parish churches (Fig. 16). As a consequence, a wide diversity of different stones can be seen in churches around the British Isles, and the exploitation of the physical characteristics of some was made to good effect. Certain stones, for example, break naturally into roughly squared or oblong blocks, while others split into elongated lengths, and some, such as ragstone, are totally irregular in shape. All this has provided some intriguing aesthetic variations throughout the regions, but the tooling limitations encountered with some forms necessitated the incorporation of freestone in those elements involving fine finishing and ornamentation. A freestone (*lapid* or *freston*) is one which has a fine grain and does not possess strongly defined laminations or bedding planes. This enables it to be more easily tooled with a chisel or a saw, making it ideal for fine carving and dressed work. The overall variation in stone selection sometimes included the use of sarsens and erratics. Sarsens are boulders of grey sandstone which appear to have no relationship to other stones in the area. In reality they are the remnants of an original sandstone stratum that has otherwise been completely eroded away. Erratics are stones which have been transported from another location by glacial action.

16. A church wall made of several different materials

The chief constituents of granite are feldspar, quartz and mica, and some also have varying amounts of augite and hornblende. The colour is greatly influenced by the crystal size and feldspar content. Those containing plagiosclase feldspar and dark micas are in relative terms less durable than those derived from orthoclase and light mica. It is these differences which determine how the stone is best used and applied. Apart from limited quantities from Leicestershire, most granite supplied for church building came from Scotland or Cumbria. Granite deposits usually have two planes of cleavage which enables them to be more easily hewn into roughly shaped blocks.

Limestones are formed from organic or chemical sources. Those of organic origin are the remains of animal organisms such as molluscs, crinoids and similar marine life which have hardened under pressure and are held together by a cementing material. Those derived from a chemical action are made up of small grains around which are concentric deposits of calcium carbonate as a result of the percolation of water carrying calcium carbonate. The oolitic limestones are aggregations of small rounded particles which in appearance are similar to the roe of a fish. The size of the grains can vary, which has a direct relationship with the texture and porosity of the stone. Magnesium carbonate is present in most limestones, but those containing a higher proportion are called magnesian limestones. If the magnesium carbonate and calcium carbonate are held in roughly equal amounts it is termed Dolomitic limestone. The areas where limestone is prevalent are Lincolnshire, parts of Derbyshire, Oxfordshire, Gloucestershire, Wiltshire, Somerset, Dorset and Nottinghamshire, with the colours in these regions ranging from white, cream, light grey, blue, buff and pink. Apart from local workings, the limestones used for building have mainly come from the larger quarries such as those in Ancaster in Lincolnshire, Bladon in Oxfordshire, Clipsham in Leicestershire, Corsham Down and Monk Park in Wiltshire, Hopton Wood in Derbyshire, Portland in Dorset and Weldon in Northamptonshire. Supplies of magnesian limestone for the large churches have probably been taken from quarries such as those at Aston and Park Nook in the Yorkshire area or Linby in Nottinghamshire.

Sandstones are composed mostly from fragments of quartz together with subsidiary amounts of other minerals such as feldspar and mica. The constituent grains may be large or small, angular or rounded. The more usual cementing materials are silica, oxide of iron, feldspar, mica or calcite, all of which determine the compressive strength and durability of the stone. Sandstones with a matrix of feldspar have been used locally in parts of Hertfordshire, Shropshire and Worcestershire. The stone is classified according to the character of the grains and the degree of stratification. Flagstones are those which are strongly laminated and split fairly readily and thickly along the bedding planes, while tile-stones can be worked in a similar fashion but produce thin pieces which may be used for roofing. Liver or knell stones are thick bedded and produce large single blocks. The term York stone is applied to sandstone from York that is particularly hard and suitable for steps, copings and similar features. Well-known sandstones for building include those from quarries at Bolton Woods, Appleton, Crosland Hill and Thornton Blue in the Yorkshire region, Dunn House near Durham, Kerridge and Runcorn Red in Cheshire, Longridge in Lancashire, and Stancliffe in Derbyshire.

Sandstone has also been widely used in parts of the South-East of England, where a thin stratum runs from the Downland areas of Sussex through to parts of Kent. There is also a narrow band which extends from Devon through to Norfolk. Slate stone occurs extensively in areas of the South-West and North-West of England and is a particular feature in parts of Lancashire and most of Cumbria. In some regions of Cornwall and Devon it was the only available material for building a number of local churches and here long lengths of slate can be seen used as lintels and beams, which over the course of time have been proved to possess a remarkably high bending tolerance.

From time to time a conglomerate called puddingstone can be seen used in church building. Composed mostly of a mixture of flint pebbles and small lumps and fragments of sandstone, it is held together by a natural cement of silicon or iron oxide. Although found in other parts it is more likely to be seen in the South-East of England along a line from Middlesex through to north-west Surrey and east Berkshire – a church in the town centre of Wokingham is partly in puddingstone. Quantities of the same stone also occur in the Church of St Lawrence in Chobham, Surrey.

Each of the various stones has had a particular impact on the quality, finish and composition of church building in the parishes of Britain. A significant change began as communication and transport links improved, resulting in an increased demand for Bath stone, which was most favoured for church work. A technique known as range work was sometimes used for facing internal walling in churches. For this, the Bath stone blocks were supplied in different heights and had to be coursed in a manner which increased the number of random vertical joints. As the stones were not finished precisely there was sometimes a need to work the surface with a drag after laying, often leaving perceptible tell-tale signs (a drag is a steel plate with serrated edges which was dragged backwards and forwards and in different directions until the required finish was obtained, as shown in Figure 15). The term range walling is also used to describe ashlar work where the blocks are in courses and are less than 7 inches (18 cm) in height.

The use of cobbles (*saxum*), pebbles (*pebyllis*) and sometimes boulders can also be found in church walling. They may differ in quality and strength and are likely to have come from a variety of rock fragments rounded into irregular shapes by the eroding action of glacial waters or the sea. Those suitable for building mostly occurred in the beds of streams, estuaries or on the seashore. Stones which are over 3 inches (8 cm) in diameter but less than 12 inches (30 cm) are termed cobbles, and those under 3 inches (8 cm) are called pebbles. These are materials which have been used extensively on the south coast of England in a similar fashion to flint. Boulder stones are those over 12 inches (30 cm) in size and are frequently set with smaller stones sometimes acting as positioning wedges. In earlier times chalk was also used as a building material where it could be transported at reasonable cost and was readily available. In the British Isles the chalk strata vary considerably in quality, with the harder and more rock-like varieties often described as clunch. The term should, however, be restricted to a particular type of chalk found in Cambridgeshire and Bedfordshire. Chalk is not usually a feature in church building except where it is used as infilling in the webs of vaulting and as infill to the hearting in composite walling.

No true marbles can be quarried from the geological formations in England, and from the thirteenth century onwards the term has been incorrectly applied to some very hard local limestones that are capable of being ground and polished. Throughout the thirteenth century they were much favoured for interior work to churches, with the main sources of supply coming from Devon, Derbyshire, Dorset and the Petworth area of Sussex. Later a wide variety of genuine marbles were imported from Italy, Ireland and elsewhere.

At around the end of the Gothic phase and in the early stages of the Rennaissance there was a move towards making exceptionally fine ashlar jointing. To achieve this some builders used a system of concave bedding whereby blocks were hollowed on the bedding surfaces to enable the visible part of the joint to be reduced in thickness. The practice became more developed during the Renaissance but it was short-lived as it created unequal stresses and made the stone vulnerable to spalling along the bed joints, especially when the mortar gradually hardened and shrank. It is a technique which is seldom found in smaller churches because of the extra

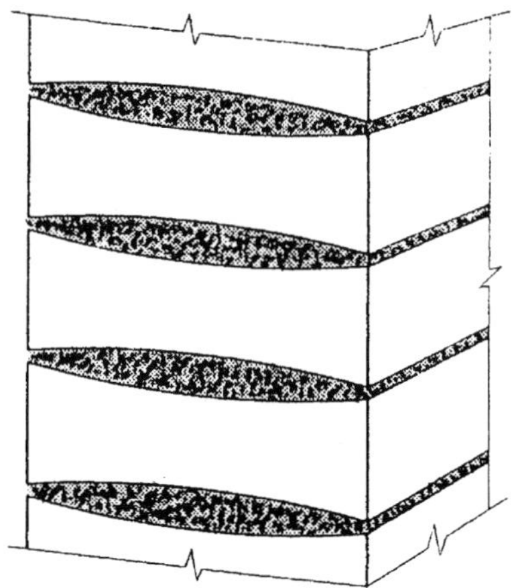

17. Concave bedding

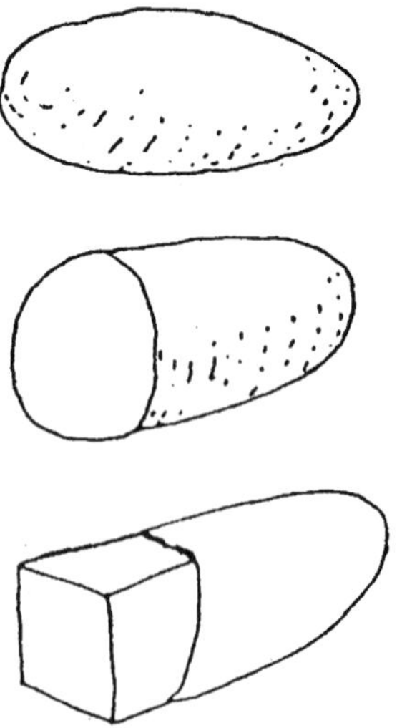

18. Flint nodules – *from top:* when taken from the ground the nodules are covered with a white crust of lime sometimes tinted because of the presence of minerals; the knapped surfaces reveal an opaque material, usually grey-black or dark brown in colour; knapped and squared flints are assembled to produce a bonding effect identical to brick or stonework

19. Flint demonstration panels, showing how flint can be worked or coursed in different styles

cost that the stone preparation incurs. At times concaving was used in some rough ashlar work, leaving blocks vulnerable to vertical cracking and often causing them to break at the middle (Fig. 17).

Flint (*flyntis*) was another favoured material for church building in the South-Eastern and Eastern regions, with the best examples being found in Sussex, Kent, Norfolk, Suffolk and parts of Hampshire. Flint should not be confused with chert, which – although similar – is never present in chalk strata and is essentially a feature in the connecting border areas between Devon, Cornwall and Somerset, but it can also be found in parts of Yorkshire. Flint can be laid as found, set coursed or uncoursed (Figs 18 and 19). It can also be used knapped or knapped and gauged. Knapping is a method of fracturing flint nodules into two or more pieces to reveal a grey-black lustred surface flecked with white, the overall result often being described as a polled face. Gauged work was a later progression whereby knapped stones were also squared (Fig. 20). Nevertheless, some of the early

20. Knapped and squared flint

21. Early Norman flint walling

flint walling in churches was particularly rough and crude – the example shown in Figure 21 is in a church in Berkshire.

The use of knapped flint first appeared around AD 1200 and opened up new horizons in terms of aesthetics and wall texturing. From about 1760 onwards, knapped and gauged flintwork became popular in church building. Flat disc-shaped flints sometimes occur naturally, and these were collected for separate use to produce a distinctive feature known as tabular flintwork. It is seldom found in the walling of churches but does occur more often in churchyard walling. The impermeable nature of flint meant that – in contrast to brick or stone – there was practically no adhesion to the mortar. This caused a particular weakness at the quoins which was overcome by using brick or stone. This could also give added strength to the main structure by the introduction of lacing courses in the same material (in this context a lacing course is an intermediate course of another material). The notion of using flint in combination with other materials resulted in the development of chequer work at the beginning of the fourteenth century (Fig. 22), accompanied a little later by a technique known as flushwork (Fig. 23). Although occasionally found elsewhere, flushwork is essentially indigenous to East Anglia. In essence, it involves cutting hollows and cavities into ashlared stone to receive an infilling of knapped or undressed flint bedded in lime mortar. It developed into a unique and highly decorative art form featuring a multiplicity of religious symbols, icons, biblical quotations and monograms. In some cases the work is of such a high quality that there is little evidence of mortar jointing. Knapped flint in flushwork is mostly found shallow bedded and there are a few isolated cases where a different stone has been used in lieu of flint.

A large number of churches in the east of the country have some splendid flushwork and are worthy of a special mention. They include the parish church at Hopton near Great Yarmouth, especially the work to the belfry, the lettering on the porch at East Tuddenham church near Norwich and the tower at Redenhall church, between Harleston and Bungay. Other notable examples are the work at Holy Trinity Church, Long Melford in Suffolk. Knapped flint set in brick occurs as a feature in the area, and this is well illustrated in the tower window at St Benedict's, Norwich. Elsewhere flint flushwork can be seen at the local churches in Bottisham and March, and at St Cyriac's, Swaffham Prior, which are all in Cambridgeshire. It also occurs at St Mary's Church, Luton and at Redbourn in Hertfordshire.

At times a technique known as galletting (taken from the French word *galet*, meaning a stone) can often be seen in church walling. Sometimes termed garnetting or garretting, it involved inserting small stones or slivers

22 Flint chequer work

(*Facing page*) 23 Flushwork

of flint into the mortar jointing of the facework before it had set (Fig. 24). It is mostly found between the North and South Downs of South-East England, covering the areas of Sussex, Surrey, Kent and east Hampshire, and also occurs in the flint-building areas of Norfolk. It was more regularly used in the seventeenth and eighteenth centuries and is only seldom found in churches of medieval origin. Throughout the nineteenth century the practice went into steady decline and was eventually discontinued.

Dressing and Working Stone

The Saxons dressed stone with an axe, which why most of the masonry from this period has not been finely worked or finished. In much of the surviving masonry the original axe-tooling marks can still be seen. In addition to the ordinary mason's axe, the hammer-axe was also in regular use, which was an implement rather like a small mattock with the blade running longitudinally. In the second half of the twelfth century there began to be a major shift away from axed dressing towards tooling with chisels for both carving and finishing. In the thirteenth century the claw tool and then the boaster appeared, and both enabled surface irregularities to be more suitably removed to give a better surface finish. At this stage the boaster was used in a manner which produced a series of fine vertical lines on the work face, but in the Early English period this changed to the lines being run diagonally across the face of the stone (see Fig. 15a). While much walling was left in this way the Gothic masons sometimes went further and finished facework with a drag (see page 36), which produced a finer finish and removed all signs of tool marks. In rubblework a smoother surface was sometimes accomplished on particularly rough pieces by wetting the surface and spreading it with sand and then rubbing with another piece of stone. This process was repeated until the desired result had been obtained.

Most church walling is composite and has inner and outer placings of stone or flint, with the core or hearting (*royboyll*), being filled with small stones well compacted in lime mortar. Sometimes an earth mortar or an earth and lime mortar was used but few examples remain. In the very early small churches and chapels the hearting has occasionally been found to have been placed dry, which made it liable to consolidate more densely at the base than at higher levels, causing unequal compressive pressures within the body of the wall. A badly packed core filling can also sometimes shrink away from the encasing stone, leaving the two skins to carry the weight of the main structure. To give extra strength, most composite walls have bonder or through stones placed at intervals, passing through the

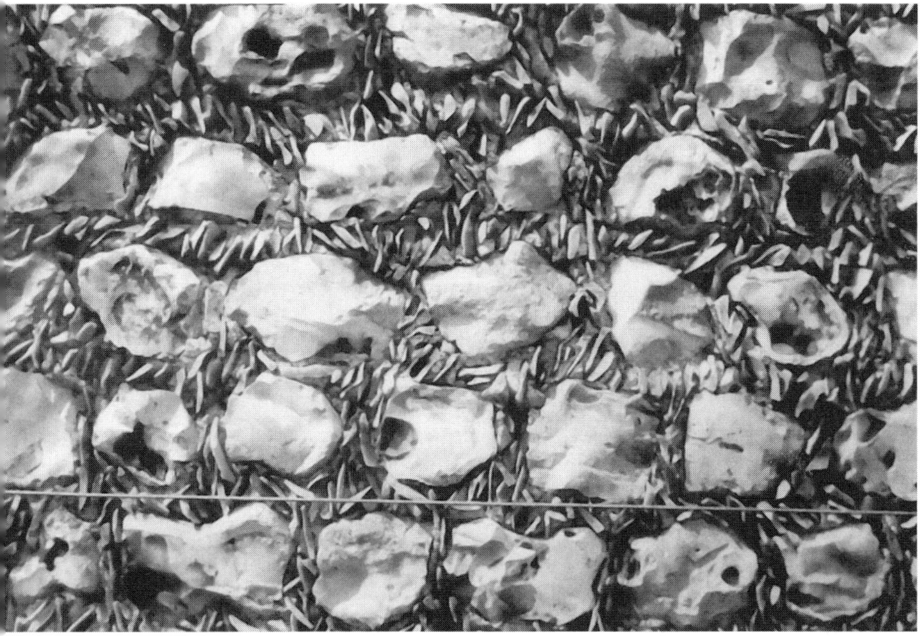

24. Galleting – *above*: knapped and galleted flintwork; *below*: galleting in the mortar joints of a stone wall

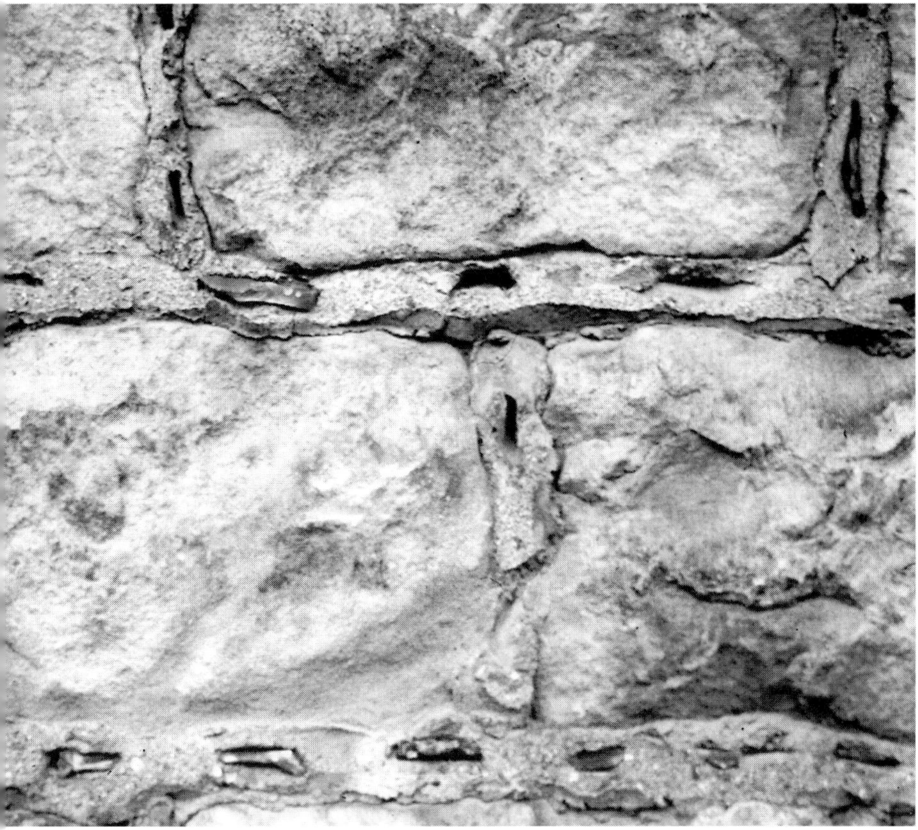

wall and are visible on both sides. In old manuscripts they are sometimes described as perpent stones (*perpeigne*), and if they are of sufficient size and number and transverse the wall thickness in a similar way it is termed parping ashlar in ashlar work.

Not all stones were suited for precise cutting and carving, and the early masons did not have the necessary tools to work difficult stones to the standards expected in the present day. The Saxons (600–1066) preferred to build in well-bonded larger stones which enabled them to make some reduction in wall thicknesses. A particular characteristic was the application of 'long and short work' at the quoins, which was achieved by placing rectangular stones flat and upright alternately (see Fig. 25). Much of the external walling was in rough ashlar often with some irregularity in the coursing, nevertheless a limited amount of more refined ashlar can be found from this period. The herringbone pattern was another feature favoured by the Saxons and appears to a much lesser extent in the early part of the Norman phase (Fig. 26). It has been suggested the technique

(*Facing page*) 25. Saxon tower with long and short work to the quoins, together with pilaster strips (lesene strips) and string courses

26. Herringbone work

may have been chosen to speed up the building process as stones could be laid more rapidly this way. Solid-stone walling was sometimes provided at selected points where additional strength was needed (see also columns, page 76). At this stage the lime/sand mortars *(Calx/sabulum)* were mostly of better quality but the sands tended to be of a coarser texture.

The Normans (1066–1199) had a preference for building walls in extreme thicknesses with small stones, using mass to resist most destructive forces. A weakness often found when cutting into this type of walling is that there is an imperfect bond between the core and the two encasing skins. The use of rubble stone on the external face was generally accompanied by the application of a lime plaster covering internally. A few Norman churches have plain projecting plinths, and a number feature continuous string courses placed immediately under the window sills (in masonry work string courses are narrow-banded horizontal courses projecting beyond the wall face). Old documents show that large quantities of oyster shells were often used to set rib stones or voussoirs and to level and wedge blocks to prevent any displacement. At the beginning of the Early English period masons built walls in slightly reduced thicknesses using more cut stone, including ashlar blocks of larger dimensions. The rubble core is generally found to have been better consolidated. In the Decorated phase (1272–1349) and Perpendicular period (1350–1593) the standards improved even further, with blocks of increased size and more accurate dimensions being used along with fine lime mortar jointing of exceptional quality. A feature sometimes found in the Perpendicular phase is decorative panelling carved into the wall faces. Church walls from the medieval period often have a slight batter (an inclined wall face or a slightly receding slope to a wall in which the wall is thicker at the base and thinner at the top) on the outer face but in the Celtic areas a batter very occasionally occurs on the inner face, with the outer face being a true vertical.

In an attempt to induce any differential settlement to be more dispersed and uniform, medieval builders sometimes inserted timbers into masonry above ground during the construction. These intra-mural timbers (sometimes termed chain timbers) were totally encased within the walling longitudinally with any necessary transverse stability being provided by good buttressing. Wilcox in his book *Timber and Iron Reinforcement in Early Buildings* (1981) describes in much detail how intra-mural timbers were used, and how they were occasionally applied as collars to hold a building square at the corners in addition to being a way of preventing distortion. His published findings also indicate that intra-mural timbers were probably used to a lesser extent in church work than in other buildings, but he does make some useful references to them being discovered in Derry Church, Co. Down, Wilmington Priory, Sussex, and St Augstine's Abbey, Canterbury. The manner and pace in which building work was undertaken also helped to minimise the effect of movement. The building process was slow, with gaps of many months and sometimes years occurring between the various stages. Work was often not progressed during the winter months, which enabled any differential movements to be consolidated and absorbed during the dormant periods. The old soft lime mortars also allowed a degree of movement to be accommodated without revealing any clear indications of settlement.

In areas where the local stone tended to be permeable there was often a need either to render externally with a lime–sand mix or to apply coatings of limewash. Limewash coatings had to be built up in stages to achieve adequate protection and required the addition of a waterproofing agent. Beeswax and linseed oil are known to have been used, but it was the more usual practice to add hot tallow tempered with alum, which helped to bind the mix because the fat was saponified by the lime to form water-insoluble calcium soap compounds. The chemical conversion also acted as a hardening agent and inhibited surface wear.

All masonry work progressed in lengths using the *virga-geometralis*, which was a measuring rod about 6 feet (1.8 m) in length. A simple plumb bob (*pedicula*) fixed the vertical and an elementary level, termed a *coaequo*, the horizontal (Fig. 27). Stones in freestanding columns should be naturally bedded but at times they may be found face bedded, which

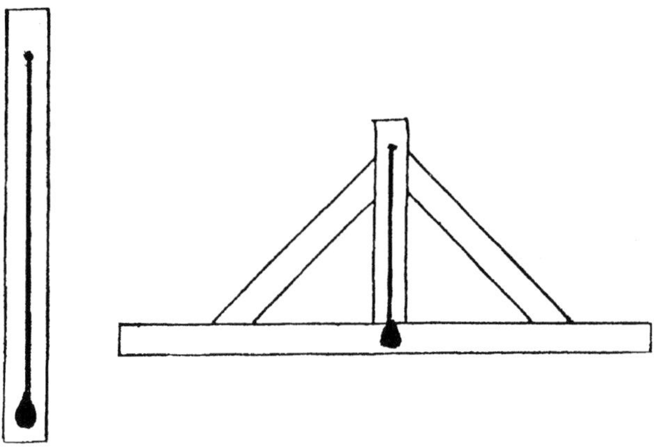

27. Plumb line *(left)* and level *(right)*

is bad practice. Similarly mullions and associated features need to be naturally bedded, but tracery has to be placed in a way that ensures it is set at right angles to the line of thrust (Fig. 13, see bedding planes). Some documents may contain references to tooth bedding, which is another term for vertical bedding.

Reuse of Old Stone

Reference has already been made to the Saxons reclaiming brick and stone from Roman works for church building (*spoila*); this habit was continued by the Normans, who in turn also reused stone that had been produced during Saxon times. Throughout the medieval period it was usual to recycle materials from redundant buildings and ruins, a practice which continued on a regular basis until quarrying developed and became more productive. Quoins that are out of proportion to the rest of the building, over-sized lintels and stones which contrast with the remainder in colour, size and texture are some of the indications that they have come from elsewhere. The emergence of a separate quarrying industry had the effect of increasing the availability of new stone at lower cost, but much of the rubble for core filling in walls (the hearting) still came from old or demolished buildings.

It is sometimes difficult to be certain of the origin of certain stones in medieval walling, but often there are subtle signs which can provide good clues and lines of investigation. A close examination may well show that various stones have been cut or dressed in a different way, and there may also be traces of another mortar around the bedding areas of the stone. Long lengths of stone taken from another building were much used as they frequently made good lintels and saved a widespread search for something of equivalent size. Occasionally pieces of broken monuments, memorials and similar are also found in walls, usually in the less conspicuous parts.

Reclamation was not only directed towards the stone used in walling but also involved various other features and elements. Parts or the complete stonework for windows, doorways, arches and similar items often came from another building. The Dissolution of the Monasteries later provided a valuable source for high-quality artefacts, including capitals, columns and bases. Some of this may have weathered differently to other stones within the same church, and the signs of this may still be discernable even after such a long period of time. It was often the practice to lay reused stone in reverse, with the original face set inwards and the back becoming the new outer face. Another technique was the recutting, trimming or the redressing of the face of the stone.

Buildings that had been badly damaged by fire invariably became a useful source of supply. When subjected to extreme heat, the structure of stone changes, usually identifiable through an alteration in colour. Stones from igneous formations, such as granite, can suffer a considerable loss of strength after a fire and are less likely to have been utilised in this way. Heat can change the colour of limestone to brown, buff or reddish brown, while sandstone normally goes pink or reddish brown, the brown/red in both stones being a reaction from hydrated iron oxide. White magnesian limestone tends to turn grey. In most cases the difference in colour only occurs on the face directly exposed to the heat of fire, it not having penetrated into the full body of the stone. If individual stones spaced far apart show signs of fire damage, and the mortar all around has been left untouched, this is a clear sign that the stone has been taken from salvage. On the other hand, if all stones in a particular area have been discoloured, it is a good pointer to a fire having occurred in that vicinity; the state of the original lime mortar should be included in any examination. Normally such a change occurs on the inside of a building only, but it can occasionally be found on the outside face if there has been close proximity to intense heat. When reclaimed dressed-stone artefacts have been in contact with fire, this will show up not only in the colour but often in fine crazing to the surfaces. Components worked from sandstone are also likely to have suffered much splitting if, after being affected by heat, they have undergone a sudden drop in temperature through watering.

Coade Stone

As industrialisation expanded and new materials began to be developed, the quest for innovative and labour-saving ideas came very much to the fore, particularly in the latter part of the eighteenth century. The introduction of Coade stone is one example and was an idea that enjoyed much popularity until production ceased in 1840. First developed in 1769 as a unique form of artificial stone, it came to the market as a ready-made labour-saving product. It was cast in a variety of tastes and fashions, and can be found in later churches and in the additions to some older churches, although it is more likely to be seen in church statuary and on memorial plaques and tombs. The wide range of available styles and units included the components for arches, string courses, door and window dressings and classical details. The exact nature of the process and the constituent materials were never revealed by the company, but investigations have suggested that it is derived from ball clay along with other ingredients such as ground flint, quartz and soda-lime-silica glass. In essence it is really a form of stoneware and chemically is very different to natural stone. Nevertheless, it has an uncanny resemblance to the genuine material and is constantly mistaken for it. A useful indication is the presence of endless repetition of a feature without the slightest sign of any variation. Ironically, Coade stone also shows less weathering or water staining than would normally be expected from natural stone. On the other hand it seldom acquires the rich patina so frequently found on mature natural stone.

The Structural Use of Buttresses (Columpna)

The way in which the very early builders used buttresses indicates they did not always know how to use them to the best effect, and it was not until the Gothic period that there was a full understanding of how dimensions and proportions could be maximised for full structural support. Buttresses counter the weight and outward thrust of roofs and vaulting and compensate for the weakening effects of window and door openings. They also contribute towards overall stability and achieve economies in material and labour costs by avoiding the need for extra-thick walling. The types of buttressing seen in the construction of churches are the angle, setback, clasping, diagonal and flying forms. Angle buttresses meet at a 90-degree angle at the corners or face of a wall. The setback form is similar but is placed slightly away from the quoins to expose the corner masonry. Clasping buttresses were used less frequently on the main structures and are more likely to be seen supporting church towers. Diagonal buttresses protrude at an angle from the corners (Figs 28 and 29).

A flying or arch buttress (*arcboutant*) is made up of an independent buttress connected to the main structure by means of an arch (the flying buttress) (Figs 30 and 31), which in the larger cathedrals and churches can occur in tiers. The counter-thrust this provides enables loads to be transmitted directly to the ground by way of freestanding outer buttresses. The system is a vital element in the design of many Gothic churches and was fundamental to the stability of a structure. The flying buttress first appeared in the Early English period and gradually developed and became more prominent from then on. The pinnacles at the terminations of the independent buttresses provide extra weight towards the resistance of outward thrust by imposing an additional compressive downward force (see Fig. 30).

In appearance, Saxon buttresses are more like pilasters and have shallow projections. They were applied as stiffening, used where there was a need to provide extra support at points which took an additional concentration

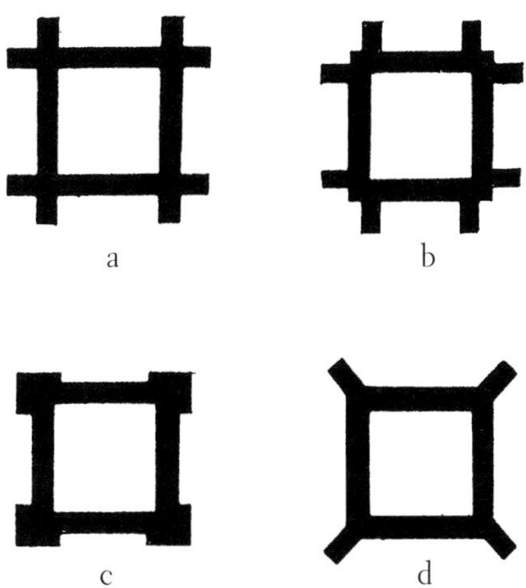

28. Buttresses – (a) angle; (b) setback; (c) clasping; (d) diagonal

29. Buttress cappings – (a) Saxon; (b) early Norman; (c) late Norman or Romanesque; (d) Early English; (e) Early English; (f) Decorated; (g) Perpendicular; (h) stepped and plain-capped buttress

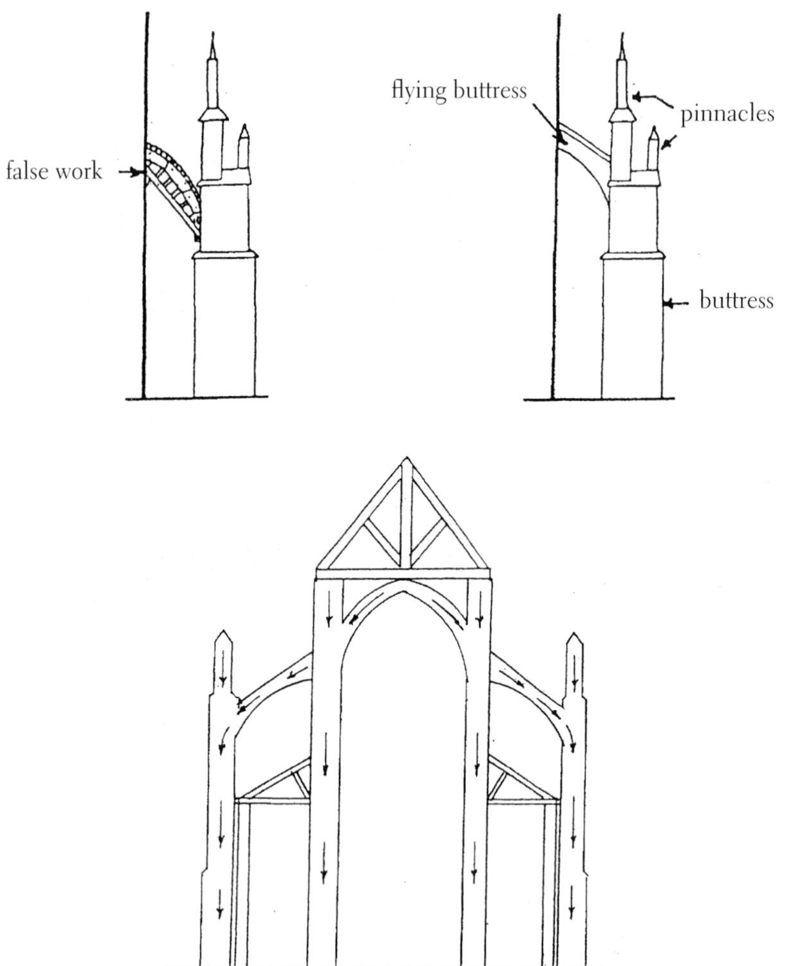

30. Flying buttresses and load paths. *Top:* false work (also called form work) is fixed in position and the inner face greased. The false work is not removed (struck) until the mortar has fully set. *Bottom:* the arrows indicate downward thrust loads from the main walls, the high-level vaulting, the buttresses and the flying buttresses. The forces created by wind loads on the roof and walls are also accommodated in this way. The flying buttresses and pinnacles require sufficient strength to resist powerful eccentric loading caused by gale force winds.

31. Flying buttresses

of weight. Buttresses of the Norman period have a generous breadth but a small projection and are usually in the same form and style from the ground to the top. They are taken up to the eaves or have been finished with an outward slope. In later Norman work the projection was slightly increased and small shafts were sometimes worked on the angles.

From the Early English period onwards buttresses took a different form and were narrower with a much greater projection. Most continued to the full height of the wall and were usually interrupted at stages with a successive reduction in the projection. The angles are sometimes chamfered or moulded. The set-offs are sloped outwards or are terminated at the head with a triangular capping which is found above or below the parapet (see Fig. 29). It is an arrangement which can sometimes give the impression of pinnacles being set into the parapets. There are three different stages of development, beginning in the Early English phase with angle buttresses being the most used. Set-back forms were occasionally provided and the clasping types were far less common. In the Decorated period buttresses were usually worked in stages, often ornamented with niches, crockets and other carved decoration. In the larger churches it was more usual to terminate the tops with pinnacles, and they are more likely to be found set diagonally. In the Perpendicular phase buttresses usually have fewer or no progressive reductions in the outward projections, and they more often go to the full height of the wall and are capped with large pinnacles. There are also differences in ornament and other decoration, and carved panelling is most common. A cap to a buttress which is pyramid shaped with finials and sometimes crockets is described as a pyramidion.

The Medieval Mason

The early builders were not skilled masons and simply assembled stone in a convenient and suitable way with little regard to refinement. The arrival of the Romans substantially altered the manner in which stone was worked and dressed; the expertise came from highly trained engineers in the legions who introduced new techniques and methods, including the use of the three-legged lewis for lifting blocks (Fig. 2c). After the departure of the Romans the Anglo-Saxons were unable to match their prowess, and the overall quality of Saxon work was much cruder and rather featureless. The credit for improvement in quality must go to the Normans for the way they raised the standard of stonework in England. It was achieved mainly through their massive church development and rebuilding programmes, which resulted in the craft of the mason being raised to a level of elite status for the rest of the medieval period. Some of our finest cathedrals and churches date from the Norman period and are the result of an influence which effectively standardised the use of many units, sizes and shapes for a long period of time.

The building process began after the masons had received from the quarry crudely cut blocks which had to be worked to the required size and finish. During the early part of the Norman period rough quarry stones were split with a jadd – a type of pick used to cut through a block. Later this practice changed and, still using the jadd, V-shaped slots were made along the cutting line into which were then inserted metal wedges. On hitting the wedges with a heavy hammer the stone separated into two pieces; the technique was the forerunner to the still-used plug-and-feather system. Feathers are specially designed pieces of metal made to receive a close-fitting wedge and when hit with a hammer they exert a force that makes for easier separation. Some stones could be reduced in size using a technique known as snapping, but this was only suited for stones of no more than around 6 inches (15 cm) in thickness. A groove was first scored on all four sides and in the same plane, and then the piece was placed on a block with one end projecting outwards. Protected by a flat wooden pallet the projecting end was given a few sharp blows with a mallet to produce a clean-faced division or snap.

The work of the mason is usually associated with a simple wooden mallet and a chisel, but in reality a range of other tools are vital, including a much smaller wooden mallet called a dummy for finer work. To obtain the correct outline to the stone the process began with a hammer and pitcher – the latter had a flat blunt working edge which was used to knock off projections and spalls. The rough straight-faced surface was then worked with a mallet and chisel, with a variety of different chisels often being employed at this stage, depending on the type of finish and shape needed. The next action involved use of the punch and, with the aid of a hammer, the mason was able to work down close to the required level. The surface was then dressed with either a claw tool or boaster and sometimes the drag, which was used for a smoother surface on softer and medium-textured stones. To get a perfectly smooth and even finish some stones were rubbed with a prepared flat stone using sand and water, the quantity of sand being reduced as the surface became progressively smoother. Because granite was so strong and dense, it was dressed using a tool called a jumper, which had a wider and flatter tooling edge. The shape of the nosing also made the jumper suitable for cutting round holes in other stones. Later a special axe was developed for tooling granite. Made up of a series of thin steel plates of equal length fitted together and bolted into an iron casting, the sharpened ends on each blade enabled a surface to be tooled to a smoother finish. Very rough undulating surfaces were first worked with a heavy pick to provide for easier axe dressing.

A block with a true face may be termed plain or half plain, the latter describing a rough form of surfacing where a smoother appearance is not material. Other forms of more elaborate finishing include boasted or droved work in which a series of bands of about 1½ to 2 inches (4–5 cm) wide are worked with a boaster and hammer. The scores may be horizontal, vertical or angular. An advance on this is tooled work, in which a series of fine chisel lines are made. This is a feature regularly found on ashlar masonry. Sunk work is the term used for the cutting and sinking of a prepared surface and includes the formation of chamfers and sloping surfaces such as the weathering to window sills. If left in a rough state it is described as being half sunk. There are many other ornamental finishes such as furrowed or fluted in which wide flutes are formed with a gouge. Batted work involves making a series of fine chisel lines, while punched work is where random depressions are made with a punch over the entire surface; picked work is a finer and more delicate version of this. It was often the fashion to cut plain margins around the face edges and these may be square or chamfered. A popular feature at the quoins was the use of vermiculated or reticulated dressing. In vermiculated work the surface has a continuous winding pattern cut into it with a gouge. Reticulated work is similar but less winding in form. Most of these different decorative and finishing techniques are shown in Figure 15.

The large volume and weight in church structures meant that jointing was necessary at points of potential weakness to overcome any tendency for blocks to pull apart or become dislodged. While most stones bedded in mortar remain in a state of compression, the mode of building and the nature of the structural design can sometimes create points of stress, some unequal loading and in places undue lateral pressure. To combat these forces a series of simple and well-tried jointing methods were devised which have changed little since earlier times. Jointing is done by using a combination of joggles, cramps and dowels (Fig. 32). Joggles are used where two plain surfaces are placed together and need a stronger connection. They are made by cutting one side to form a projection while the corresponding other face is cut and sunk to receive the projection. It is used to prevent movement between stones and to help to distribute weight evenly. A tabled joggle is one which has been formed along the bed joint where there is a danger of strong lateral movement. In fine ashlar work uniform and accurate mortar jointing is vital for the correct aesthetic result. Blocks can be laid on thin and carefully prepared mortar beds with a trowel, but the same result cannot be obtained with the perpends (vertical joints). Adequate mortaring and cohesion could only be achieved through the provision of cement joggles in the form of an inverted Y, with the grooves being cut into the meeting surfaces of the stones. These then had to be filled with a mortar grout, the grooves having been roughened to ensure a good bond between the grout and the stones.

Lateral connecting pieces known as cramps are made from hard stone, slate or iron and are used to resist the stresses which cause stones to pull apart. The slate and stone forms are made by cutting grooves into connecting stones – similar to the dovetail joints used in carpentry – into which are fixed identically shaped pieces of slate or stone, which are bedded in mortar. Iron cramps are simply flat wrought-iron strips bent to right angles at the ends and set into a matching recess with mortar. The early use of wrought-iron in this way has ultimately done extensive damage to much historical stonework. The laminated nature of its make-up enabled rapid oxidation to

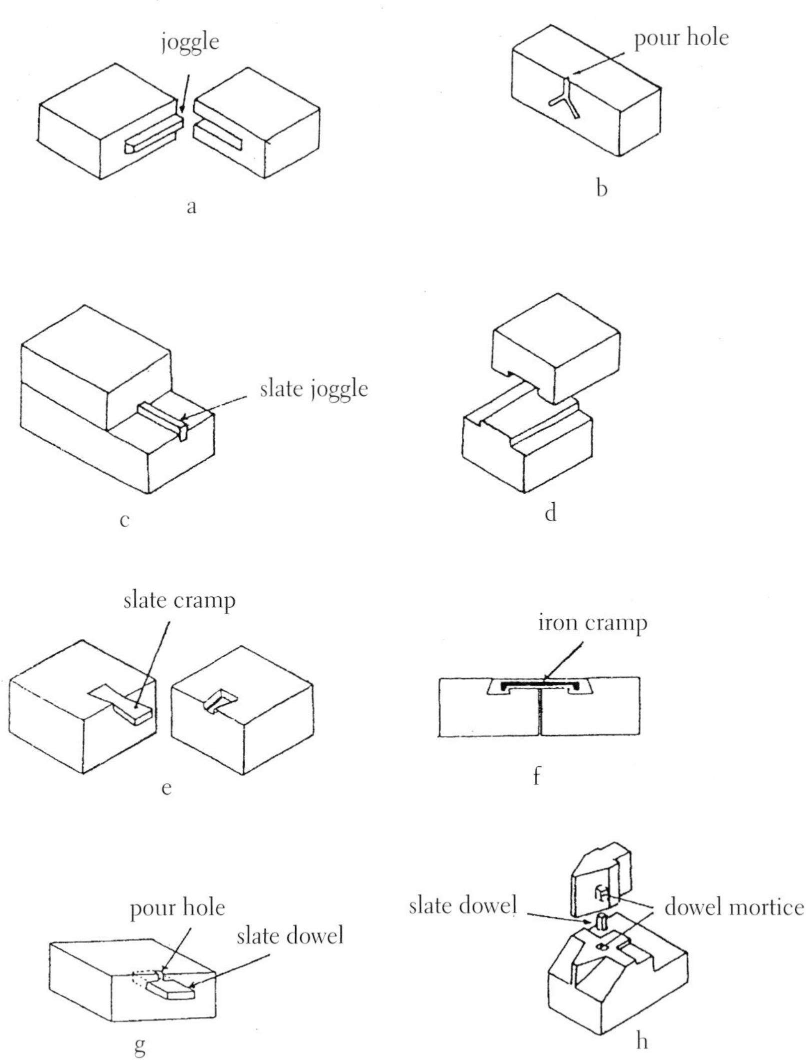

32. Masonry joints – (a) joggle joint; (b) cement joggle; (c) slate-bed joggle; (d) tabled-joggle joint; (e) slate cramp; (f) iron cramp run in lead; (g) horizontal dowel joint; (h) vertical dowel joint

take place, and the resultant expansion from rust caused serious disruption within the body of the stone. References to this problem have been found in manuscripts as far back as the thirteenth century. The efforts made to ameliorate this were never successful, but various attempts were made, including grouting the iron seatings with molten lead and later the tinning of each cramp. Dowelling is also used to prevent lateral movement, with dowels made from stone or slate measuring about 1 to 2 inches (2.5–5 cm) in section and about 5 inches (13 cm) in depth. Sunk into corresponding mortices with mortar, dowels can be used in both vertical and side jointing. In church building adequate dowelling is essential in the high exposed parts where the weight is reduced and the various components are less able to withstand strong wind pressures without additional strengthening. This is especially applicable to the tops of spires, pinnacles and finials.

From the Norman period onwards it was the practice for the mason to put his individual mark or cipher on every stone he dressed before it left the banker (work bench) (Fig. 33). The system served as both a check on his output and to identify his work in relation to his remuneration. The marks found on ashlar work should not, however, be confused with those made for the stone setters, which are known as position marks or the trade signs created by some merchants. Quarry marks were also made to enable the origin of the stone to be checked, a practice which often provided a guarantee of authenticity and quality.

A particular feature of interest in stonework is the masons' mitre. When two pieces of a material are joined at right angles they normally meet at an angle of 45 degrees, but during the medieval period it was often the practice for a mason to work the appearance of a mitre from a single piece of stone (see Fig. 35 below).

A masonry team also needed a carpenter proficient in stereotomy, which is the making of templates (*fourmers*) to enable stones to be cut to the correct shape and size. Made mostly from wood, the templates were particularly important to ensure uniformity in the mouldings, tracery, ribs and similar features, but it was also the general practice to produce full-sized working drawings onsite, from which the masons and carpenters could work. Many drawings still remain inscribed on workshop floors and walls, which were painted or limewashed so that the inscribed work could be more clearly seen and followed more easily.

Elaborate and heavily enriched carving usually required the services of a sculptor (*sculpo*). The blocks in question were roughly prepared on the banker first, and then when they were in position the sculptor would exercise his skill, working from clay or plaster models. Some developed

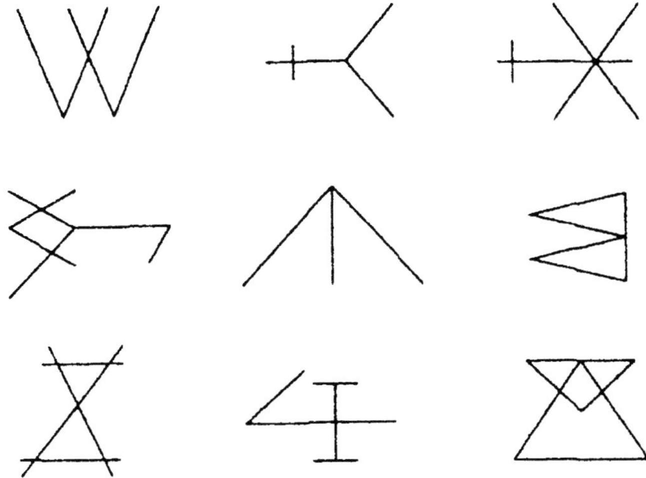

33. Some examples of masons' marks

a speciality of certain features and became renowned for the delicate and accurate carvings they produced, and were engaged as *imaginators* or *entraylers* to distinguish them from sculptors. Shaping in relief passed through a series of different fashions and forms such as bas-relief or basso-relievo, where the figures project only slightly above the surface. When the figures project to half of the correct proportion they are described as half-relief or mezzo-relievo and if more than half they are called alto-relievo. Cut work below the surface is sometimes termed counter-relief.

Stone Stairs and Steps

Except where there were extended widths, rectangular stones each cut as one piece formed the steps (*gradus*) to church entrances, the more common dimensions giving a rise of 5½ inches (14 cm) and a tread of 12 inches (30 cm). Two methods of assembling steps are found: the first is the plain overlapping form shown in Figure 34a; the alternative has rebates between each connection as in Figure 34b. In later work nosings were introduced and rebates improved in design to be more resistant to movement (Fig. 34c). In church towers and turrets a circular staircase (*scalae*) with winders was the more general form of access to the upper levels. Earlier documents also refer to a stone spiral staircase as a vise (*vys* – meaning a screw), the circular part of each winder being equal in diameter to the newel from which the staircase was built up. This continued for the full flight, with the outer end of each step bearing on the wall (Figs 34d and 34e). The method of construction was sometimes varied by the building of a cylindrical shaft, with the inner end of each step being let into the shaft while the outer end was set into the wall as before (Fig. 34f). Where there is no evidence of original stonework open-tread staircases in timber would have been provided.

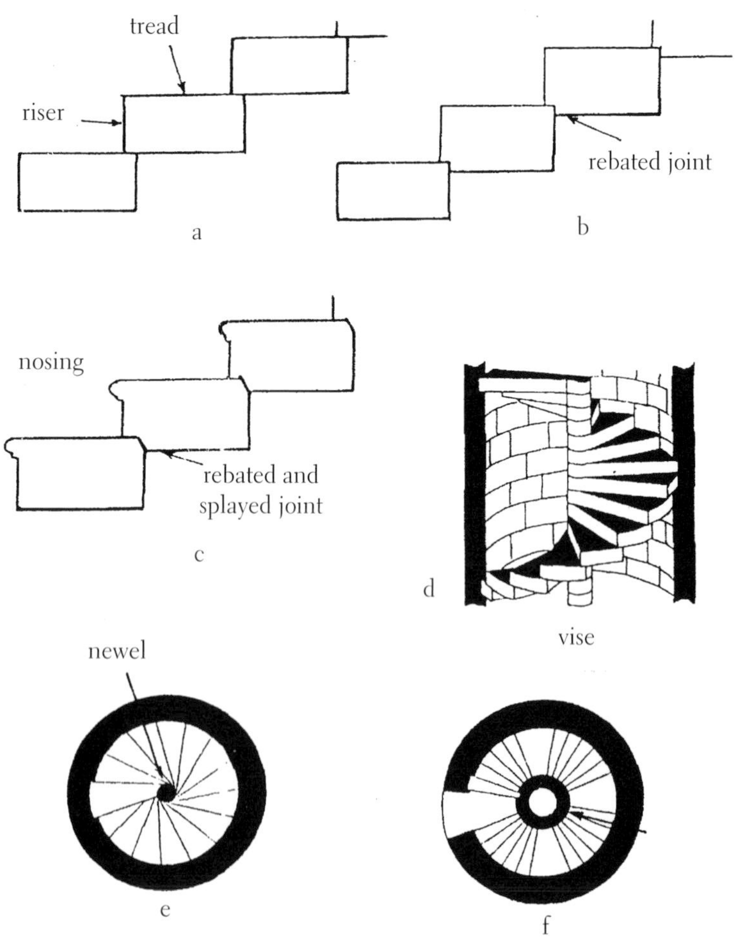

34. Stone stairs

Stone Windows

Without mechanisation and more advanced tooling medieval masons could only use the most basic techniques in the formation of architectural detail and other features. The tracery windows of the Gothic period were especially time consuming, but the outcomes were often of the highest quality. All the mullions (*monielles*) and transoms, including any tracery were made from a series of small component parts pieced together by dowelling the vertical pieces, usually resting on stoolings. These are plain horizontal surfaces which are formed on sills (*soillii* or *suyll*) to make seatings for jambs, mullions and similar items (Fig. 35). All this was first achieved by drawing the required shape on to a specially prepared plaster surface, followed by making templates to match. The masons then inscribed the profile of the template onto each end of a block so the unit could then be cut to the required shape. In work involving tracery the cutting

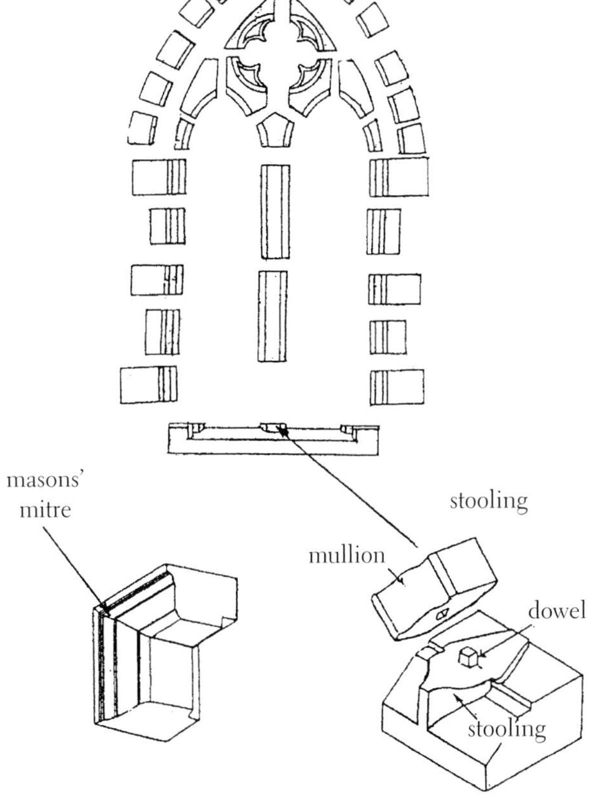

35. Exploded view of a Gothic stone window, showing the individual components

and setting of each stone had to be extremely accurate to ensure the joints were true, otherwise this diminished the strength. In addition to dowelling, connecting stones at the window heads are sometimes found with vertical dovetail-shaped mortices with pouring holes. The mortices were made to correspond with each other, which created a series of small cavities between adjoining stones. After they were placed and positioned, molten lead was poured into the mortice cavities and caulked after cooling. Craftsmen also realised that large areas of window space with little or no overhead weight were more vulnerable to wind pressures, the self-weight often not being sufficient to resist the stronger forces of thrust. As a result it became the practice to load a sufficient amount of masonry above window heads to ensure the mullions were put into a constant state of compression.

Vaulting

The use of vaulting was known to the Egyptians and the Babylonians but it was left to the Romans to develop and improve the way in which it could be used and applied. The earliest type of vaulting (*volutus*) was barrel vaulting (Fig. 36a), a simple semicircular arch similar to that seen in tunnelling, which exerted a downward and outward thrust along the whole length of a wall. When two of these vaults met at a right angle it produced the groined vault, the groin being the connection between the intersecting vaults. A fine example of early groining can be seen at Rochester Cathedral. This method of vaulting not only involved large quantities of building materials but also imposed severe practical constraints on design, application and width of span. If the arcs were taken from the diagonal of a square a problem immediately occurred, as it meant the rise went to a higher point and resulted in vaulting of varying heights. This was partly overcome by using domical or elliptical ribs, but they had the disadvantage of being structurally weaker and often involved stilting the arches (see also Arches, page 71). Nevertheless, improvements by the Normans in semicircular rib vaulting (*ogivis or ogeus*) enabled the use of groins and cross-vaults to be discontinued. The semicircular ribs ran at right angles and diagonals to form a structural skeleton of raised stone bands which sprang from the wall. In addition to giving added strength to the arches, they also supported the infill panels of stone.

The next significant change came with the pointed rib, which – once fully mastered – steadily advanced to create a fascinating range of interconnecting rib patterns. At first the pointed rib was used for transverse ribs only, with those worked to a diagonal continuing to be semicircular.

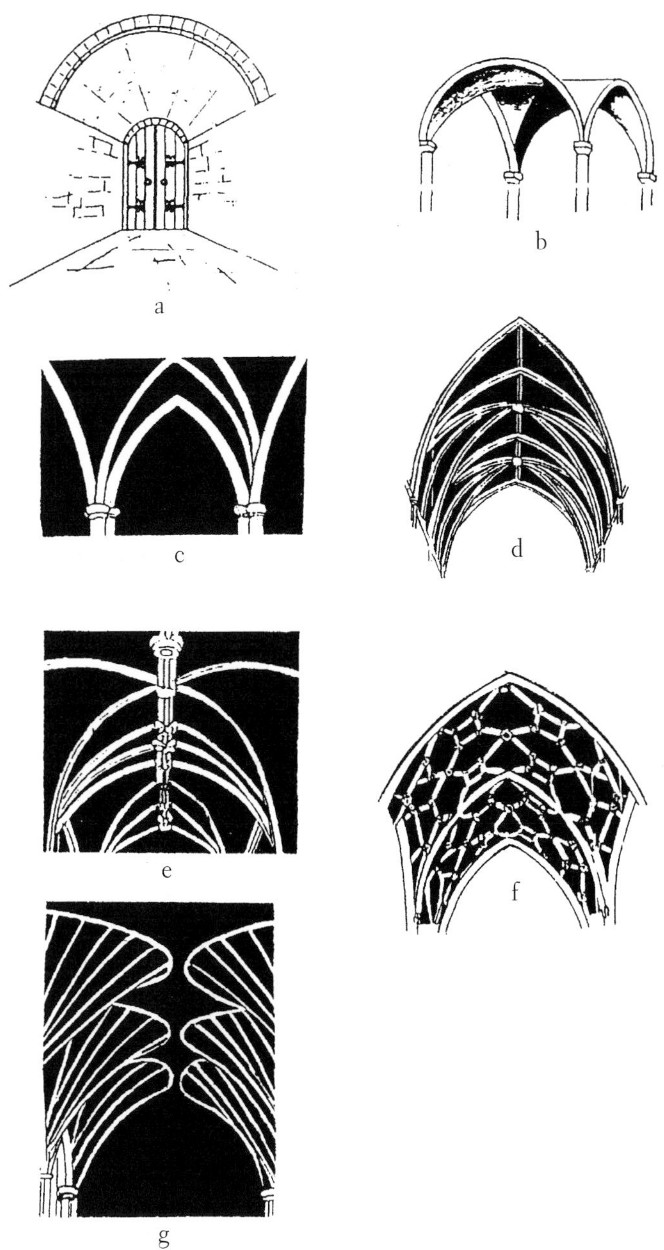

36. Vaulting – (a) barrel vaulting; (b) groined vaulting; (c) quadripartite vault; (d) sexpartite vault; (e) tierceron rib; (f) liene rib; (g) fan vaulting

Some of the vaulting at Durham Cathedral has pointed transverse ribbing, believed to be the earliest example of pointed-arch vaulting in England. Another unusual feature in the cathedral is the use of flying buttresses internally. In ribbed vaulting most of the forces are concentrated directly into the ribs, and then on to the heads of the columns on which they are seated. The weight of the purpose-cut stones placed in the webs between the ribs was often reduced by using chalk or tufa.

Church design is based on a series of bays (*severey*) and with barrel vaulting these needed to be square. The introduction of the pointed arch and flying buttress altered everything and opened the way for the advancement of the Gothic form. Whereas the structural bay had hitherto needed to be a true square, it could now be square or rectangular and for the first time it became possible for all vaulting to be taken to the same height throughout. Empirically it also became possible to use different arch forms by varying the radius of the curvature of an arch, which could be either tall and narrow (lancet type), medium sized (equilateral style) or wide (obtuse), all of which could be applied to varying heights and spans. Nevertheless, while the radius was not tied to the span it was subject to the span not being more than twice the radius. The significant advancement this achieved enabled loads to be taken to selected points instead of the need to distribute them equally. Initially pointed-arch vaulting was quadripartite, that is each part had four intersecting divisions; a later variation was sexpartite vaulting. Both types were often worked in association with a ridge rib that ran between each apex, thereby joining the different bays at the bosses. An example of pointed-arch vaulting linked by ridge ribbing is shown in Figure 37.

The stones making up the ribs were first placed on a temporary wooden structure known as a centring and then set in mortar. The rib stones (voussoirs) were started from a stone at the base termed a springer, and were gradually built up until they connected to a keystone or boss (*bosse* – a lump) at the apex, which formed the intersecting point for the ribs in each bay. Once the mortar had set firmly the centring could then be struck (removed). Apart from being decorative, the boss had an additional function in that it could be used to conceal any errors or discrepancies connecting the ribs. With vaulted ceilings the top surface was screeded with a thick layer of lime mortar as a protection against fire breaking out in the overhead roof space

When vaulting was constructed in series it often meant the same capital and springer had to be used for more than one seating, a feature which was a constant source of weakness. The problem was overcome when the

37. Pointed-arch vaulting with ridge ribbing

capital and connecting voussoirs were formed from a single block of stone termed a tas-de-charge. In the fourteenth century tiercerons appeared fixed to the ridge rib and not to the central boss, a feature which helped to subdivide the load and give added strength (Fig. 38). The next step involved the introduction of the lierne (*lien* – a tie) rib, which formed a series of transverse interconnecting ribs between the vertical ribs and provided additional bracing and stability. Vaulting in a semicircular apse is termed multipartite work. In the early stages of development all ribs were plain and lacked decoration, but the artistic creations so associated with the Gothic style soon extended into rib work with some interesting profiles being produced.

38. Ribs-to-roof vaulting

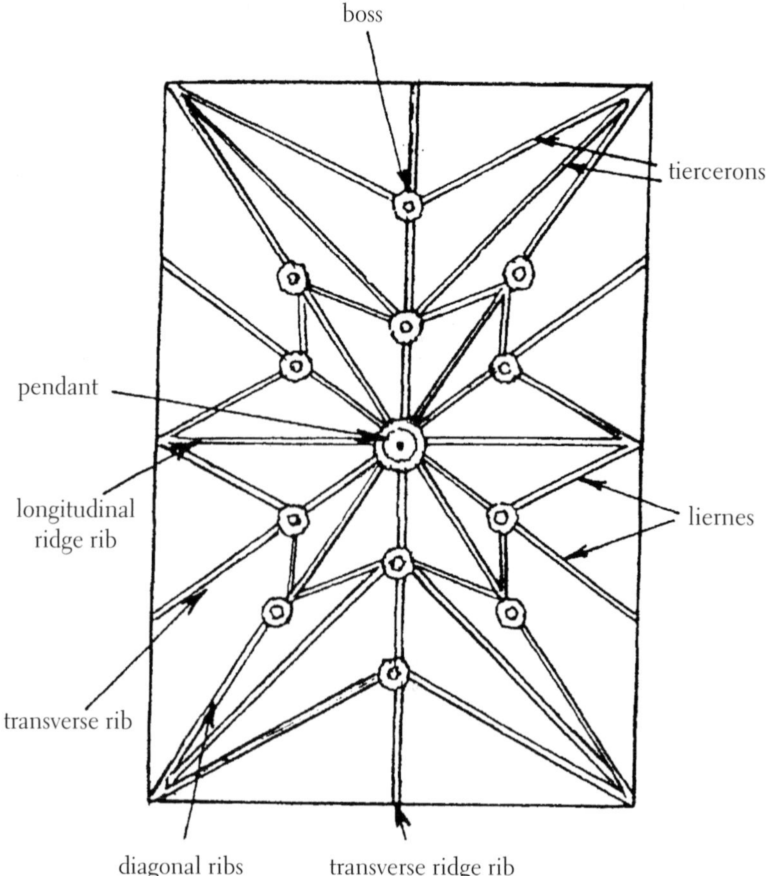

The exceptionally heavy thick masonry walls of the Norman period were strong and robust and possessed more than the required capacity to carry the normal gravitational downward loads and the inclined forces from winds or outward thrust. The innovations which came in with the Gothic form heralded an enormous change and resulted in a new concept in architectural proportions and new methods used in construction. The application of new counter-thrust techniques enabled loads to be transmitted directly to the ground in a way that had hitherto been impossible. In addition, the deliberate imposition of weight at pre-determined points gave improved stability and helped to prevent movement away from the vertical. Once this was established the earlier Norman reliance on mass stonework was completely replaced by the imaginative application of columns, pointed-arch vaulting and deep buttressing in a manner that was nothing less than dramatic. It resulted in walls gradually becoming taller and thinner and in windows and other openings becoming wider and more expansive. In circumstances where heavy pinnacles cap independent buttressing the added weight not only contributes to improved vertical stability but also helps to resist sideways shear at the point where flying buttresses connect to them. In locations where flying buttresses have been used in tiers, the forces taken by the

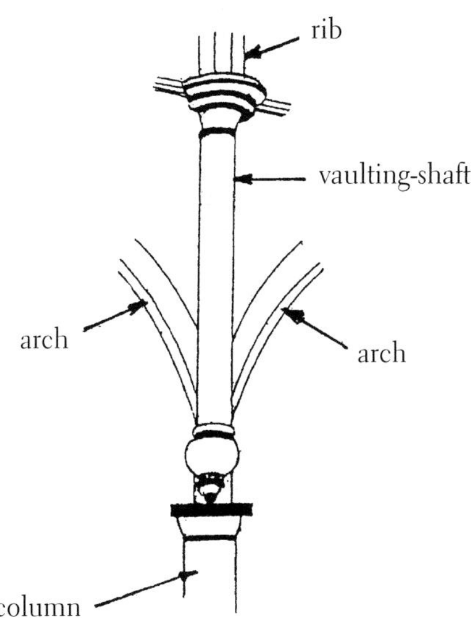

39. Vaulting shaft

lower buttresses reduce the function of those at the higher level to being more of an added restraint against wind pressure.

During the Perpendicular period lierne vaulting improved to become stellar vaulting, which is easily identifiable by its distinctive star-shaped pattern. As the application of vaulting grew, it was found that some loads could be conveyed to the tops of columns without the need for prolific ribbing. The progression to fan vaulting was the ultimate achievement, with the concave curvatures of the ribs radiating out to connecting semicircular ribs. Fine examples of this can be found at Gloucester Cathedral and Sherborne Abbey in Dorset. Individual ribs sometimes rest on vaulting shafts (Fig. 39). In the Norman and Early English periods vaulting shafts were taken from floor level, but in later work most are found resting on the capitals of columns or on corbels. In a few cases they have been placed between the springing of juxtaposed arches; a particularly good example of this is at Netley Abbey.

~

Key Points

Saxon	Remaining evidence indicates all vaulting was based on the techniques used by the Romans.
Norman	Roman system used until the introduction of transverse and diagonal ribs. A great advance was made with the appearance of pointed ribbing.
Early English	The adoption of the pointed arch surmounted the difficulties previously encountered with semicircular vaulting. Intermediate ribs known as tiercerons introduced, followed by ridge ribs.
Decorated	Lierne ribs introduced. By this stage vaulting was made up of transverse, diagonal, tierceron, ridge and lierne ribs, which decreased the size of the panels they supported.
Perpendicular	Intricate stellar vaulting introduced, along with fan vaulting.

~

ARCHES (*ARCUS* – A BOW)

The arch is of ancient origin and was known to the Egyptians and the Babylonians. The Etruscans (800–200 BC) also constructed fine buildings with arches and are believed to be the first to introduce purpose-cut voussoirs. The methods they devised were continued and developed by the Romans, so that they were able to achieve impressive feats in the construction of aqueducts, bridges and other large structures.

In masonry walling the structural function of an arch is to support the imposed load from above, and to transmit it to the abutments in a manner sufficient to create an equilibrium or balance. The wedge-like units that form the arch sustain each other and hold the components together. This in turn allows the load to be transmitted down to the arch supports while the abutments must have the capacity to withstand outward thrust. It is also essential for an arch to be under compressive stresses only and for there to be a complete absence of tension. The various parts which make up an arch are illustrated in Figure 40. The wedge-shaped blocks are called voussoirs and rest on base blocks known as springers, which meet at a specially shaped keystone at the apex. The springing line is the level at which the arch springs, which is usually taken from a projection called the impost (*impositus*). The sections of walling immediately below the springing points upon which an arch rests are the abutments. The outer curve of the line of the voussoirs is the extrados and the inner curve the intrados. The under-surface is termed the soffit. The span of an arch is the distance between the supports or abutments. The rise (height) is measured from the centre of the springing line to the highest point of the intrados. Medieval arches appear in a great variety of forms and are scribed from arcs, as shown in Figure 42. The various components were formed to the correct size and shape from wood or metal pieces termed templets, and were then set in mortar on a temporary timber framing known as a centre (*syntres*) (Fig. 41). After the mortar had set the framing was removed.

Mention has already been made of how the height of a pointed arch can be taken to almost any degree, a development which was to have a profound influence on the progression of Gothic architecture. In relation to a given span a pointed arch also exerts a lower outward thrust. Nevertheless, in some work the early medieval masons did not always follow practices which we regard as necessary today. Various elements, especially the voussoirs, can be found badly placed and of irregular size, while the keystones have not always been adequately fixed, and on occasions springers can be seen to be poorly set. The illustration in Figure 43 is an interesting variation in

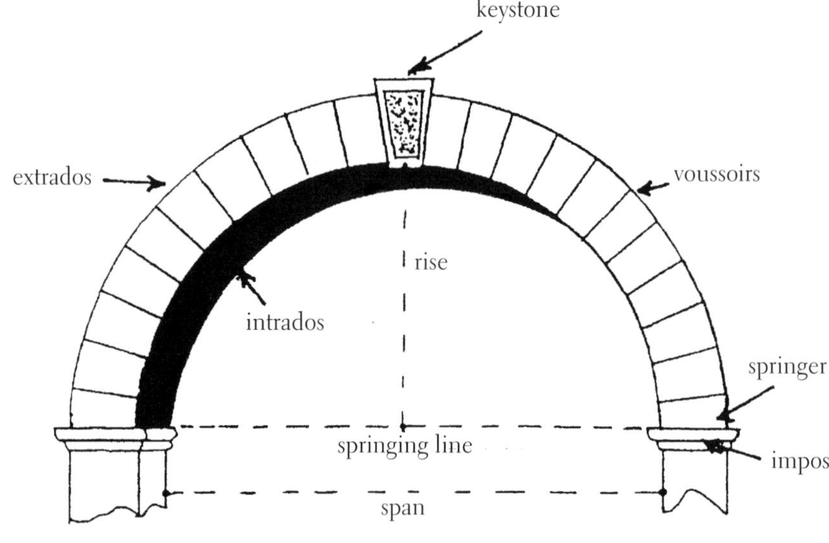

40. Parts of an arch

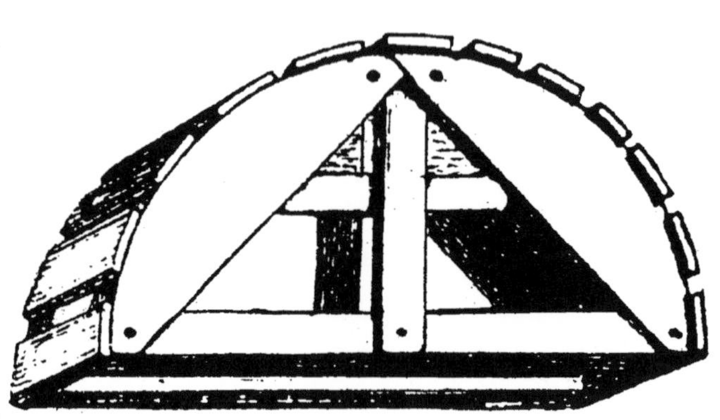

41. Timber centring used to build an arch

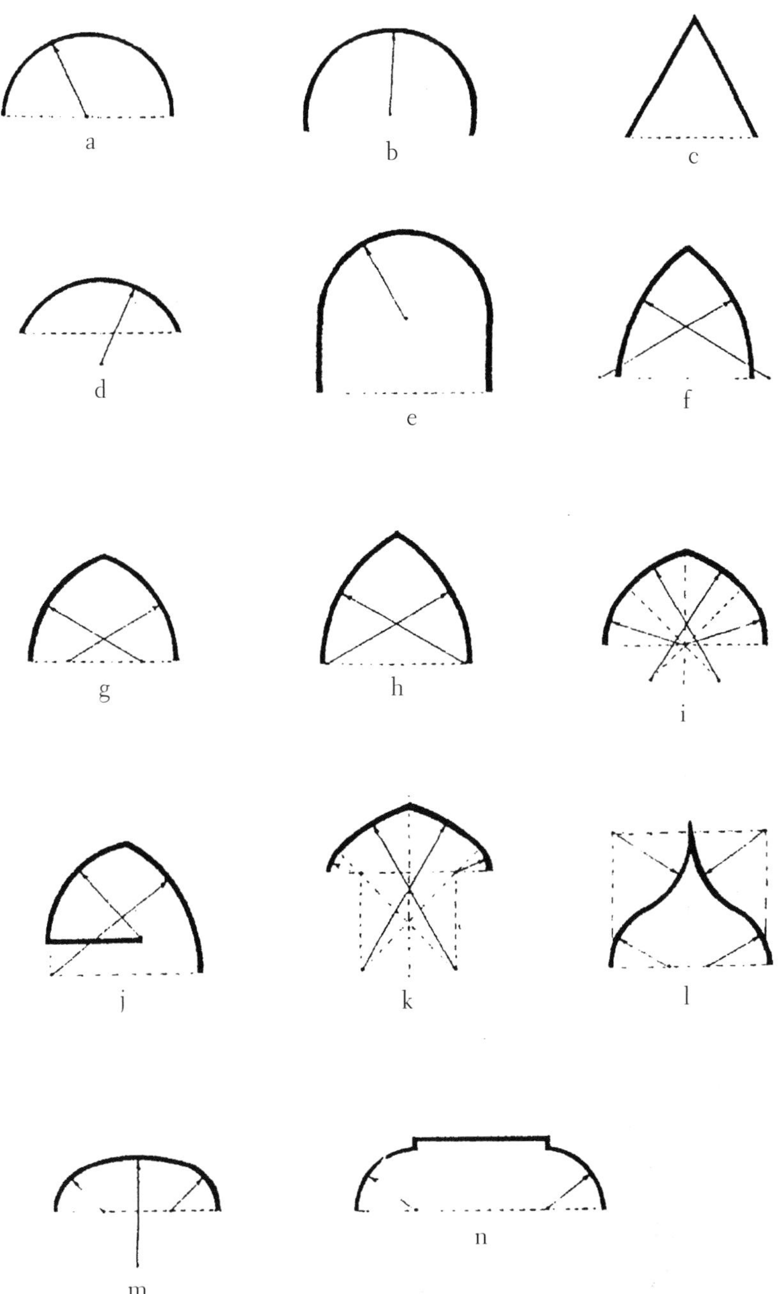

42. Different arch forms – (a) semicircular; (b) horseshoe; (c) triangular; (d) segmental; (e) stilted; (f) lancet; (g) obtuse; (h) equilateral; (i) three centred; (j) rampant; (k) four centred; (l) ogee; (m) basket; (n) shouldered

which an early pointed arch has been made from four large pieces of stone. Conversely, in good-quality work the components can sometimes be found strengthened with special joints run in molten lead (see also Windows, page 63). Over time, arch construction has proved to be extraordinarily stable and tolerant to structural movements, capable of enduring considerable pressures before entering into a state of distress. The evidence is to be seen in the ruins of the old priories, where arches have been able to withstand the forces of destruction when other components have failed.

Many of the early Saxon arches are simply two stones set at the head to form a triangle, which causes them to be subjected to transverse stress as well as direct compression. Saxon half-round arches are often rather crude and unfinished in appearance and are plain and lack decoration, the exception being those which have some narrow moulding. The way the stones have been placed, especially when they extend from the front face

43. Stone arch made of four pieces of stone

to the back face, is usually a reliable pointer towards their date. The early Norman arches are semicircular or segmental and as the style progressed they became more decorated with enriched ornament and mouldings. Window arches and doorways also started to become recessed, with some being given double or treble recessing. There are also clear differences in construction from the Saxon style. Due to the extra wall thickness Norman semicircular arches seldom have individual stones running from front to back; it was more usual to confine the use of cut stone to the face, with the remainder being in rubble.

The lancet arch was dominant throughout the Early English Gothic period (c. 1200–72) but the equilateral, obtuse and segmental forms were also in use. Towards the end of this phase arches with trefoils, along with other foil designs, began to appear more frequently in church building. The shoulder arch also came in at around this time for use over doorways, a feature which went on into the Perpendicular period. While the lancet arch continued to be used during the Decorated period (c. 1272–1349) which followed, the equilateral arch and the obtuse arch along with the segmental arch are particular features of the phase. Ogee arches also came in at about this stage, with the design confined mostly to secondary doorways, niches and similar features. An ogee arch is a pointed arch formed of two convex arcs above and two concave arcs below (see Fig. 42l). The obtuse arch and the equilateral arch continued into the early part of the Perpendicular period (c. 1350–1539) before being replaced by the four-centred arch. In church work Saxon and Norman half-round arches are often found stilted. Stilting is where the the vertical sides of an arch opening are lengthened before the beginning of the arch curving at the impost (Fig. 42e). Many arch forms are built this way; it is normally used to achieve conformity in the visual line between window heads.

A separate arch known as a rere-arch (*arriere-voussure*) is often found supporting the inner part of a pointed arch opening. It is very much a feature of the lancet window openings of the thirteenth century, and has subsequently been perpetuated in many other door and window openings throughout various phases of the Gothic period. They are readily identified by the clear variations in shape and profile compared to the arches in the external face. A squinch arch is a small arch formed across the angle of a square to support a superimposed polygonal or rounded structure (Fig. 44). In churches it is more usually found where either an octagonal or broached spire or an octagonal overhead lantern combine with a square supporting tower. This form of construction is at times also described as a sconce.

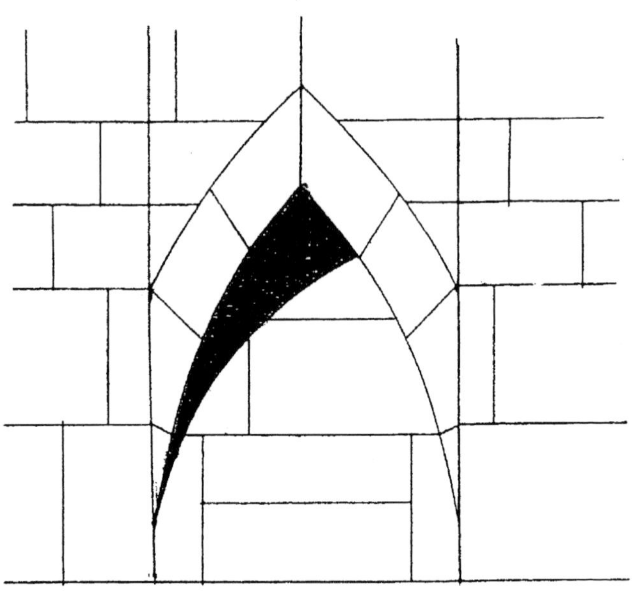

44. Squinch arch

Pillars, Piers and Columns

Church pillars, piers and columns have been used both as a means of support and as decorative features for different architectural styles. A pillar is a simple upright support carried from the ground; a pier either sustains a dead load from a beam or lintel or takes the thrust from an arch. An arch which springs from a pier is known as a pier arch, and a pillar which divides a doorway to house two smaller doors is termed a trumeau. In church building piers or columns are mostly used to support the arches that form the arcade between the nave and the aisles. A column is a vertical support consisting of a base, shaft and capital. The base is the lowest part of a column or pilaster upon which the whole rests. A pedestal is the structure supporting a column and has three elements: the base, the dado and a cornice upon which the column stands. The shaft is the section between the base and the uppermost part, which is the capital. An engaged, applied or attached column is one where a part is attached to the wall, and in any situation where they are used in pairs they are described as coupled. Shafts on engaged columns and extended shafts to vaulting are termed *en delit* if they stand in front of a pier and are not worked from the same block. A small or miniature column is termed a colonnete. Entasis is where a slight convex curve is made in a shaft's vertical profile and is formed to counteract the optical illusion of concavity. It occurs some distance above the base, and the difference in the line is only slight. Depending on how they have been arranged, central shafts surrounded by slender columns are described as being grouped, clustered or compound. Intercolumniation is the set distance between columns. When columns are set as a group of four, it is known as tetrastyle; a group of six is hexastyle; groups of eight and ten are octostyle and decastyle respectively.

Columns that feature a twist similar in shape to a rope are termed solomonic whilst those which have entwined decorative vine leaves are known as wreathed. Prominent features in the Classical orders such as vertical fluting and narrow annulated bands around a shaft are also found in other styles.

Most columns and piers constructed in early church building are composite, the outer ring being cut in stone, with the inner core filled with small stones compacted and set in lime mortar. An alternative method involved a series of smaller stones being cut to shape in each course, rather like a jigsaw, and the whole was then set in lime mortar. Later this changed so that each section or lift in the column was cut from one large piece of stone. Known as drum work, this gave much greater strength and stability. In order for the base to be set at the correct level, plain stone blocks – occasionally described as scamilli – needed to be placed between the top of the foundations and the underside of the blocks forming the base (note that the term scamilli is also used in a different but similar context in Classical architecture).

Pilasters and Responds

A true pilaster is a projecting rectangular column attached to the wall, the design of which is in accordance with one of the Classical orders and includes an entablature over the abacus (see page 79). An entablature is part of the horizontal superstructure and is supported by columns. It has three components: an architrave, frieze and head, which terminates in a cornice. The term pilaster, however, is often applied to any column or pier which projects from a wall and is shallow and rectangular in

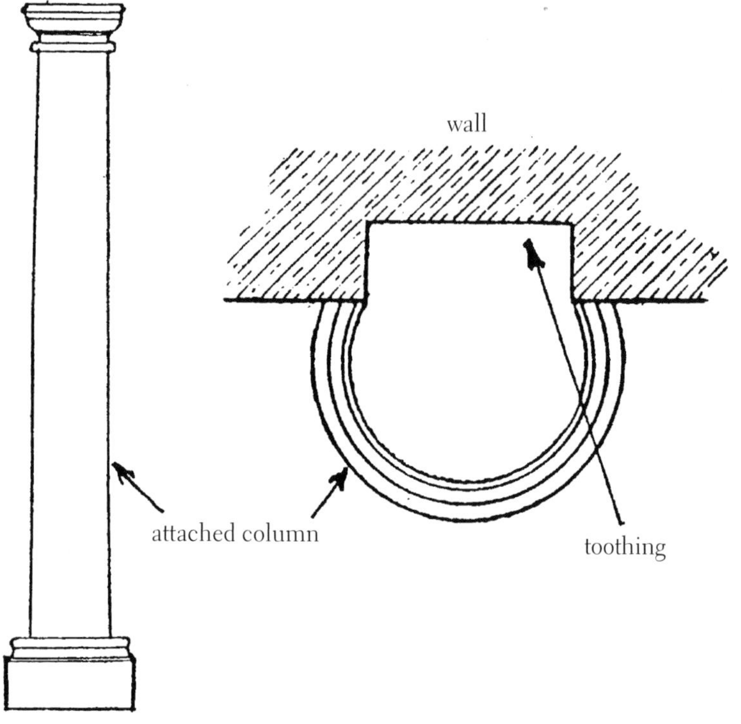

45. Attached column

shape. Pilasters should not be confused with pilaster strips, which are sometimes seen in churches as narrow projecting vertical strips. They are mainly decorative and are usually cut from local freestone and do not have either capitals or bases. While they are a particular feature of the Anglo-Saxon period they are also associated with Neoclassical designs, where they are termed lesenes or occasionally piedroits. A respond is a half-column or pilaster set against the wall face. In churches responds are often engaged to support one side of an arch springing from the end of an arcade. As with pilasters they are toothed into a wall by precisely cut rectangular projections at the back of the stones that form the respond. A corresponding recess of the same dimensions is then cut into the wall, enabling the two units to be firmly bonded together with lime mortar (see also attached column, Fig. 45).

Capitals, Bases and Plinths

A capital (*chapiter*) is the head of a column, pier or pilaster and provides the springing for an arch or the seating for a beam or lintel. The main function of the capital is to provide a larger bearing area than the supporting column. The base is the lowest part which receives the foot of the shaft. In medieval architecture the forms and proportions of the base and plinth were not regulated by arbitrary rules, as in the Classical orders, and a number of variations and individual designs can be found. In the same way, capitals were sometimes made especially decorative and prominent as a crowning feature.

Some bases rest on a block known as a plinth, a feature more regularly seen in Classical architecture. When used in the Gothic styles the plinth is occasionally divided into elements, with the top splayed or worked in a series of rounds and hollows, sometimes with indentations. The true Classical forms are always in accordance with one of the orders but from the Norman period onwards different themes generally developed as a feature of a particular period. Masons and sculptors often created their own images for bases, which sometimes makes it difficult to relate them to a particular period. Identification can also be made more problematical because of the transitional phases between the advent of one style and the passing of another.

At the top of a capital is a thin slab called an abacus, often with some narrowing underneath called a necking, all of which can be plain or carved according to the fashion of the time. Sometimes the abacus widens into a series of upward steps and usually finishes with a projecting edge. Those produced in Saxon times are flat, with a chamfer or moulding, and most Norman forms are square with a plain chamfer on the lower edge. In the Early English period the abacus is more often circular but sometimes octagonal or occasionally square. In the Decorated phase they are mostly circular but can be polygonal, while the Perpendicular period generally had octagonal and more occasionally circular abacuses.

A common form during the Norman period was the cushion capital, which rather resembles a bowl with the sides truncated, the upper part changing shape to form a square. In the Gothic phase the form frequently changed to a shape rather like a chalice, although many variations are to be found. The different styles affecting capitals and bases are illustrated in Figures 46, 47, 48, 49 and 50, and further explanations are given in the sections on Saxon, Norman and Gothic architecture below.

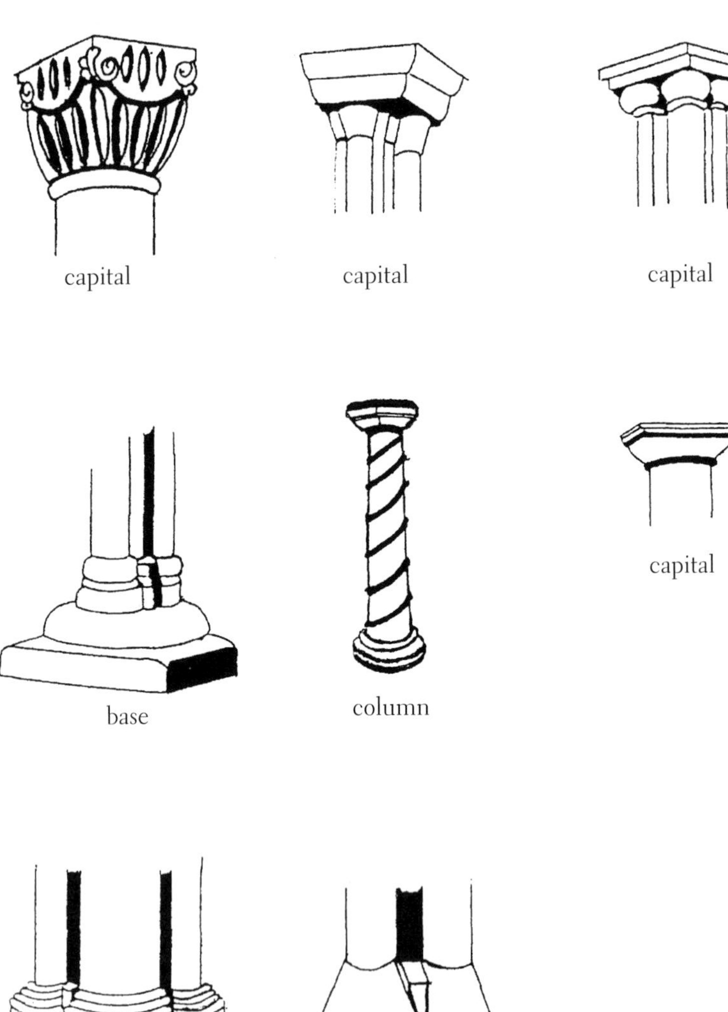

46. Saxon period columns

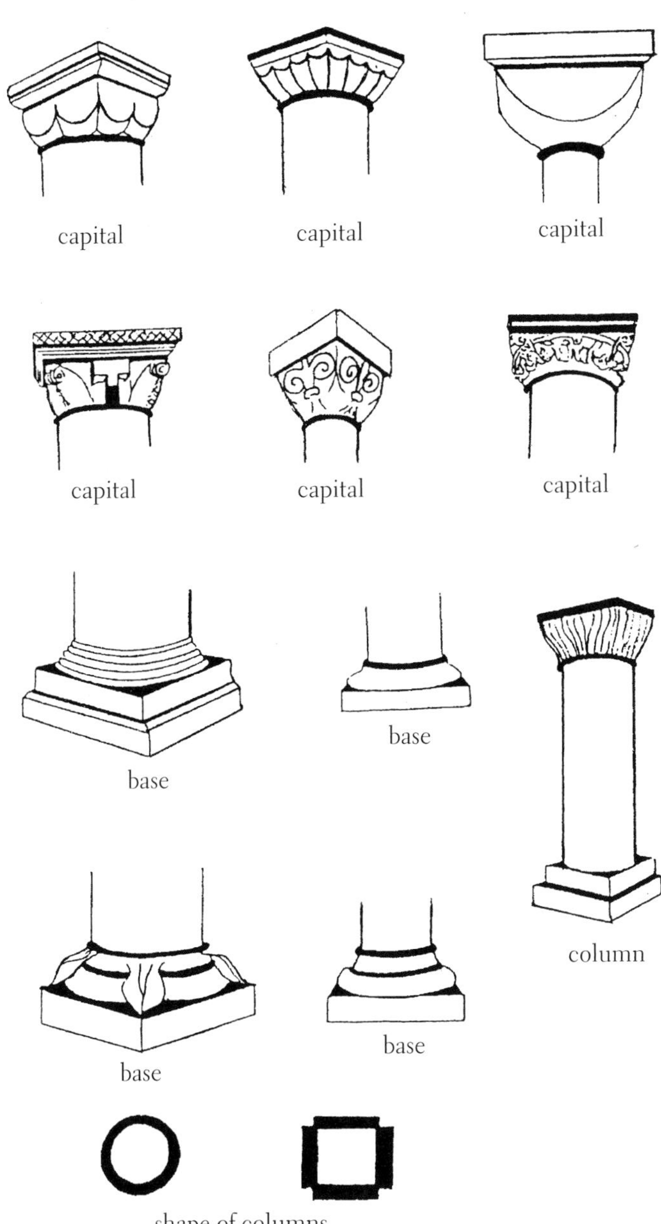

47. Norman period columns

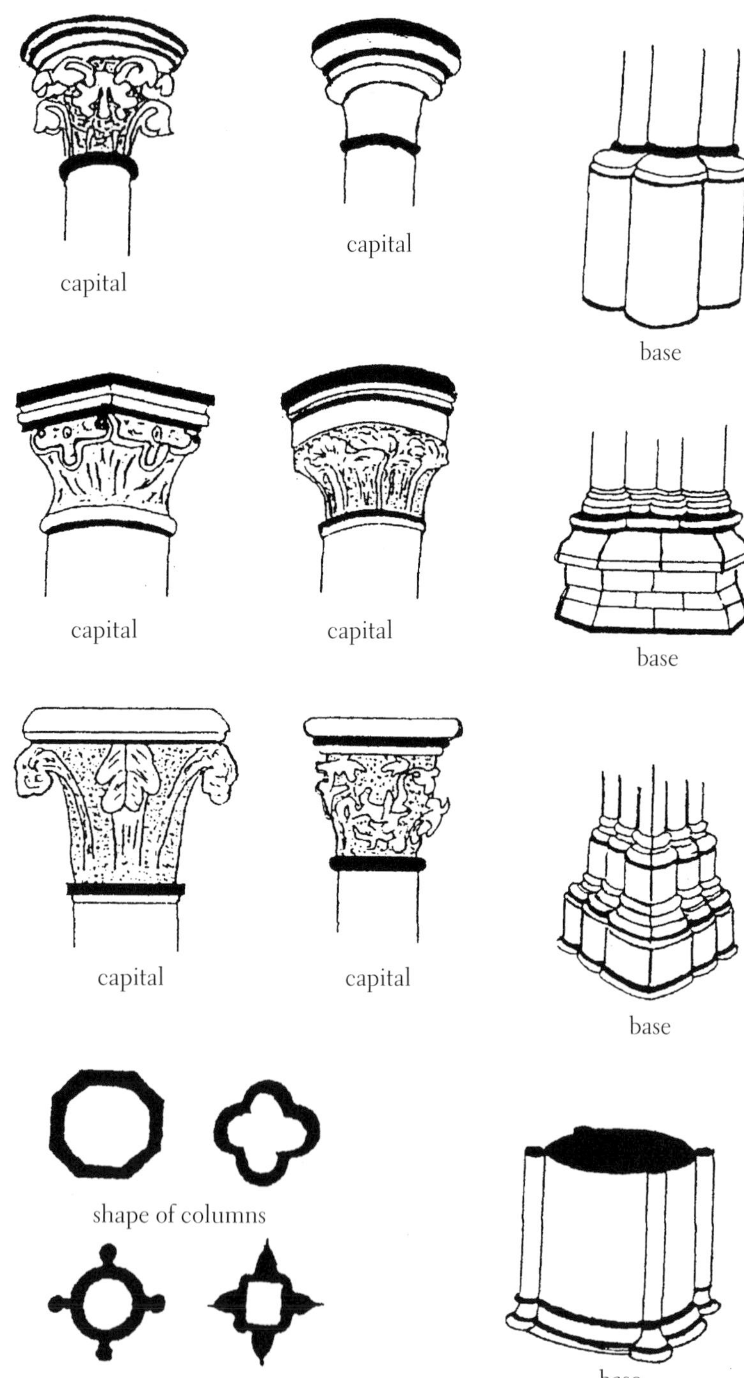

48. Early English period columns

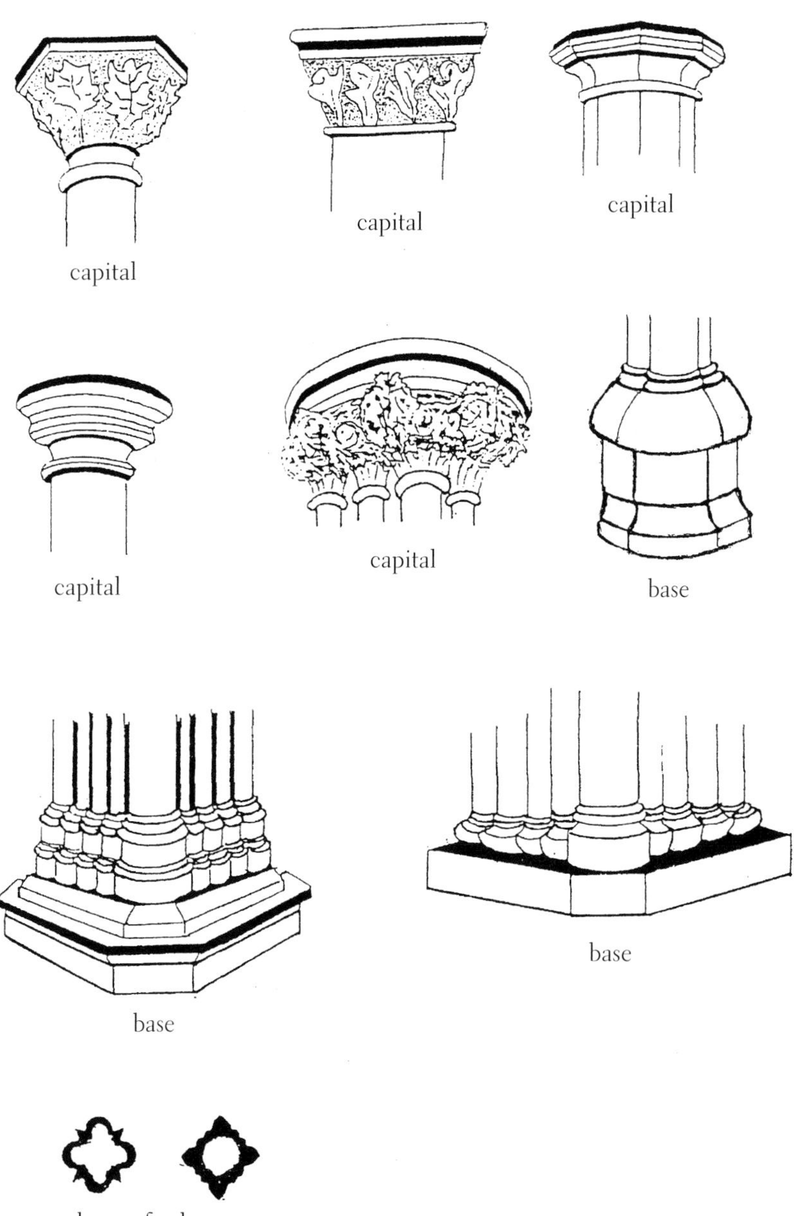

49. Decorated period columns

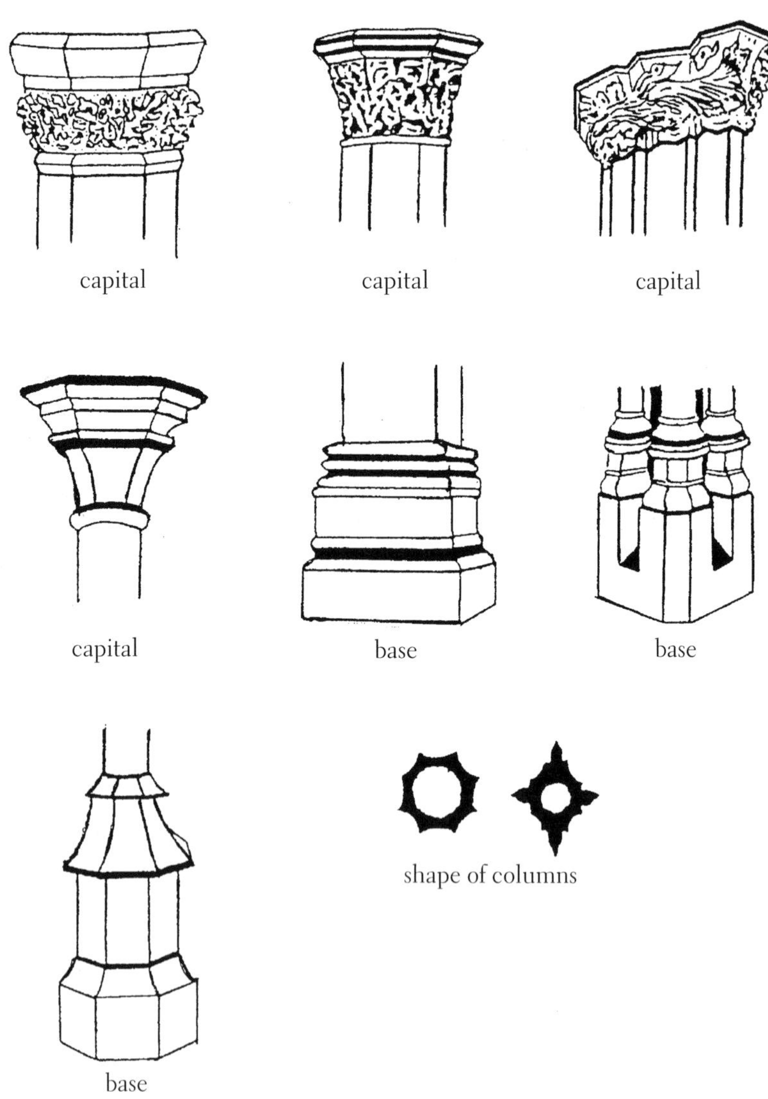

50. Perpendicular period columns

Floors

During the medieval period many small churches had earthbound floors formed from a mixture of broken-down clay and water which had been turned over and worked until it had reached a state of plasticity. Lime or gypsum was sometimes added for improved durability, and then the whole was laid and beaten down to a smooth finish and allowed to dry. Chroniclers also mention small animal bones sometimes being added as aggregate to give extra strength and resistance to abrasion; the process was described in old parish records as *terrare* flooring. To help prevent the accumulation of dust and uneven wear the surface was either covered with rushes or mats or treated with a mixture of soot and water to harden the surface. Fresh soot was put into a Hessian sack and soaked in water for a number of days, the resultant liquid was then drained and applied as a wash. There are also references to animal bones being driven into the clay surface in patterns and then being cut back to give an even face.

The application of lime concrete offered an improvement. It was compounded from broken-down clay bricks and tiles mixed with lime putty and brick dust, and could be laid directly onto an earth sub-base. In areas where chalk was easily obtainable it was used for flooring by smashing larger lumps into small fragments. After being well trodden it was then rammed and compacted until firm. This was followed by a light watering-in that enabled the natural action of compaction to continue and for the particles gradually to re-cement together. In the greater churches the use of clay-brick or tile flooring became well established during the thirteenth century, and by the end of the century it was also a regular sight in many medium-sized churches. A clay tile known as a pamment (*paventy*) appeared as a feature in some areas, especially in the eastern counties of England. The tile sizes normally ranged from 9 to 12 inches square (23–30 cm square) and were between 1½ and 2 inches (4 to 5 cm) in thickness. They were invariably a local product and so the colours and textures varied according to the composition of the clay used. From the eighteenth century onwards brick and tile paving was being used in all churches if more durable local options were not readily obtainable.

As early as the twelfth century marble and mosaic were being used in the floors of the great churches and monasteries. Mosaic work (*opus musivum*) is usually formed from small square pieces of marble ranging in size from ¼ to 1 inch square (0.6–2.5 cm square) bedded on a lime–sand screed. After the various pieces had been fixed in place the surface was washed with a grout and wiped clean with a damp cloth. Once it had set any high spots were ground down to a smooth finish with rubbing stones. Westminster

Abbey has a magnificent example of a mosaic pavement, which was laid by order of a Papal Charter for the coronation of Henry III. The work was carried out by the Cosmati family, who used a prized collection of precious and semi-precious stones together with a range of different coloured pieces of glass. Much of the mosaic work found in ancient churches is *opus tessellatum*, in which small cubes of marble and stone are arranged in geometric patterns. A variation is the *opus vermiculatum* style crafted from different-sized cubes of marble or stone. A contrast to both is the *opus Alexandrinum* technique, where a specified variety of different coloured pieces have been inlaid into marble slabs to form intricate designs and patterns.

The use of natural stone for flooring has a long tradition, it being widely used in the districts where supplies were plentiful and easily transportable. This was especially so in the slate-producing districts where hard impervious slabs with proven wearing qualities could be laid directly on to the soil. In some districts, more notably Cornwall, local slate was sometimes set vertically into the soil and then pared down to a level surface. This avoided surface flaking if the slate was prone to laminating. Certain limestones and sandstones could also be used for cutting into stone flags, but they were not all durable. In the granite-bearing regions roughly hewn flagstones made ideal flooring but the cost of splitting and working them to shape normally restricted use to the larger churches. Cobbles and pebbles set in a lime–sand mortar provided another durable option. A more unusual type of flooring was pitche stone, where stones were 'pitched off' from a large block to form a wedge shape. These pieces were then rammed side by side edgewise into the ground using a beetle (a large wooden hammer).

Decorated floor tiles first appeared in the great churches and monasteries around the tenth century, but initially the high cost prevented them from being available for general use. As supplies became more plentiful the tiles gradually started to become a feature in the less prestigious churches, including in a limited number of small chapels. In churches of lesser importance the use of floor tiling was usually confined to the chancel and sanctuary areas. The tiles produced in the medieval period were lead glazed and contained impurities which produced a yellow tinge with white, brown and red clays, and olive green with grey clays. They can be readily identified by their lack of clear definition and absence of sharp edges, in contrast to those of a later date. The designs were produced in different ways, with the relief in some being raised above the surface of the tile.

Counter-relief was also used, which involved the design being sunk into the surface of the tile. Inlaid tiles are often described as encaustic (meaning burnt in) and were impressed at the surface, and then a contrasting clay slurry was poured into the depressions; the tiles were then glazed and fired in a kiln. Line-impressed tiles were made in a similar fashion, with the design being lightly scored with thin lines into the surface. As the fourteenth century advanced, the use of decorative tiling became fairly widespread and could be found in a large number of churches around the British Isles.

By Victorian times tile manufacture had made big advances and tiles were being produced to standards of fine precision and quality. They were also readily available in various shapes and sizes and in a wide range of colours, making them ideal for use in the extensive church restoration programmes of the time. Apart from being decorative and long lasting they were also easy to clean and maintain. On the minus side the change resulted in many of the original floorings being lifted or obliterated, which resulted in a large number of valuable relics being lost. As a general rule most restoration works at this stage involved chancel floor levels being raised, with the sanctuary floor being lifted slightly higher. It became the fashion to mix plain quarry tiles and decorative tiles of different colours into geometrical patterns, with most paving work being confined to the walkways, the chancel and the sanctuary. The pews were given raised timber platforms fixed over the original flooring. Not all church floors are found to be even or level: one such example is the floor at St Hubert's Church, Idsworth, Hampshire, where the floor follows the contour of the land. In St David's Cathedral there is a rise in the floor from west to east at a perceptible angle, and is believed to have been an attempt to use the rules of perspective to give an effect of greater length.

Church Towers

Church towers regularly dominate the surrounding landscape or roofscape and often reflect the architectural features of the time when they were built or altered. In many situations they are later additions or have been remodelled or extended; some have undergone changes many times over, while others may have origins dating back as far as the seventh century. The early detached towers often doubled as lookouts and as places of refuge and safety from attack, an aspect that is particularly apparent near the English side of the border with Scotland and around the Welsh Marches, where the shape and style can often suggest a clear defensive purpose. This is well illustrated in the tower situated in the churchyard of the parish church at Corbridge, Northumberland, where the exceptionally thick masonry walls, the narrow loop windows and the generous provision of floor space are a clear indication of the original use. In some locations detached towers were built for a different reason: as a way of overcoming the poor bearing capacity of the soil by limiting the concentration of loads on the main body of the church structure. Any tower with a belfry which is substantially detached or isolated from the main part of the church is more correctly described as a campanile. Communities with insufficient funds to finance the cost of a tower usually opted for a single or double bellcote (Fig. 51). This should not be confused with the sanctus bell, which is fixed to the apex of the roof immediately above the connection between nave and the chancel.

Large churches often have more than one tower, especially where the plan is cruciform, and in some circumstances there may be as many as two at the west end and a larger one over the crossing. Few parish

51. Bellcote

churches have more than one tower, but a number have a porch entrance that goes through the ground floor of the tower, and is a feature more regularly seen at the west end of a church. Church towers first appeared in the later Saxon period and at that stage were narrow and square and not particularly tall. They can be identified by small round-headed or triangular window or belfry openings divided by balusters, with the different floor levels often defined externally by plain horizontal strings or bands around the base of each lift. Most had long and short work at the corners, together with pilaster strips. Internally they did not normally have an integral stone staircase, in contrast to towers from the Norman and the following Gothic periods. Particularly good examples of surviving Saxon towers can be seen at Earls Barton, Northamptonshire, and St Peter's Church, Barton-on-Humber, Humberside. At times the mystifying presence of an original doorway, or evidence of one, can be seen part way up the height of a tower. Stepping out at such a level would have meant falling a considerable distance to the ground as there is never any sign of an original staircase internally or externally. Why this doorway should exist is not known, but it is likely access was gained from the outside by means of a moveable ladder and the chamber at this level would probably have been used to keep safe precious relics, jewellery, plate and other valuables. There are also indications in some of residential use in the past – the occupants are likely to have been priests or acolytes. It is thought many of the original Saxon towers had a Rhenish helm similar to the one surviving at Sompting in West Sussex. A Rhenish helm has four diamond-shaped roof slopes which go down to gables.

Norman towers are mostly square and seldom any taller than one tower's breadth above the level of the church roof; some also have the typical broad, flat buttresses of the Norman period (see also Buttresses, page 52). These towers are also wider and more expansive than the styles before and after. Typical features are massively thick masonry walls with round-headed belfry openings, usually divided by a shaft in the middle, over which is a semi-circular arch which spans the whole. In the early examples decoration was kept to a minimum, and there were few or sometimes no window openings below belfry level. Later Norman work often has more prolific decoration, including blind arcading with carvings around some of the windows. When using the cruciform design for their church the Normans had a strong preference for an axial tower over the crossing. An unspoilt Norman tower can be seen at Weatherthorpe Church, not far from Scarborough, and another, which is much less austere, is the central tower over the Church of St Nicholas at Old Shoreham in West Sussex.

Many of the surviving Saxon and Norman church towers have flat-cap or pyramidal spires (Fig. 52). Where flint was the only local material it was easier to build towers rounded as this avoided the need for dressed stone at the quoins, which could incur considerable extra expense, in addition to the cost of cartage over long distances. When correctly assembled this form of construction is strong and seldom requires further support such as buttressing. The round towers of East Anglia are a distinctive feature of the region and a number date back to Saxon times (Fig. 98).

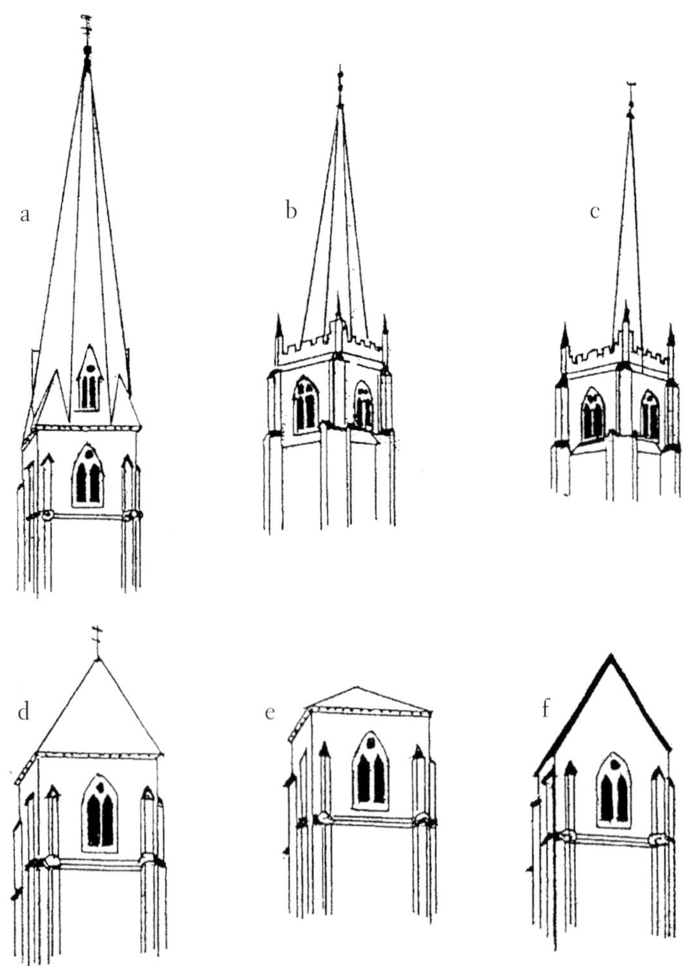

52. Spires – (a) broach; (b) parapet; (c) needle; (d) pyramidal; (e) flat cap; (f) saddleback

The Early English towers are of much greater variety and proportion. While they are mostly square and have reduced widths, a few constructed during this stage are octagonal and a more limited number have a square lower base with the upper part an octagon. They also tend to be taller than the preceding styles and most were built with a projecting stair turret (*toreles*). Towers were terminated with parapets and pinnacles, with small lancet-type window openings, with the louvred belfry openings becoming slightly larger than before. A particular feature of the period is the use of angle buttresses at the corners. In the Decorated style, clear differences from earlier work emerged, especially in the range, type and amount of enrichment and in the scale. An additional item was the use of large heavy pinnacles at the corners. In an attempt to extend the range of the sound from the bells it was sometimes the practice to form small rounded openings known as sound holes in the walls of the belfry. Records seem to suggest the saddleback roofs of the Gothic period first appeared between the end of the Early English phase and the beginning of the Decorated phase. Many are thought to have been intended as a temporary expedient until funds could provide for something more ornate. Towers then became taller and slender, and buttressing changed to the diagonal form, accompanied by more diversity in the arrangement of subordinate parts such as pinnacles, and in the general application of the ornamentation, which included the use of niches.

In the Perpendicular phase, towers tended to be arranged in lifts and there was a tendency for the window openings to be square headed and for stair turrets to be octagonal, the height sometimes extending above the parapets. It became a regular practice to crenellate parapets and the spire was eventually dropped in preference for the flat roof. Parapets also became taller and the pinnacles had crockets (Fig. 53); the extra decoration also extended into the buttresses, which included niches and carved panelling. This is a feature which can also be found in some of the pinnacles. Parapets which have been heavily carved or pierced and give the appearance of a balustrade are more recent and are from the seventeenth, eighteenth or nineteenth century. Axial towers over a crossing generally have a well-proportioned lantern: a good example is the one under the fourteenth-century broach spire at St Mary-the-Virgin in Ketton, Leicestershire (formerly in Rutland). The term lantern is used in church architecture to describe that part of a tower that has been designed to admit extra light, or any other structure such as a dome or polygon with the same function.

a

Parapet spire with pinnacles supported by flying buttresses

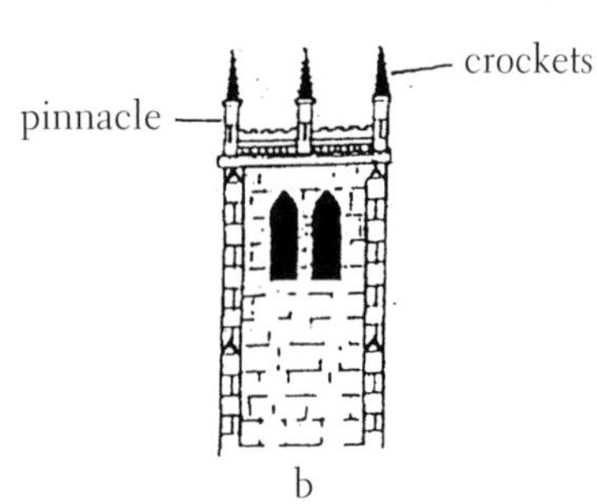

b

Tower with decorative parapets and pinnacles

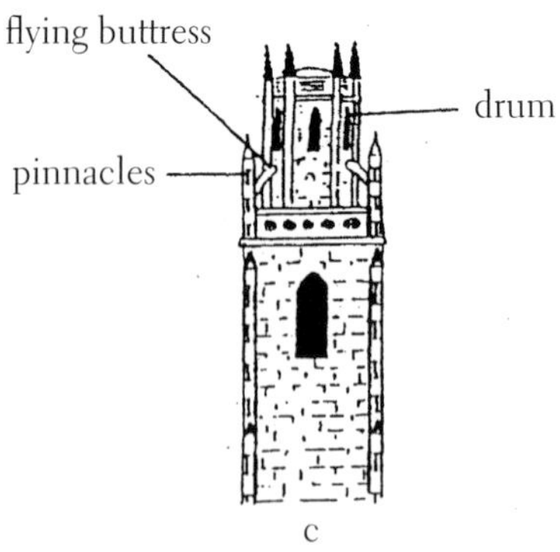

c

Parapet tower with octagonal drum

d

53. Terminations to church towers. Note the difference between the drums in c and d: c has a parapet with low pinnacles connected to small flying buttresses, while d has no parapets and the drum has small diagonal buttresses and tall pinnacles.

Spires and Steeples

Spires are generally recognised as a progression from the early pyramidal roof and are one of the splendours from the architecturally rich medieval Gothic period. Those more regularly seen are the broached and parapet forms, with the needle and pyramidal styles being much less frequent. A needle spire is acute and extremely slender and rises from the centre of the tower in a form which is sometimes described as a Hertfordshire spike (Fig. 52c), well exemplified by the fourteenth-century spire at St Mary's, Ashwell, Hertfordshire. Other examples of needle spires are at the Church of St Peter, Oundle, Northamptonshire, and the Church of St Mary at Radwinter in Essex. A spire becomes a steeple if the construction between the spire and the tower cannot be clearly identified as being in separate parts, and a crown steeple is an open or pierced spire which in outline resembles a crown or helmet. The Church of St Mary at Faversham in Kent has a delicately carved crown steeple with profusely decorated pinnacles. At All Saints' Church in Leighton Buzzard, Bedfordshire, there is a particularly fine example of a medieval steeple which dates back to 1290. A fleche is a small slender spire rising from the ridge of a church roof, and if it houses a bell it becomes a bell-fleche. A good example of a fleche can be seen at St Edmund's Church, Southwold, Suffolk. A spirelet is a miniature spire. Spires referred to as pierced are those which have an intrusion in the sloping face in the form of either a lucarne or gablet or both. A lucarne is a small window projecting from the face of a spire in the form of a dormer and may be capped with either a miniature gable termed a gablet or a decorative finial. The primary purpose of a lucarne is to provide ventilation within the spire and to reduce wind pressure. They are always spaced equally apart to ensure wind is evenly dissipated through the openings in order to reduce pressure uniformly.

The design for a spire had to take into account the forces acting upon it, including wind pressure, the swinging movement of the bells and the pull of gravity. The greatest threat was from strong winds: the force causes a higher proportion of loading to be taken on the leeward side. At the apex there is an additional danger which arises out of a lifting action by the wind. This is the reason for the vane rod, which not only gives support to the weather vane but also helps to keep surrounding components more secure (Fig. 54).

Where spires have been built in timber, the carcassing would have been assembled in one of several ways, with differences sometimes occurring in constructional techniques between the regions and over periods of time. Figure 55 is a general representation of the main parts which most of the

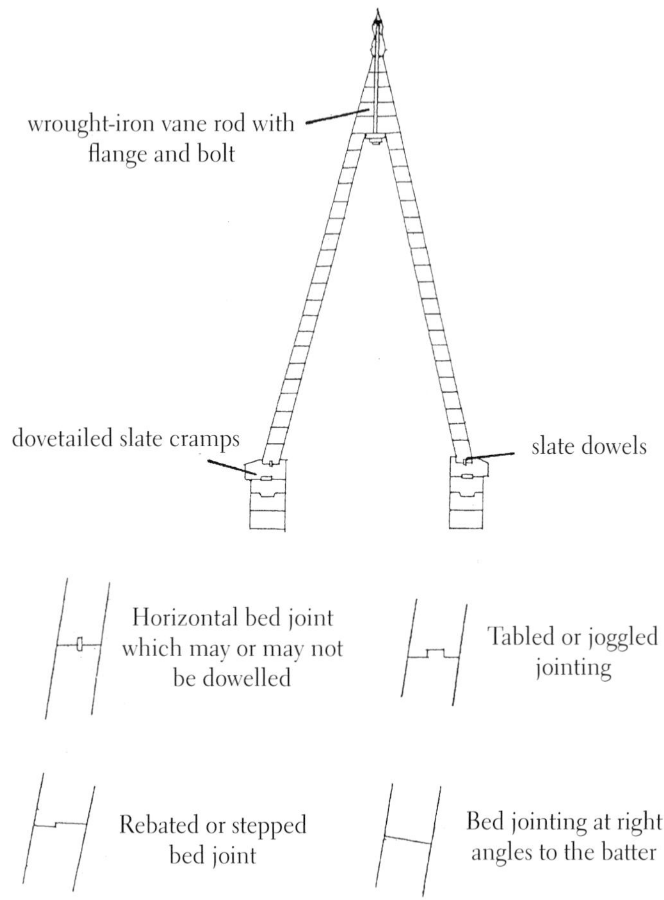

54. Stone spires; various bed joints were used in the construction of stone spires

various methods share. It features a frame base with corner posts resting on beams which take a central spine arranged in a series of incremental lifts. The spars are linked to the main frame by a range of braces and cross-braces notched at the feet to beams or beam plates (*thebes*), together with additional fixing to sole pieces (beam plates are enlarged wall plates resting on either offsets forming part of the thickness of the wall or corbelling). Originally timber spires were mostly covered with shingles, with lead sheet occasionaly being used. A church that is believed to have the oldest lead-covered spire in England is the parish church at Long Sutton, Lincolnshire.

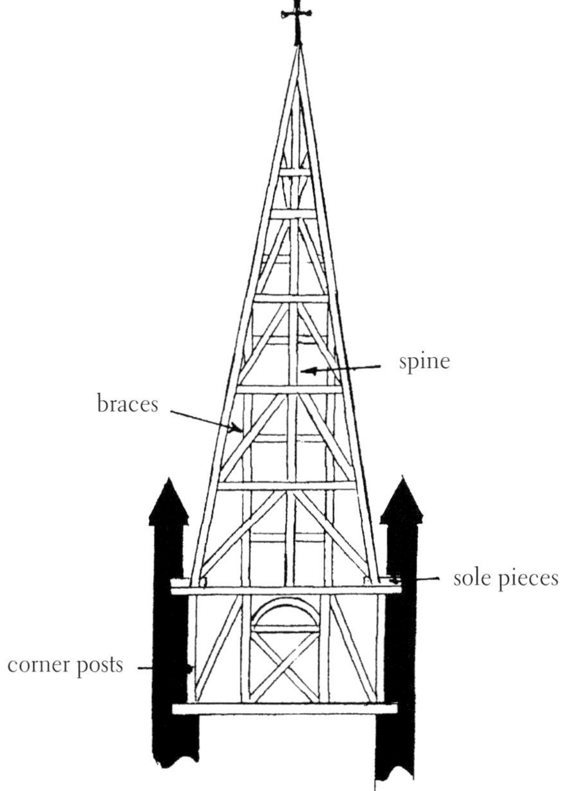

55. Timber spires

In the course of time the shingles were gradually replaced with slate, but nevertheless there is a surviving timber spire clad with shingles at All Saints' Church, Monkland, Herefordshire.

The construction of spires in stone was an intricate operation and every credit must go to the medieval masons who achieved so much. The cutting and placing of each stone required a high degree of accuracy and necessitated good jointing between the blocks (See Fig. 54). It was also important that the spire seating was on properly cramped and joggled horizontal receiving courses well bonded throughout. With tall spires the buttressing was generally taken to the full height of the tower to ensure adequate resistance against thrust. The early stone spires are much lower in height, a good example being the spire at Oxford Cathedral, which was built at the beginning of the thirteenth century. In the South-East of England, where timber was plentiful, the smaller churches often opted for timber belfries placed on the roof at the west end of the nave. Most have a flat cap, with the belfry clad in shingles or weatherboarding such as that seen at Tangmere, West Sussex, Alford, Surrey, and Brenzett, Kent.

The Early English Gothic spires are mostly octagonal and stand on a square tower. They were built to rise from the external walls of the tower in a form known as broached; the octagonal dimensions of the spire were linked to the corners of the tower by means of inverted triangular splays (Fig. 52a). Broaches differ in size and style according to the shape and proportions of the tower, and in some cases are supported underneath by squinches – see also Arches (page 71) and Figure 44 above. The broached spire is essentially an English innovation and most date from the thirteenth and early fourteenth centuries. A rare example of one being built in the Perpendicular phase is at Irchester, Northamptonshire. A rather unusual and somewhat stunted broached spire can be seen at Frampton Church in Lincolnshire, which was built in 1350, and is very much in contrast to the tall slender spire seen at Leckhampton, Gloucestershire. Most broaches overlap the tower underneath and the size of the projection can vary from deep to slight. Nevertheless, an isolated number are found with the spire base flush with each wall face of the tower.

During the Decorated period a different design became popular in which the base of the spire rested behind parapets. Parapets are generally battlemented with string courses, copings and merlons. Merlons are the solid parts between the crenels; the crenels are the open areas of a parapet. There are two main parapet forms: one is the collar type which over-sails the tower walling, the other is the straight-sided type where the parapet runs flush with the tower wall. Both were constructed during the fourteenth and fifteenth centuries and gave much easier access for maintenance to the spire. When the spire was constructed from stone small flying buttresses were often used between the spire and the pinnacles to the tower (Fig. 53a). In the Perpendicular phase which followed, additional ornamentation appeared, apart from the few towers capped with an octagonal lantern (Fig. 53c). A parapet spire of particular interest can be seen at Louth, Lincolnshire, which is 294 feet (90 m) in height and has tall crocketed pinnacles – the height of the spire is equal to the height of the tower. Once the fashion for the parapet had become firmly established the broached spire was more or less abandoned and did not reappear until Victorian times. It was then resurrected by the revivalists who believed it gave a greater impression of height.

Gables

A gable is the triangular upper part of a wall at the end of a pitched roof, although in Classical architecture the same area is always described as a pediment. Old documents suggest that a reference to a gable (*poynyon*) applied to an entire end wall, but over time this gradually altered to describe that part contained within the slope of the roof. The features which are normally present in a church gable are a specially prepared apex stone that meets the inclined faces of the gable (as shown in Fig. 56); kneelers should be set midway along the incline to help resist thrust, and springers normally need to be placed over the top of the quoins. Where it was necessary to provide further restraint against inclined forces in the gable, slate joggles were inserted between the springers and the quoins (Fig. 56).

56. Gable features

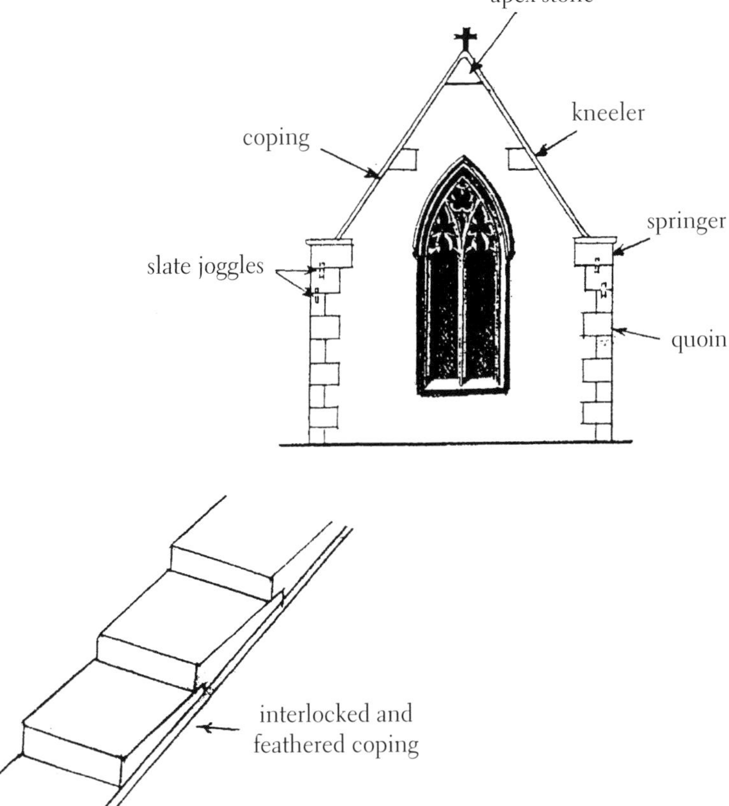

A close examination of a gable will often reveal past alterations, with the profile often having been reset to conform to the pitch of a new roof. Those built in Norman times generally, but not always, have a steep pitch – a feature which continued into the Early English phase. During the Decorated period pitches tended to be lower, especially in the later stages. This fashion continued in the Perpendicular phase, when they went even lower, a practice which was sometimes accompanied by the gables being stepped. Although usually plain, the copings can occasionally be found interlocked and feathered for improved weathering, the lower part thinning towards the top to give a more angled incline for water run-off (Fig. 56). In the Gothic phases some were moulded and in all cases good practice required that the copings were given a projection from the face of the gable with a throating (a groove) underneath to prevent rainwater running down the face of the wall. A variation of the springer known as a shoulder block can sometimes be found, with the upper part specially formed to receive and house the first coping stone.

Plasterwork

Surviving medieval wall plaster (*dauberium*) has a different quality to later work; in addition to being extremely thin it always follows the contouring of the wall face. This is in contrast to plastering from the seventeenth century onwards, which is much thicker and is reinforced with horse hair. A distinctive feature of medieval plastering is the way it is taken flush to the edges of dressed stone windows and door openings; later work has overall coverage and masks most features of this nature. At one stage the Victorians embarked on an extensive policy of stripping the original church plaster from earlier periods and in so doing destroyed many items of historical value.

The early wall plasters are of a lime–sand mix, usually in the ratio of 1:3 and are made from a lime putty derived from almost pure calcium carbonate. Plaster of Paris (gypsum) first appeared in Britain in the mid-thirteenth century and came from France, but the prohibitive cost made it unaffordable in most circumstances. Once suitable deposits had been found in Britain, the use of the material gradually increased, especially from the late eighteenth century onwards, and by the late nineteenth century mass production had made it a readily available material.

During the sixteenth and seventeenth centuries plastered ceilings began to appear in a limited number of churches, and it was an item which steadily became more ornate, especially in the eighteenth century. By this time gypsum was often the preferred material for the plain surface areas because of its rapid set, with lime plaster being more suited for modelling. Much of the latter comes under the heading of stucco-duro, worked from equal parts of fat slaked lime, finely powdered white marble together with lime water and a small quantity of gypsum. Mixes containing lime were particularly suited for ornamental features as the set could be controlled as needed. Plasterers (*daubators*) were able to speed up the setting time by adding alum or potassium sulphate, or they could retard it with the addition of animal glue or urine. The strength could also be increased by including a small quantity of magnesium.

During the Renaissance a few churches built in the Classical style were rendered externally with stucco, which became a low-cost substitute for stone as a similar effect could be achieved by working wet render to look like stone. There can be no doubt that the dexterity and skill used in applying the plaster made an important contribution towards the adoption of the Classical form. Some of the natural cements proved to be ideal for this purpose: Roman cement in particular was not only hydraulic but also had durability, good resistance to damp and could be worked to fine detail. The mix could be tempered to replicate various coloured stones by adding dilute sulphuric acid into the mixing water along with ochres and other colouring materials of natural origin.

A further development with similar properties was oil mastic: the basic component was linseed oil to which was added an inert filler such as well-ground porcelain clay or clean fine sand. Some formulations also included additives such as litharge, lime and turpentine. Application was by way of an initial coating of linseed oil painted on to the background surface, followed by the oil mastic, which was worked in one coat. The first recorded patent appeared in 1773 as Liadet's cement, only to be generally known later as Adam's cement. Subsequently other patents appeared, such as Dahl's cement (1815) and Hamelin's (1817). This latter was made from a mixture of earths, different lead oxides and pulverised glass or flint, which was crushed down to a fine powder and mixed with linseed oil. An additional option was the use of hydraulic lime mortar after it had been suitably adapted by adjusting the setting time. This could also be speeded up with additives and hardened by adding small quantities of magnesium, which made the finish much harder and stronger and more weather resistant. Finer sands were also used, but coarser varieties were unsuited and less workable for intricate detail or a smooth finish. In 1838 a new product known as Keene's cement came onto the market. Produced from hard-burnt anhydrous gypsum and other ingredients, it combined the advantages of a harder surface finish which a much slower set. This gave added time for trowelling and made it especially useful in working intricate detail. If needed the set could also be accelerated with an additive.

Prior to the introduction of fibrous plaster it had long been the practice to work cornices and other forms of enrichment in solid plaster. The traditional method of forming a cornice was done with an appliance known as a horse and runner (or slide), which enabled a continuous moulding to be run in situ. Old records show that the ingredients of a mix varied, the most favoured probably being compounded from mature lime putty, fine sand, some gypsum and animal glue. In 1856 an innovation by a Frenchman, Leonard Desachy, introduced a new technique which quickly became established practice. Known as fibrous plaster, this was produced from gypsum reinforced with hessian mesh and wooden laths cast together into moulded sections. The whole was then firmly secured in position with counter-sunk screws with the joins concealed with hessian over which was laid a covering of plaster.

Smaller churches can sometimes be found to have been rough-cast externally, a feature which is generally perceived as being a modern development as much speculative building has been finished in this way. In parts of the British Isles the use of rough-cast has a long tradition, with the original renders being a mixture of stone chippings, sand and slaked lime. Pebble-dashing is similar, the difference being that the small stones are left out of the render but are then thrown on to the surface later while it is still wet.

Metalwork

The building of cathedrals and large churches could not have functioned without a blacksmith being permanently onsite, which required the provision of a covered workshop nearby together with a stone forge (brick not being used until later). Until the thirteenth century the production of iron could not be properly controlled and the quality varied, although by the fourteenth century advances steadily ensured a much-improved material with good reliability. Apart from those used for the making of armour, medieval anvils were always square, although some had at least one cone-like projection at the side for the shaping of curves. This changed in the eighteenth century, and since then the rectangular London anvil has been the most used. The standard equipment of a blacksmith included bellows, hammers, tongs, cutters, chisels, punches and a selection of swages. Swages were grooved or moulded blocks used for shaping and forming a range of metal objects of various sizes and variety.

The making, maintenance and tempering of the tools used by the other trades was an activity vital to the running of the entire building operation. In addition to clean water, a brine solution and sometimes oil were also used for tempering as they caused the metal to cool more slowly, giving the blacksmith more effective control over the process. Brine was mostly used for axes and oil for knives – the oil was often a refined form of tallow. It was the practice that the brine was kept in a tub held by supports over a larger tank of clean water. After the forged metal was quenched, the salt deposits were then washed off in the clean water.

Brazing was another much needed skill; it was used mostly for the repair of broken tools, and involved the placing of the broken ends in the forge until they glowed orange-red. The broken parts could then be reunited by hammering and annealing them together, the ends first being coated with a flux, followed by a scattering of spelter (fine metal filings of zinc or brass). In the early medieval period salt was applied as a flux but either borax or a mixture of borax and sal ammoniac were used later. The sprinkling of spelter around the parts to be joined reduced any tendency to oxidise, which could otherwise have a weakening effect on the connection.

Throughout the middle ages lead, brass, bronze and iron were all used for the making of church artefacts. Blacksmiths displayed exceptional skills in the working and application of these metals and turned many utility items into objects of high artistic value. Hinges, handles and door knockers were all highly ornamented. Blacksmiths produced a great variety of nailheads, with two, three or even four different pieces being used for decorative studding (see also Church Doors, page 121). Door handles and knockers made during the Early English period are usually rather plain, apart from some twisted spiral work, with most escutcheon plates (*scutum* – a shield) having a projecting boss with perhaps a decorative leaf design. In the sixteenth century and into the seventeenth century door knockers changed to vertical strips hinged at the top, and by this time important monuments in churches were often enclosed with protective iron railings. At this point security doors in churches started to take the form of flat iron bars riveted together to make a protective grille. In the Early English period door hinges were especially elaborate and conspicuous, often bifurcated and taken across the full width of the door. This form of ostentation continued into the Decorated phase, but not with the same exuberance or regularity. During the Perpendicular period door hinges became much plainer, except for the occasional and modest fleur-de-lis design or similar at the strap ends.

The first tapered iron screws (*twystis*) were made by blacksmiths in the late seventeenth century and were filed to shape individually. The time this took – and hence cost – meant they were seldom used, but by the late eighteenth century screws were being produced using lathes. This continued until they were mass produced by machines from the mid-nineteenth century, although threads did not become interchangeable until Sir Joseph Whitworth introduced his standard BSW system of threading in 1841.

Brass was mostly used for memorial purposes, including inlaid work on incised stone slabs. In this form it appeared as latten, which is a brass alloy made from copper, zinc, lead and tin. Sepulchral brass is usually a particular feature, with incised delicate designs and tracery often picked out in an assortment of various coloured enamels. In the fifteenth, sixteenth and seventeenth centuries many lecterns were made out of brass, the majority taking the form of an eagle, although some featured a pelican. The few surviving early pre-Reformation lecterns have slots into which coins could be dropped. They were used to collect Pentecostals – more commonly known as Peter's Pence – a tax levied in support of the Holy See. It was paid annually on Lammas Day (1 August) and was abolished by statute in 1534.

The bronze used in ornamental work is usually 90 per cent copper and 10 per cent tin, which oxidises to a dark brown. It is very stable and corrosion resistant and produces a protective coating called a patina nobile. In the twentieth century many ecclesiastical items were mass produced in bronze and were given a dark-brown patina to simulate the effect of age through a special heat process. Important leadwork was sometimes tinned to improve durability and appearance. This process involved laying tin foil over heated lead at a temperature which caused it to fuse into the surface; it was often finished with a coating of natural resin.

Carpentry

The medieval carpenter (*carpentarius*) had an important role in nearly every stage of the building process, including the setting-out, the making of centres for arches, the formwork for vaulting and the provision of moulds for casting. The biggest difference between present-day and medieval carpentry is in the type and application of tools, the most fundamental variation being that the axe and the adze were used regularly. The axe is now normally seen as being suitable for rough work, but in the past it was also used with great dexterity in the fashioning of timber. Carpenters (also called wrights) used the broad axe (*dolabrum*) for dressing large timbers and a small hand axe (*securis*) for other work. Also in regular use was the side axe, which had a sharpened edge bevelled on one side only and a slightly cranked handle to give hand clearance for working close to a surface. The long narrow-bladed thrust axe also formed part of the tool kit. The adze (*ascia* or *addice*) is like an axe but has a curved blade fixed at right angles to the handle and was used for the skilful shaping and smoothing of timber. It can sometimes be difficult to differentiate between an adze-worked surface and one that has been planed. The axe and the adze were used in preference to the saw as saw blades were prone to bending or buckling on the push stroke. The softer quality of the steel would have also necessitated frequent re-sharpening of the saw teeth, and jamming was a constant problem from the rapid wearing of the serrations. Once steelmakers found the means to overcome this difficulty the saw came into more general use as durability and the strength of the blade gradually improved. Mouldings were originally produced by dragging a specially shaped plate known as a scratch stock over a surface until the required outline was achieved. Later the process was speeded up and made easier through the introduction of moulding-planes with interchangeable soles and irons.

The tools mostly used to make joints were the auger (*terebra*), various shaped chisels, the brace (*wymby*), a selection of gouges (*goug*), the twybil (a type of chisel with an elongated shank) and a small hand-held axe known as the thrust axe, which had a narrow extended blade. The now-familiar brace and bit with a cranked handle was not devised until the early part of the fifteenth century, but it made a big improvement in wood-boring, making it faster and easier to undertake. The plane (*planetorium*) is Roman in origin and has changed little in basic terms from the designs used in medieval times. The cross-cut saw (*twortsawe*) was used for cutting large sections of timber and a hand saw (*handsight*) for smaller work. In order to help prevent blades from bending the early versions were set in hardwood frames so that they could be tensioned and kept taught.

Nailing was not used and many joints were held firm with wooden pegs, using a technique known as draw boring. The holes for the pegs were always drilled slightly out of alignment, so that when the peg was driven in it drew the members closer together to make a much tighter connection. The practice also ensured that mortice and tenon joints were fixed in a manner that held the shoulder of the tenon hard on the mortice member. The mortice and tenon joint is one of the most commonly used joints in carpentry, made by cutting a projection on one timber in a manner that fits into a corresponding sinking in the other. Figure 57f depicts a stopped tenon, which is when space is provided in the mortice to take two wedges, that were driven home after assemply to make a firmer joint connection.

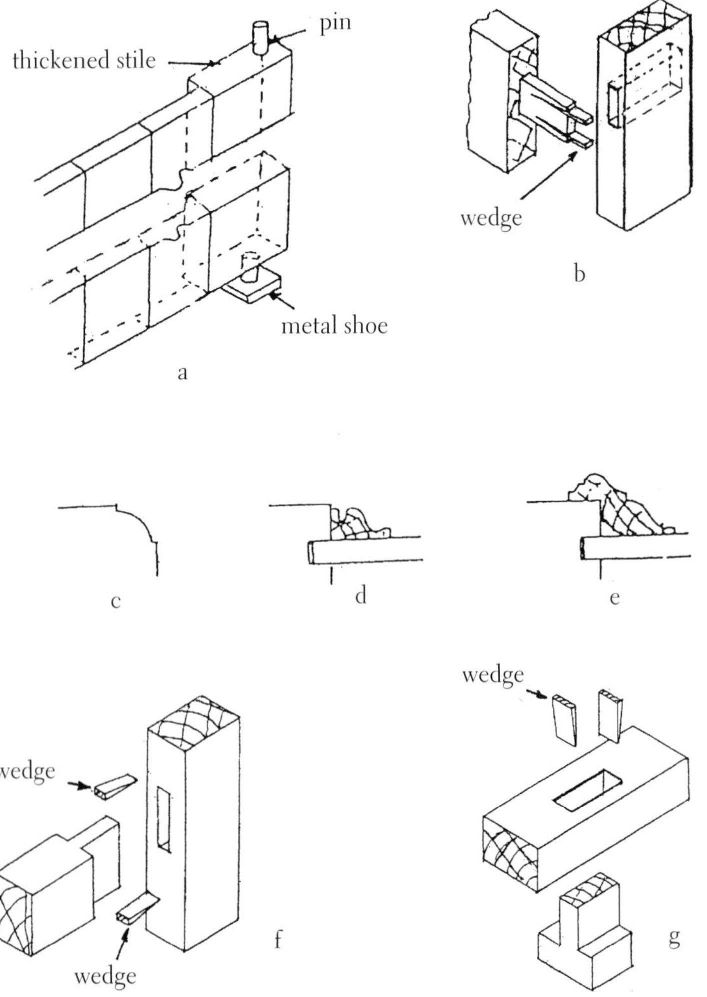

57. Carpentry joints – (a) harr door hanging; (b) foxtail wedging; (c) stuck moulding; (d) planted moulding; (e) bolection moulding; (f) stopped tenon; (g) closed mortice and tenon

This is in contrast to foxtail jointing (Fig. 57b), where the wedging is inserted into slits in the tenon.

This type of work was always done when the oak was still in a green state as it is extremely difficult to work English oak after it has been properly seasoned. As a result of drying out, all unseasoned wood warps and twists to a greater or lesser degree; to minimise this effect oversized timbers were often specified. A tool called a mitrum was used for setting mitred joints. Riven work was done with a froe, which is similar in appearance to a long-bladed axe. In addition to chisels and gouges some decorative work was carried out with a small sculptor's adze which has two different curved blades. If a surface could not be smoothed by tooling it was rubbed with a lightly moistened soft leather and fine clean sand. Pumice was sometimes used too – sandpaper was not developed until around 1860.

In basic terms the purpose of timber jointing is to connect two pieces together in a manner that will withstand stress – the load or force acting upon the timber and any adjoining materials. In this, jointing has three primary functions involving lengthening, bearing or shouldering, the latter being designed to accommodate forces imposed from an oblique angle. The method of preparing and assembling carpentry joints was governed by long-standing traditions; some notable innovations and changes were only accepted after they had been in general practice for a long time. Two important systems which went through exceptional evolutionary periods are scarf and lap jointing.

Scarfing was used as a way of extending structural timbers to a length that could not otherwise be obtained from any available timber. To be effective it was essential for the joined parts to have a strength comparable to that found in any unjoined lengths of timber of the same size and type. In his penetrating and extensive study on medieval timber jointing Cecil Hewett (in *English Historic Carpentry*, published 1980) has traced the development of the scarf joint from modest beginnings through to a high level of sophistication and reliability.

Figure 58 illustrates simple scarfing that depended on timber pegging to resist movement or separation; also shown is a tabled and splayed variation, which can be seen in the side purlins at Chichester Cathedral. In carpentry, tabled joints have projections in each piece which connect with each other to make a more secure join, and help relieve any stresses that may occur in wood dowelling or metal fixing-bolts. More developed versions are also illustrated, one is described by Hewett as stop-splayed and tabled, including a face-halved and bladed scarf. Included in Figure 58 is a

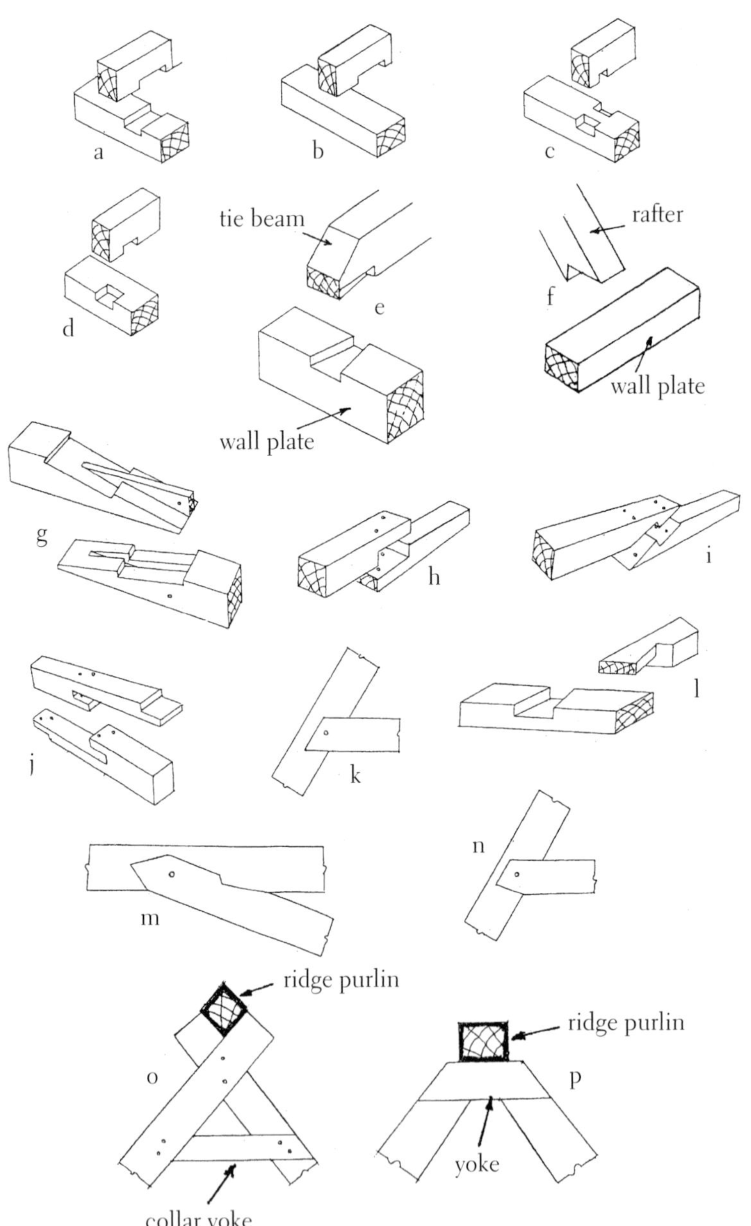

58. Carpentry joints – (a) double-notched joint; (b) single-notched joint; (c) double-cogged notched joint; (d) single-cogged notched joint; (e) tie beam and wall plate; (f) birdsmouth; (g) stop-splayed and tabled scarf joint; (h) edge-halved scarf joint; (i) through-splayed and tabled scarf joint; (j) face-halved and bladed scarf joint; (k) pinned lap joint; (l) lap joint; (m) angled and notched lap joint; (n) pinned lap joint; (o) ridge purlin with collar yoke; (p) ridge purlin with yoke

range of different joints, together with a number that were used for bearing such as notching and cogging.

The earliest lap joints, such as the pinned type shown in Figure 58k could be vulnerable to withdrawal under various movements and stresses. The drawing at Figure 58n shows a lap joint that Hewett discovered at the Saxon church in Sompting, West Sussex, which, although clearly designed to resist thrust, nevertheless remains vulnerable to withdrawal. The other lap joints shown in Figure 58 are later modifications designed to resist separation. Bridle joints are used where one member runs into another at an angle, the receiving member having two rebates with a projecting middle part that engages a recess cut into the connecting member. An oblique joint is similar, the difference being that a single tenon is inserted into the receiving member (Fig. 59).

Before the introduction of the spirit level the simple plumb line was the only way to ensure verticality and a gauge (*livel* or *coaequo*) for the true

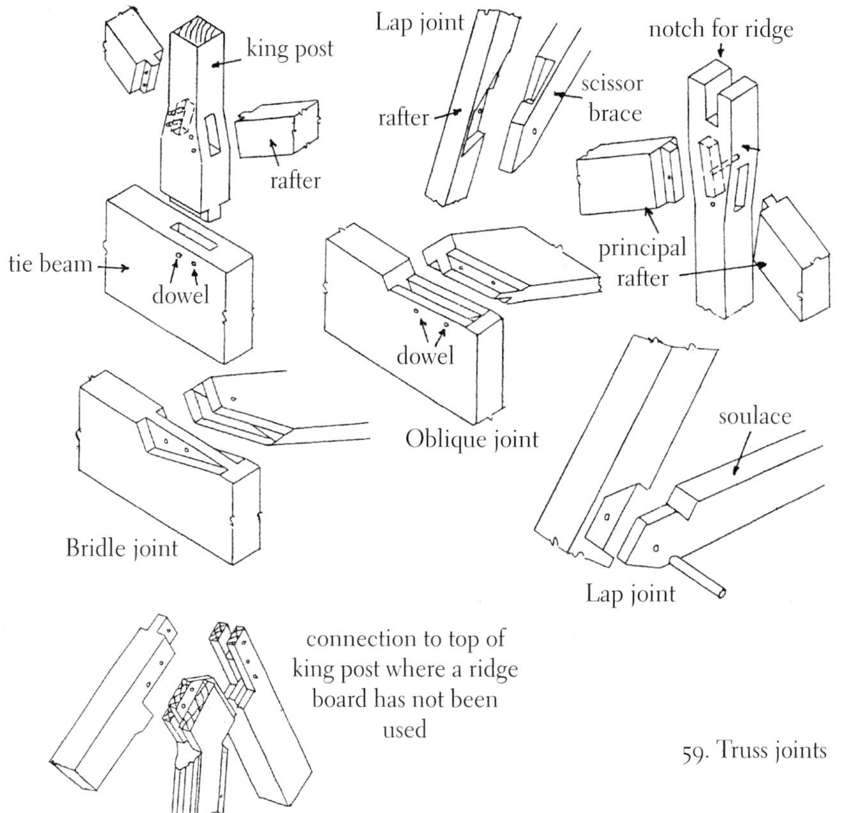

59. Truss joints

horizontal (Fig. 27). Certain features such as scores, indentations and knife cuts can be significant in dating and analysing original work. When everything was ready for assembly it was the practice for carpenters to mark preformed timbers with a system of identification resembling Roman numerals (Fig. 60a). Known as carpenters' marks, these should not be confused with hewing marks used for the conversion of logs into timber baulks (Fig. 60c). Plumb and level marks are also likely to be found on the face side of timbers and on the tops of tie-beams (Fig. 60b). With principal rafters these usually appear in a mid position close to the seating of the purlins.

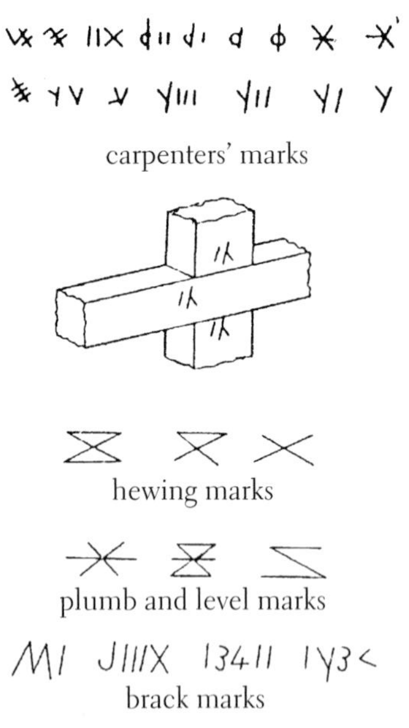

60. Craftsmen's marks – *from top*: carpenters' marks, showing the form and style they normally take on members and frames; an example of how carpenters' marks were used; hewing marks: a number of variation and permutations of these symbols can be found; plumb and level marks, showing some examples of the different forms – many can be easily mistaken for hewing marks; brack marks: letters, signs and numerals are painted, scored or burnt on timber, particularly on timber imported from the Baltic as part of the sorting and assessment of timber at source. Brack marks continued to be used in the style illustrated here until well into the nineteenth century.

Roofs

Roof Construction

In the majority of English cathedrals and in many of the larger churches the ceilings have been constructed in stone vaulting as a barrier to the spread of fire in the roof space. The carpentry in the roofs which cover and protect the vaulting are nevertheless superb examples of craftsmanship and for obvious reasons are not decorative. In the early stages of the medieval period there are indications which suggest some parish churches had plastered or boarded ceilings with a few having clues that suggest the roof space was used for storage. Later it became normal practice for the roofing timbers to be visible from inside, a feature which continued until the seventeenth century when there was a sporadic tendency towards the reintroduction of the ceiling; this lasted until the eighteenth century.

Roofs are broadly classified as being of single, double or triple construction. Single roofs consist of rafters (*sparrys*) fixed at the ridge and to wall plates at the base, a form only used for minor works. Double roofs have purlins which carry the rafters, but in addition to the purlins triple roofs also have trusses. Trusses are spaced apart in a series of bays of usually between 12 to 15 feet (3.6–4.6 m) and house the purlins, which in turn support the common rafters. Truss designs are always triangular and are used where additional support is needed for uninterrupted wider spans, the triangle being the only polygon that is unalterable in form when stressed within the limits of its resistance. All three of these categories of roof are to be seen in church construction, the type depending on the overall size of the structure and the nature of the roof covering. There are some variations in technique between the regions but the basic roof designs for most churches are the tie beam, trussed-rafter, collar, braced and hammer beam forms (Fig. 61). In a few older churches which have subsequently been remodelled the original roof framing can sometimes be found hidden from view by boarding or a plastered ceiling. Little is known about Saxon roofs as none has survived. Many of the illuminations in old manuscripts do, however, show a conventional sloped construction but it is not possible to determine the likely pitch or the type of assembly from information of this nature.

All pitched roofs need to be able to resist outward movement at the eaves and withstand wind pressure, together with the weight of the roof covering and any snow loading. For this to be achieved, shallow roofs require greater lateral strength than those with a steep pitch. The truss system was a major advance in roof design and evolved out of a need for buildings to be bigger and more expansive. While similar in appearance to the traditional rafter roof it is nevertheless very different when considered in terms of structural theory and practice. The desire to increase height internally resulted in a number of variations in roof design which involved the omission of tie beams or ceiling joists in favour of collars fixed further up the roof slope. Left like this a considerable loss of strength could occur; the problem was overcome by providing additional support which included bracing, the use of ashlar pieces and the insertion of supplementary collars (ashlaring is the term given to the short vertical timbers at the base of the rafters, see Fig. 61r). A favoured way of dispensing with the tie beam was the arch-braced collar truss which is seen more in churches built during the sixteenth century. This method involved substantial principal rafters, supported on the underside by curved and robust arched braces let into heavy collars. This could be further strengthened by extending the arched braces from the collar down well past the eaves and then on to strong stone corbels (Fig. 61p). The now much-admired hammer beam truss is a development of the arch-braced system.

All surviving Saxon churches have been re-roofed, but it is apparent that the original pitches in Norman churches varied from moderate to steep, with little or no ornamentation to the timbers. Early English roofs were generally made to a steep pitch, but this was not always so, and any ornamentation tended to be restrained. Minimal change occurred during the early part of the Decorated period, but there was a tendency towards lower pitches in the later stages with ornamentation becoming a feature. A further difference came in the Perpendicular period, when pitches were again lowered, with many roofs being considerably flatter than earlier ones. The exposed timbers were often profusely moulded, and some roofs were ceiled with decorative oak panelling between the rafters, sometimes enriched with bosses and other ornament. A fine example is at All Saints' Church in Martock in Somerset. A strong preference also developed for hammer beamed roofs.

One of a number of fundamental differences between past and present roof construction is in the method of fixing the purlins. In the present day purlins are normally fixed strutted under the rafters. This differs in basic terms from earlier practices, as shown in Figure 62. The clasped purlin in Figure 62 is held between the principal rafter and the collar, the latter cut to take the shape of the purlin as part of the housing – a feature seen mostly in the Midland areas of England. The trenched purlin is trenched into the outer upper face of the principal rafter and the butt purlins have been morticed and tenoned into the principal rafter, a characteristic more commonly found in the southern parts of England. An adaptation of this is the threaded purlin, in which openings are cut into the principal rafters, allowing the purlin to be passed through.

A helpful feature in dating roof assemblies is in the way the common rafters have been fixed at the ridge. Up to around the beginning of the eighteenth century it was the usual practice to couple each pair of rafters with a pinned lap joint; later it was more common for there to be a ridge

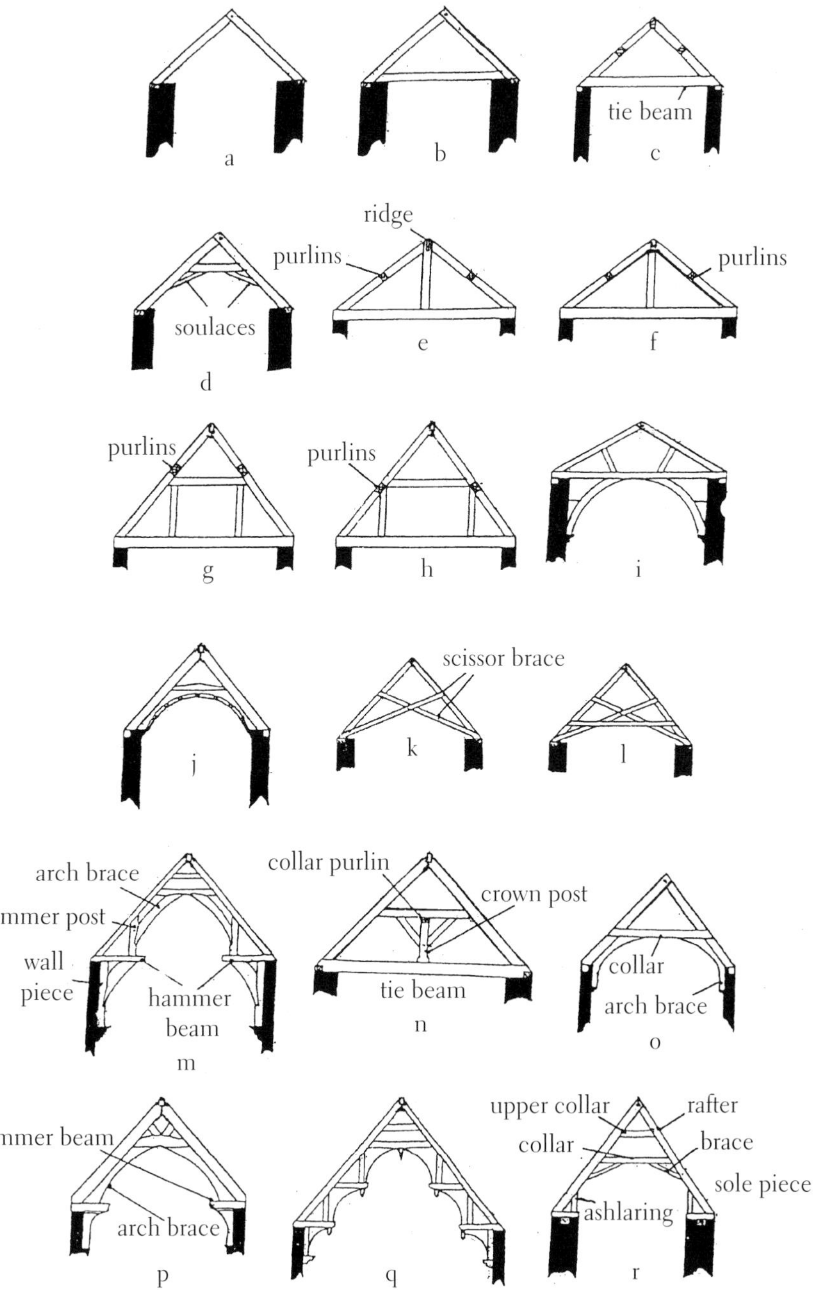

61. Roof construction – (a) coupled rafter; (b) close-coupled rafter; (c) tie beam; (d) soulace; (e) king post; (f) king strut; (g) queen strut; (h) queen post; (i) aisled; (j) barrel; (k) scissor; (l) scissor and collar; (m) hammer beam; (n) crown post; (o) arch-braced; (p) false hammer beam; (q) double hammer beam; (r) trussed rafter

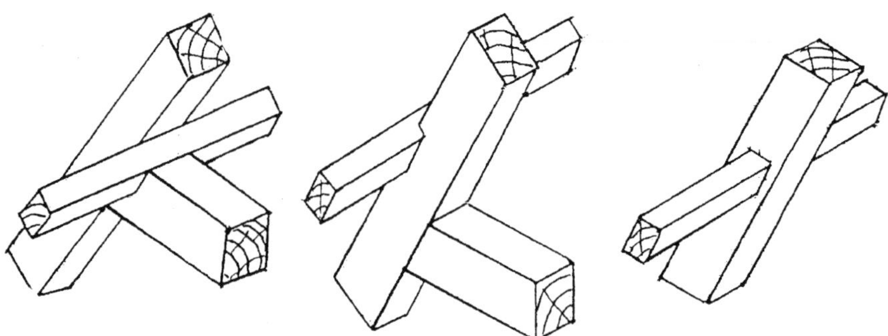

62. Purlins – *left to right*: clasped purlin; trenched purlin; butt purlin

board. This means that there is also a difference in the way principal rafters are connected at the apex in truss assemblies, as shown in Figure 59. The use of either a board or purlin at the ridge produced more integrated and stronger framing and enabled roofs to be constructed at much lower pitches. A number of different methods were used in the fixing of ridge boards and ridge purlins. Some are found set into the rafters diagonally, with a collar yoke occasionally fitted immediately underneath. An alternative system involved securing the purlin on top of a yoke, which was a small timber piece linking the rafters at the apex (Fig. 58p).

The illustrations in Figure 61 give a range of the different roof types found in churches and chapels of all sizes and categories, but it is important to keep in mind that roof work in some older churches may be a later replacement. In many cases the original roofs have not withstood the test of time and in others changes have been made as the result of alterations and additions involving entirely new roofing. In the early medieval period tie beams were generally not needed in the small churches because the exceptional thickness of the walls was sufficient to resist thrust and roof spread. As the population expanded larger parish churches were built and many roof designs changed to the scissor truss to prevent outward movement. Scissor roofs can be identified by having braces (*ligamina*) attached to the lower part of rafters intersecting centrally with the corresponding opposite brace before linking with the middle part of the opposite rafter (Fig. 61k). The technique should not be confused with the use of soulaces, which are shorter diagonal braces fixed between common rafters and the collars (Fig. 61d).

Carpenters originally had a problem with home-produced timber as this grew to relatively short lengths and in practical terms imposed limitations on the span of a tie beam. The difficulty was mainly overcome by using the hammer beam truss, which enabled widths of exceptional note to be spanned, the best example being Westminster Hall, which extends to 67 feet 6 inches (20.5 m). The hammer beam roof is a system whereby principal rafters are connected to sections of cantilevered timber (the hammer beams) upon which is a hammer post let into the principal rafter. The triangulation this forms is further supported by an arch brace, and the rigidity of the assembly is sufficiently tenoned and pinned to resist outward thrust. Variations on this type of roof construction occur regularly.

The illustration in Figure 61p shows a hammer beam roof with a collar beam into which the arch braces are fixed, an example of this can be seen in the parish church at Little Welnetham, Suffolk. This contrasts with the roof structure at St Botolph's Church at Trunch in Norfolk, where the collar beam has been omitted and the curved braces have been carried up to a triangular connecting piece at the apex. In many churches these assemblies are tiered to form double hammer beams, which have hammer beams and hammer posts arranged in two stages, the hammer posts sometimes being carried down to form decorative pendants (Fig. 61q).

Use of the design was not confined to large churches; it can also be found in middle-sized and smaller ones. The absence of a continuous tie beam gave an enhanced impression of height and a sense of space, a feature which was of particular aesthetic importance during the Gothic period. When pursuing this for reasons of appearance some designs did not always follow the correct principles of hammer beam trussing. Known as false hammer beams, these can be readily identified by the absence of proper hammer posts and are a feature more likely to be found in small churches (Fig. 61p). A similar situation is apparent in the small Lynne Chapel at the Church of St Clement, Outwell, Norfolk, where there is a miniature hammer beam roof; no doubt this was also used to create an impression of height. A fine hammer beam roof with carvings can be seen at the Church of St Agnes, Cawston, Norfolk and there are excellent examples of carvings to the double hammer beam roofs at St Wendreda's Church, March, Cambridgeshire, and the Church of St Nicholas, Castle Hedingham, Essex.

In essence, the truss form of construction is a triangular-framed structure consisting of two principal rafters held by a tie beam, with the purlins sustained by the principal rafters, which in turn support the common rafters. A variation is the aisled roof whereby braces fixed to wall pieces connect to the centre of the tie beam. This is a technique that should not be confused with the trussed rafter system, which involves each rafter being connected to a collar and brace together with ashlar pieces, the latter occasionally being called under-strutting. It is a feature seen more in the South and East of England and became popular at one stage as an alternative way of providing greater internal height. Queen post trusses have two vertical members rising from the tie beam which connect to the principal rafters and help support the purlins. In contrast, the queen strut roof is similar in appearance but the queen struts do not carry the purlins directly.

In the king post truss a single king post rests in the middle of the tie beam and connects into the principal rafters at the ridge; king posts are seen more in the northern parts of England. In medieval times pitches never went below 45 degrees, but in later periods shallower pitches are not uncommon. There are usually inclined struts extending from the tie beam to the middle of the principal rafters, although they can be absent from some of the early trusses. In general terms the use of inclined struts came more to the fore as roof pitches became lower. The main difference between this and the king strut is that the king strut does not receive the ridge as it connects into the underside of the principal rafters.

A feature which is more regularly seen in the South-East of England is the crown post. The assembly can be readily identified by a centrally placed post fixed to a tie beam, upon which is secured the collar purlin with a collar between the rafters placed immediately above it (Fig. 61n). In all triangulated roof trusses the posts act in tension and are used to prevent sagging in the tie beam. The barrel roof is a trussed-rafter roof in which the rafters have been given curved braces, which are more usually covered by plaster or boarding. Where church ceilings are of wood they are sometimes coffered, which is a form of recessed panelling. A selection of methods used in the jointing of roof trusses is shown in Figure 59.

The purpose of bracing is to provide diagonal strengthening, and it was often made to be decorative, with the members sometimes being worked to concave or convex shapes. The decorative carpentry work now regularly seen in parish church roofs began in a relatively modest fashion during the Early English period but as time progressed a greater emphasis was placed on ornamented finishing. At this stage tie beams and cornices were frequently moulded and king posts were worked to different shapes, with some also given carved capitals and bases. The dressed finishes on these posts are more usually chamfered, octagonal, cruciform or rebated. As the Decorated style advanced, tie beams were regularly provided with curved under-braces. The ultimate in carving and ornamentation came in the Perpendicular period with corbels and pendants being intricately worked and other items being enriched with features such as tracery and feathering. Many other items were also elaborately carved, including bosses, crockets and finials. A church worthy of special mention is St Oswald's in Malpas, Cheshire, which has exceptionally fine decorative carvings to the roof timbers in the nave. The parish church of St Peter and St Paul in Knapton, Norfolk, also has a series of elaborate and unusual roof carvings featuring angels with large outstretched wings crafted in fine detail.

In general terms, the highly decorative and artistic roof carving of the fifteenth century became less of a feature in the sixteenth and seventeenth centuries, with more churches having plastered ceilings, often with detailed cast ornamentation.

Oak was the most used timber for roofing until the later importation of Scandinavian fir, which was classified through a series of signs termed brack marks, which continued to be used until well into the twentieth century (Fig. 60). Where oak could not be afforded, other timbers were sometimes used in the small churches and chapels. The suitable alternative options were willow, hornbeam, elm or Spanish chestnut, all of which were used for construction purposes but none has the lasting properties of oak. Although the Saxons had different ways of working timber, very little has survived and most of the carpentry techniques now in use are in substance a legacy of the Normans.

By the beginning of the eighteenth century, fir had replaced oak as the most used timber for roofing but the change was not without problems. Softwoods do not have the same strength as oak and are weaker in tension. Loading could cause fixing pegs to be crushed and tenons to split along the grain. Carpenters overcame this loss of strength by fitting metal straps or stirrups at the base of posts to prevent deflection. Bolts were also passed through lap joints and similar connections, including the joints between the principal rafters and the tie beam. Occasionally hybrid forms of roof trussing can be discovered in parish churches, usually the result of remodelling and adapting the original early medieval construction with reinforcing timbers.

Whatever form of roof used, a complete variation in technique had to be made over the chancel if the sanctuary terminated with an apse for this required a conched roof termination. The base of a conch roof is semicircular, with the roof a semi-dome. Construction normally began by making curved sections for assembly into wall plates using a technique similar to that adopted by wheelwrights. Wall plates (*peces*, *palnas* or *resons*) are horizontal timbers fixed on the top of walls to receive the roof carcassing. An alternative method involved fixing the foot of each rafter to a right-angled sole piece set into the masonry. If purlins were necessary the more usual form seems to have been the butt type. The conch shape meant that not every rafter could be taken to the apex, which resulted in the remainder being secured to those fixed at the apex or interfixed to adjacent timbers (Fig. 63a)

Roof Coverings

Throughout the medieval period, including the time of the Saxons, roofs to the larger churches were covered in cast lead sheeting which was produced by melting pig lead in a crucible and then carefully pouring the molten lead over prepared moist beds of fine well-compressed sand. As the casting table needed a slight incline for the fast spread of the molten lead, this always resulted in a small variation in the thickness of the lead sheet between the low and raised ends of the table. This process also had the effect of creating a stippled surface on one side, which is the distinguishing feature for this type of casting. The sheets were originally shorter, much narrower and thicker, which meant they could not be manipulated with the same ease as the later milled sheeting. Casting did, however, give better resistance to the effects of expansion and contraction because the natural formation of the molecules remained largely unaltered. Local tradition or the preference of the plumber (*plumbarius* – the lead worker) seems to have determined whether the sheeting was used with the sand-face up or down.

Much of the lead derived from the local mines around Britain contained traces of silver, which gave improved durability, but the method of casting was particularly prone to flaws from air bubbles and sand holes. By the end of the seventeenth century sheet lead was being milled or manufactured by passing cast lead slugs between large steel or cast-iron rollers which compressed it into sheets. This process resulted in the finished product having a uniform size and thickness, making it nominally free from defects.

Most woods contain vegetable acids, and when lead is placed in direct contact with them it can deteriorate through a chemical reaction. This is why it was common practice to put a layer of earth or sand between the two materials. With pitched roofs dried moss was used as an alternative. Copper sheeting was not used as a roofing material in Britain until well into the first post-medieval phase.

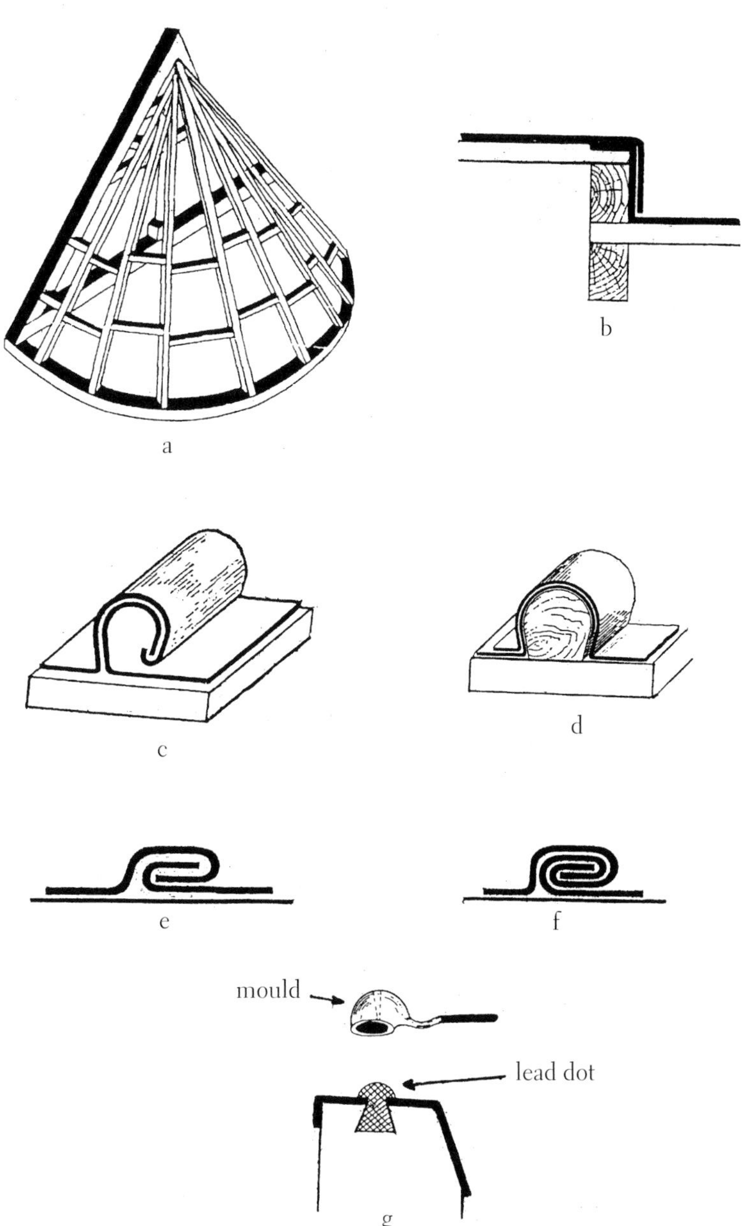

63. Sheet-lead jointing – (a) roof termination over an apse showing a conch end; (b) lap joint; (c) hollow roll; (d) solid roll; (e) single welt; (f) double welt; (g) lead dot

When laid as a roof covering, lead sheets are fixed together by a series of different folds in the form of laps, rolls and welts. Laps are formed by dressing one piece of lead over another, as shown in Figure 63b. Rolls are used as a way of jointing by working the sheet ends into a tubular formation (Fig. 63c). In medieval times the roll was always made hollow but in the post-medieval phases it became the practice to join sheeting over rounded wood strips (Fig. 63d). Welts are formed from upturns which are bent over and worked into an interconnected flat joint (Figs 63e and 63f); this method is not suitable for flat or slightly inclined roofs and where lead sheeting was dressed over masonry there was often a need to guard against the lifting action of the wind. This was done by forming a square or circular dovetail-type joint in the stone to receive a lead dot, which was essentially a rivet of lead. The sheet lead was first embossed into the opening, and then molten lead was poured in, as illustrated in Figure 63g.

In the medieval period the only other method of jointing lead involved the use of solder (*soldura*), which is an alloy of tin and lead; the most probable composition at the time would have been three parts of tin to one part of lead. This would have had a much lower melting point than the more recent plumbers' solder, which is one part of tin to two parts of lead. The earlier burners were not very adaptable, which made working at a higher melting point more difficult to control and increased the risk of damage to the lead. It is the reason why the solder with a lower melting point was always used. Old documents also refer to the use of a solder of pewter, which is an alloy produced from tin together with small quantities of lead and brass. The application of a flux over the cleaned and prepared parts has always been essential to prevent the surface from oxidising or corroding. Tallow seems to have been the preferred material in the past but old records also refer to the use of salt or the resin from conifers dissolved in spirit.

Zinc sheeting also has a place in church history as a roofing material. Chosen only occasionally and mostly in small churches, it was first manufactured in England in 1740, but does not appear to have been a commercial success until the early part of the nineteenth century, when it was used either as roof sheeting or in the form of a patent interlocking tile. A well-recorded example is at Canterbury Cathedral in 1835, when zinc was chosen to re-roof the cloisters. The specification describes how the sheeting was laid between wood rolls finished with lead cappings.

In medieval times the selection of a suitable roof covering at parish level seldom permitted many choices and much depended on the availability of materials and the cost of transport. Riven oak shingles (*scandulae*) were often used and are a lasting legacy from the time of the Romans. Cut and shaped rather like a clay tile, they were a favoured material for small and medium-sized churches, especially in the counties of Kent, Sussex, Surrey and Essex. The practice continued until the price of oak increased, whereafter usage steadily declined, finally ceasing in the eighteenth century. Mostly around 16 inches (40 cm) in length and about 8 inches (20 cm) in width, the shingles were riven by being split along the grain, which avoided the disruption of the natural fibres and enabled them to channel rain along the grain in a similar fashion to thatch. Fixings were made with oak pegs with the shingles for spires being much longer and narrower in shape. St Peter's Church at Newdigate in Surrey is one of the few remaining churches with a shingle roof, another is the spire at the thirteenth-century Church of All Saints in Monkland, Hertfordshire. There is evidence to indicate that in some districts larch was used in this way. During the early 1800s locally grown pine was tried as an alternative but found to be unsuitable, leading to the strong preference later for cedar.

It is also clear from the steep pitches seen in many surviving medieval roofs that thatch was a frequent church roof covering. In the districts where reeds were used it is sometimes listed in old accounts under the intriguing name of fleakage (this should not be confused with the term fleeking, which is a layer of material placed against the roof timbers to help support the thatch covering). In the poorer regions the minor churches and chapels were regularly obliged to adapt a variety of materials, including bent (marram grass), furze, meadow rushes, ling (heather), bracken roots and broom. It is probable that at times turf thatch was selected, with the grass laid uppermost. The more widely used materials were nevertheless wheat, rye, barley and oat straw. Few churches are now seen with a thatched roof – a rare example is All Saints at Icklingham in Suffolk.

In certain areas limestone could be split into sizes suitable for slating (*sclats*), and they were laid to a pitch of 50 degrees or more. As the stones did not always dress into regular dimensions they were more usually fixed as diminishing courses, the sizes being graded with the largest at the eaves and the smallest at the ridge. This enabled them to be used more economically and avoided excessive waste. Once the quarry sap has dried out, limestone slates can become extremely hard; many of the more suitable types are found in Dorset, Somerset, north-west Yorkshire, the eastern half of Gloucestershire, parts of Oxfordshire and Worcestershire. They can also be found in some parts of Northamptonshire, Rutland and the Kesteven area of Lincolnshire. A few sandstones were also used in this way but they produced heavier and thicker slates. Sandstone suitable for roofing can be found in a belt running from the Pennines into Yorkshire and Scotland and the regions of the Derbyshire Peaks and parts of North Wales which border the Midlands.

True slate is shale that has been under metamorphic pressure which has caused it to change into a hard state. As it can be cleaved into thin sheets it makes an ideal roofing material and has been used extensively all over Britain. At one time it was only used in areas where it could be easily quarried. Most of the roof slating in Cornwall has come from the quarry at Delabole, which produced fine-grained strong and compact slates with good durability. In Leicestershire the well-known Swithland slates became a noted local feature until they were replaced by cheaper slates from Wales, a change which eventually swept across the whole of the British Isles.

Some old slate roofing can be found shouldered, which is where the slate heads are bedded in mortar to tighten the fixing nails and prevent wind penetration. A similar technique was torching, whereby slates or tiles were mortared on the under surface as a form of weatherproofing. The climate conditions of an area largely dictated the manner in which natural local slate was used. The wrestler slates of the Lake District are a good example and are cut in a manner that enables them to be interlocked, and provide greater resistance to uplift and slippage from wind. These variations gradually became less pronounced after the Industrial Revolution when improved road, rail and waterway communications enabled Welsh slate to become a cheaper and more suitable option. In the course of time it resulted in church roofs in most regions being re-covered in high-quality slating from the Welsh quarries.

During the thirteenth century the first plain clay roof tiles started to become a feature in many parts of South-East England, later extending into the Midlands as far north as the Welsh border and into the southern parts of East Anglia. The tile size was standardised in 1477 to 10½ x 6½ x ½ inches (26.6 x 16.5 x 1.2 cm). The original tiles were fixed with small wooden pegs through holes at the top, but in lieu of pegs the knuckle bones from sheep were sometimes used as an alternative. In the eighteenth century knibs (small studs which project on the underside of a tile for hanging over the roof batten) started to replace peg holes, reviving a practice that had previously been introduced by the Romans. It was not until well into the nineteenth century that production-made machine tiles appeared and brand names entered the market. There is, however, a very important difference between the early tiles and those made in more recent times. The early tiles have a cross-camber devised to convey rain water onto the middle surface of the tile directly underneath – a factor which is missing in the more modern equivalents. This makes modern tiles incompatible for repair and replacement work in roofs which still have the earlier tiles. Much of the original tiling also had irregular gauging, sometimes varying from 4 inches (10 cm) to 8 inches (20 cm) in the same roof (in this context gauging refers to the depth of each slate or tile course between the nail holes of one course and the next).

Single-lap tiling has a different origin and first appeared in the eastern counties of England towards the end of the seventeenth century as a result of trade links with Holland. The tiles are much larger being around 13 inches (33 cm) to 14 inches (35 cm) long and about 9 inches (22 cm) to 10 inches (25 cm) wide and are fixed to a gauge of around 11 inches (27 cm). In contrast to plain tiles they are laid with overlapping side joints and have only two thicknesses at the head joints and a single thickness at the un-lapped portions. As they are lighter than plain tiles they became popular for replacing roof coverings of thatch and were eventually made locally. Thatch is a comparatively light roofing material and so thatch roofs were assembled with timbers of smaller dimensions that would have been overloaded by the heavier plain tiles; single-lap tiles overcame the problem. The introduction of single-lap tiling had a limited impact in other parts of England but eventually regular use did extend into Yorkshire (excluding the Dales).

Doors

Most surviving church doors from the early medieval periods have been constructed from heavy oak planks (*valvas*) placed vertically on the outside and horizontally on the inside (Fig. 64). This resulted in the grain of the wood between the two leaves being at right angles, which helped to reduce distortion and splitting. In much of this work the boards are found butt jointed and are often covered externally with a chamfered or moulded strip along each connection. In some examples rebating and counter-rebating techniques have been found between the boards. Large wrought-iron nails with ornamented heads were used in the fixing, driven from the vertical face into the timbers behind and then clenched (clenching was when the exposed ends were bent over with a punch). Few examples remain of Saxon door carpentry, but some interesting variations have been found that depart from the usual medieval practices and in the transitional phases which followed.

Hewett's *English Historic Carpentry* (1980) contains some highly revealing findings, especially on his investigations at the Church of St Botolph in Hadstock, Essex, which give a clear insight into some unusual techniques.

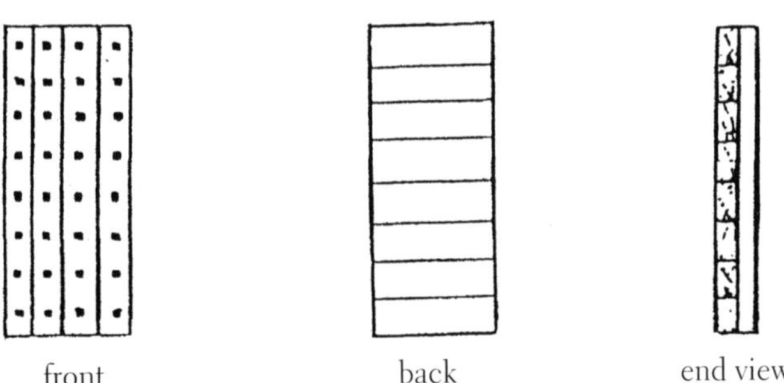

64. Basic medieval door construction

His further studies also show that many methods not in accordance with the general practices of the time were used in other churches. One of the best examples believed to be Saxon is the north door (*hostium*) at St Botolph's, which was constructed from four wide planks held together by D-shaped lengths of oak, and the whole was fastened by a series of iron roves and clenches (Fig. 65a). Hewett also made a valuable analysis of a Saxon door in Westminster Abbey. It is formed from five vertical planks joined by square rebated edges, all held by concave ledges housed into the back of the planking (Fig. 65b – which has a single ledge in the middle of the reverse face). His work on the west door of the parish church at Kemply, Gloucester, which he dated as early Norman, is of particular interest. This door is made from three large planks counter-rebated together, with the middle plank being shouldered into the two on either side, and all held by a series of free tenons (Fig. 65c) (free tenons are independent slips of wood which join timbers by means of mortices in each). Also covered by the Hewett study is the south door at St Nicholas' Church, Castle Hedingham, Essex. Here the use of nailed narrow planks and the liberal application of stepped counter-rebating between them is highly innovative and, apart from the west doors at Ely Cathedral, nothing has been discovered to date which really compares with this particular form of assembly (Fig. 64d). It is probably the outcome of a craftsman with ingenuity being given a free hand to develop an idea that never caught on.

In many parish churches the earliest doors were set on harrs (*cardones*), a method which is a legacy from the Romans (Fig. 57a). The harr was formed by extending a pin from the upper part of a thickened hanging

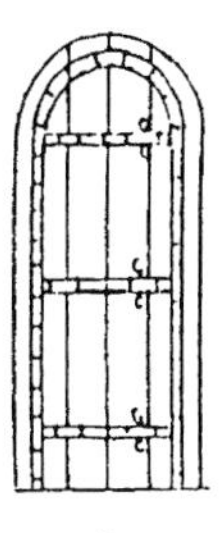

a

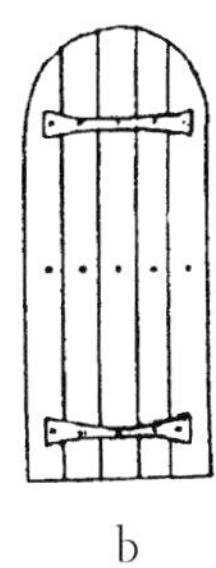

b

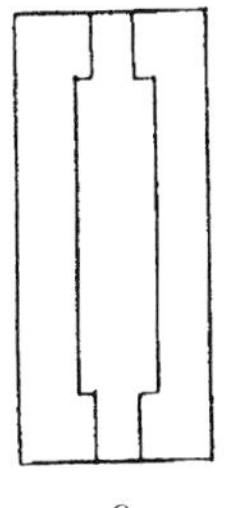

c

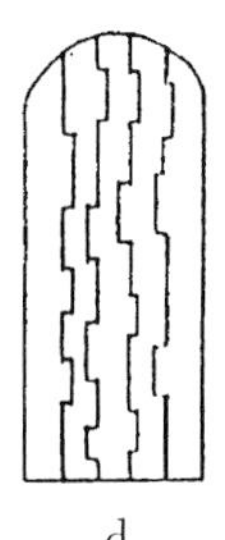

d

65. Variations on standard medieval door construction (after Hewett, *English Historic Carpentry*, 1980)

stile into a hole in the lintel immediately overhead. This was repeated at the base, which fitted into a hole in the threshold or a specially made iron shoe. This enabled the door to turn on itself and in some instances an iron pin can be found driven into the base of the hanging stile in lieu of a wood pin. The method involved a different building sequence as it was necessary for the door to be assembled and put in place at the same time as the lintel. Many of the early doors closed directly onto the doorstead (a stoneworked jamb made by cutting into the walling). In the middle and later Gothic phases pointed arch doors were fixed to a durn, which is an arch-shaped frame made from a naturally curved piece of timber split to form two matching pieces. Stiles used in early door framing are described in old manuscripts as *lynia*.

In the later medieval period most church doors were ledged (*legges*) or ledged and braced. The ledged doors were made from vertical planks fixed by wrought-iron nails to horizontal ledges (Fig. 66a). To reduce the tendency for doors to sag or drop at the outer edge, bracing (*ligamina*) was introduced at a diagonal from ledge to ledge (Fig. 66b). Later, the design was improved to become the framed, ledged and braced door (Figs 66c and 66d). Once framing had taken hold, especially from the fourteenth century onwards, framed panelled doors gradually became the fashion, although a large number of church doors continued to be in vertical oak planking until around the beginning of the seventeenth century. This change also heralded the appearance of the Classical six-panel door with prominent mouldings, the top panels later being made smaller than the others – no doubt reflecting the Classical notion of vertical progression. The method

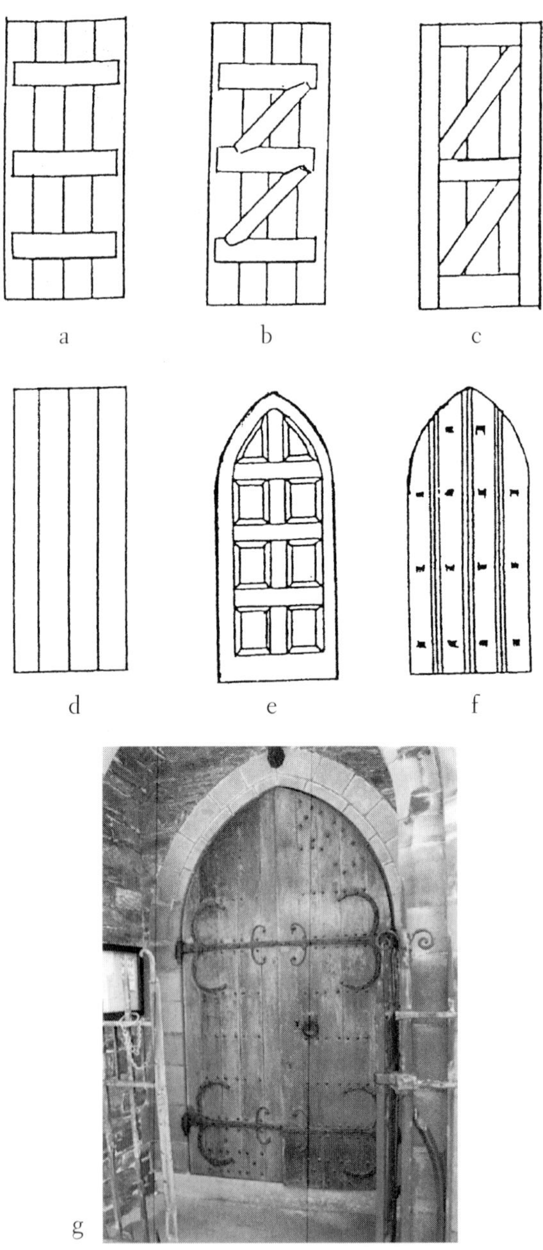

66. Later medieval door construction – (a) ledged; (b) ledged and braced; (c) back of framed, ledged and braced; (d) front of framed, ledged and braced; (e) panelled; (f) framed door with vertical planks and chamfered cover strips at the joins; (g) framed, ledged and braced door in the Gothic style with decorative hinges

also enabled shrinkage and expansion to be more suitably accommodated by cutting grooves into the framework into which the panels could be slotted, with sufficient allowances being made for movement.

During the eighteenth century it was often the practice to hang the main entrance doors to a church in pairs. The carvings found on these and on those from an earlier period can often give vital indications to their date of origin. Mouldings usually followed the fashion of the time and most were stuck – that is they were worked on the edges of the framing which received the panels. Planted mouldings are made separately and do not form part of the same fashioning, while those described as bolection moulds are a later feature and overlap and hide the connection between the panels and the framing (Fig. 57e). During the nineteenth century many old church doors were replaced, some in a replicated form with the original ironwork often being refitted. Crosses scored into the jambs of the entrance doors are the legacy of a medieval custom which believed this kept evil away from the church.

The Normans seldom ornamented doors except for the hinges, which were regularly scrolled with bifurcated ends. Elaborate metal design work to church doors began in the thirteenth century, some of it being most flamboyant, especially in the formation of the hinges. In the fourteenth century more use was made of artistic wood carving, but the application of featured metalwork so prominent in the previous century still continued. By the fifteenth century intricate carving appeared more regularly, with hinges becoming less of a feature. A most remarkable door from the Perpendicular period can be seen in the Church of St Mary, Stoke-by-Nayland, Suffolk. Made from solid oak, it has a magnificent carving of the Tree of Jesse. The door in the porch of St Saviour's Church, Dartmouth, Devon, has exceptionally fine medieval ironwork, and other notable examples are the fourteenth-century work to the south door of St Mary's Church, Meare, Somerset, and the fifteenth-century door with hinges at St Mary's Church, Twyford, Buckinghamshire. After the fifteenth century, hinges generally changed to a plainer form and the decorative elements tended to be more subdued. In addition to having a functional use, nails were also made for decorative purposes, a practice which perpetuated until around the time of the Industrial Revolution. They were often produced by local blacksmiths and can be found in a wide variety of designs in the studding to church doors.

Nail-making later became a cottage industry and no doubt some of the surviving decorative nail work originated from this source. The locks (*cera*) made during this time have decorative patterns and mouldings and display heavily enriched escutcheons over the keyholes, which are mostly in the form of a shield.

Many of the large circular pendent handles with ornamented bosses so often seen on church doors originated as sanctuary rings. At one time churches could offer sanctuary for a period of forty days to any fugitive from justice or to those undergoing persecution or threat from an enemy or a hostile source. During this time fugitives were safe and could only be persuaded to leave the premises at their own choosing. The right of sanctuary was abolished during the seventeenth century but many of the original brass rings (*hagodays*) attached to large bosses have survived, with most displaying grotesque images of animals. One such example is to the ring attached to the door of St John's Church, Adel, West Yorkshire; another at Durham Cathedral is from the twelfth century and features a lion's head. During the early medieval period 'witches marks' were engraved into door latches in the belief that they prevented witches from entering a church. They took the form of a saltire within a triangle and are sometimes still clearly visible in the few remaining examples.

The Structural Use of Iron

Throughout the medieval period iron was severely limited as a building material as it could only be produced in small quantities; this is why its use was confined to the making of small artefacts such as door handles, hinges, catches and similar items. The wrought iron made in this way had a very low carbon content and was prepared for use by a process of repeated heating and hammering which expelled most of the slag content. This gave the finished product a laminated fibrous structure, distinct from the various crystalline forms found in cast iron. The laminations make it easy to identify, but they also have a tendency to separate. Wrought iron is malleable and ductile and can be worked hot or cold. The structural use of wrought iron before the eighteenth century was limited to the fabrication of items such as stirrups, strapping and bolts, or as additional reinforcement to tie beams. As the scale of production changed from small localised furnaces to mass output in the industrial locations, it was possible for rolled beams and stanchions to be manufactured widely and by 1845 wrought iron had come into use as an important structural material.

In 1774 the development of Wilkinson's cupola blast furnace enabled cast iron to be produced on a highly competitive basis and this heralded a major change. The switch to cast iron started to escalate and by 1840 the material was being seen by many as superior to wrought iron. It was used for both beam and column work, with the latter being cast in distinctive circular, octagonal and hexagonal shapes. Most columns had a hollow core which helped to alleviate the differential stresses which occurred during cooling. Many of these units were joined using spigot and socket joints. At the time there were varying views about the structural application of iron, and many plans were misconceived and failed. The first known application of cast iron in church building goes back to 1770, when cast-iron columns were used to support the gallery in St Anne's Church, Liverpool. During the nineteenth century cast iron was often used for decorative detail and in the making of church windows, with some even having opening lights. These windows are readily identifiable from their thick, heavy profiles and slightly blurred detail. The first church to have cast-iron windows is believed to be St Alkmund's, Shrewsbury, where they were installed in 1794.

The Making and Use of Stained Glass

There is clear evidence from old documents to confirm that by the middle of the twelfth century the windows in many churches were glazed (*vitreolas*), and a number had at least one stained-glass feature, although many at parish level continued to have little or no stained glass until the early part of the nineteenth century. Much of the original stained glass came from the Mediterranean region. Known as 'pot metal', it was produced in the hot climate areas in deep colours to reduce the brightness and glare from the sun, but when used in the duller skies in Britain it caused the intensity of natural light in churches to be much reduced. The glass was made by infusing metallic oxides into plain glass, but the manufacturing process had limitations and it could only be suitably adapted in small pieces, mostly because the finished sheets had excessive irregularities in thickness which made shaping to precise sizes difficult and wasteful. After a design had been drawn on to a work table, selected pieces of glass were placed over it, with the various outlines then being traced on to the glass using a mixture of crushed chalk and water. This was followed by drawing a hot iron rod along the chalk outlines, causing the glass to crack roughly into shape. The jagged ends were then broken off and the edges trimmed with a specially designed tool called a grozing iron which produced a characteristic finish to the edge. Post-medieval glass was cut with a diamond-tipped or hardened-metal tool that gave a clear definitive finish. The stained glass was assembled by fixing the various pieces into a carefully contrived lead network that followed the artist's design. The lead for this had cast H-shaped strips called cames which were then cut and bent to the required shape and soldered together.

In the medieval period the cames had a rather convex profile but they became flatter and wider from the eighteenth century onwards. At the fitting stage grooves were chased into the stone window reveals and the completed glass framework was then positioned and pointed in with lime mortar. The glass was made weatherproof and held firm in the cames by embedding it in putty, tallow or graphite. When it was assembled in panels, larger areas of leaded glass needed to be held in an iron framework to prevent bowing and distortion. This framework is termed ferramenta and was made up of vertical iron supports called stanchions and horizontal ones termed saddlebars; the glass panels were then tied to it with lead strips and soldered on.

An alternative method of making coloured glass involved burning pigments into the surface. Stained glass was also produced by a process called flashing, whereby white glass was coated with a layer of coloured glass while both were in the molten state. This created glass with one coloured surface and one clear surface, which had the effect of making the glass much more transparent than that made by the pot metal process. Fine detail (*pictura*) was achieved by painting in images with a mixture of powdered glass, metallic oxide and gum arabic. A small quantity of water was added, together with vinegar or urine, to render the gum arabic insoluble after it had dried. On completion the cartoon was fused into the surface of the glass by subjecting it to intense heat.

In the thirteenth century the reaction against subdued church lighting grew and a consensus developed for improvement. The initial change came with the grisaille window. This was a type of opalescent greyish stained glass which gave a mother-of-pearl effect through which considerably more daylight could pass. A much admired example is the lancet window in York Minster known as 'The Five Sisters' (Fig. 67). In the early fourteenth century a yellow pigment produced from silver oxide or silver chloride was discovered, which began a process known as staining. This led to important changes in production and enabled a much wider range of yellows and oranges to be made, which extended the scope and options through which artists could work. It also became possible to obtain variations and greater depths of the same shade by applying extra colour coatings on parts of the same cartoon.

The small pieces of coloured glass produced in the twelfth century created a visual impression somewhat like a mosaic, which has resulted

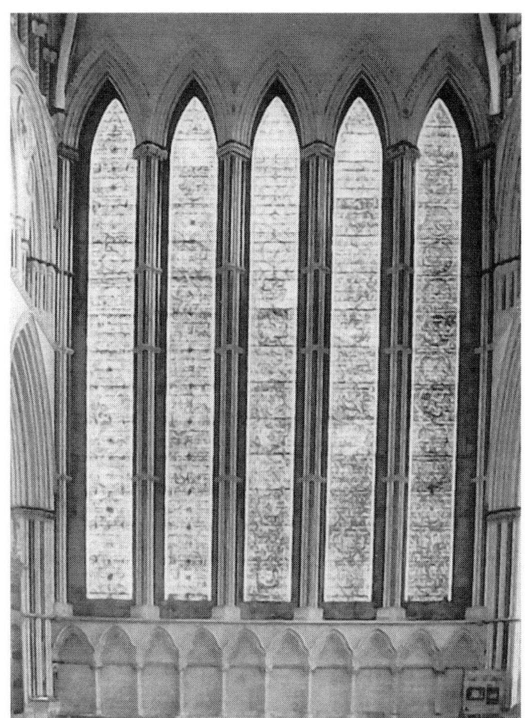

67. Stained-glass windows – *top*: the grisaille window, York Minster; *bottom*: brighter colours from the Perpendicular period, Shinfield, Berkshire

in the windows from this period being described as mosaic windows. Some original examples have survived, more notably those in Canterbury Cathedral and Lincoln Cathedral. Some of the grisaille windows of the thirteenth century are masterpieces, with delicately formed geometrical patterns and interlacing decoration. Salisbury Cathedral has some particularly fine examples.

In the Decorated Gothic period there were marked changes in the application of stained glass, with considerably more light being admitted through windows which had larger proportions and coloured glass of lesser intensity. Moreover craftsmen produced stained glass in brighter colours in contrast to the dark sombre effects which came from the earlier pot metal glass. The most prolific time for stained glass in England was in the Perpendicular period, when brighter glass was produced in a range and variety of different colours to create a more invigorating and inviting environment (Fig.67).

In the first half of the sixteenth century the remarkable splendour that had already been achieved rose to even greater heights. The whole gamut of colours now produced increased to a level where a new range of presentations could be made. From then on quality gradually started to decline. During the Victorian Gothic Revival phase the use of stained glass returned as an architectural feature but in a number of parish churches it is unimaginative, sombre and dull. Much of the Victorian church window glass was housed in wood sub-frames, some with opening lights.

In many of the early minor churches and small chapels the cost of glazing would have been unaffordable, and to overcome the extremes of the weather window openings are likely to have been screened with an assortment of materials. This would have included parchment, oiled cloth, greased linen and undaubed wattle, but a more permanent solution could always be found by using animal horn. Mostly taken from cattle, the horns were boiled until soft and then slit and rolled flat, after which they were cut to the required shape and allowed to dry. The trimmed pieces were then fixed by overlapping in a similar style to roof slating or tiling. In locations that needed ventilation and little light slatted or fretted panels were normally fixed over a window opening.

2 Church Architecture

The Greater Churches

Most churches in this classification needed to cater for the wide range of ceremonial and the many services which were linked to or revolved around the monastic orders. By the eleventh century all churches of this type had layouts with recognisable similarities, although they were not standard or uniform in any way (Fig. 68). The various internal arrangements which developed all proved to be highly functional and, apart from a few notable exceptions, most were cruciform or part-cruciform in plan with a central tower. One of the fundamental differences between the monastic and the parish churches was the arrangement of the presbytery and the high altar. It was necessary for the presbytery to have considerably more space for the functions and activities of the monastic orders, and this included the need for a lady chapel and various side chapels. At this stage the saints also had more prominence in the celebrations, which created an additional demand for enlargement as a result of growing attendances and increased processional activity.

The presbytery is the area within the immediate vicinity of the sanctuary and is connected to the eastern extremity of the space known as the choir, the demarcation often being made by several steps raising it above the choir. It was also the place of the high altar, and the space behind this was sometimes included as a part of the presbytery. The choir was the part immediately east of the nave and west of the presbytery, originally separated from the congregation by a screen. This divide was further emphasised by the provision of at least one step, and some churches also had aisles running alongside the choir. There is nevertheless a vagueness to be found in the use of these terms, with presbytery or choir occasionally being applied to the entire eastern end, and in the Roman Catholic Church the term presbytery is now used regularly to describe the residence of a priest. At one time the whole of the eastern area was assigned only to the bishop

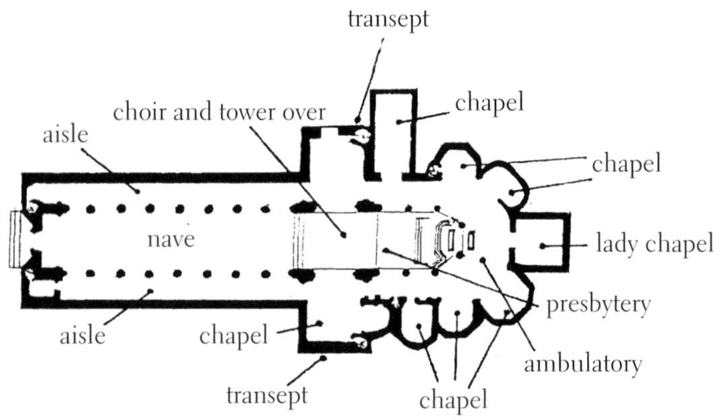

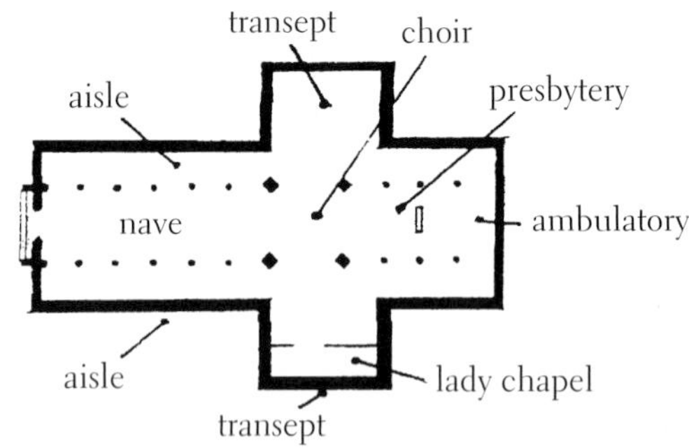

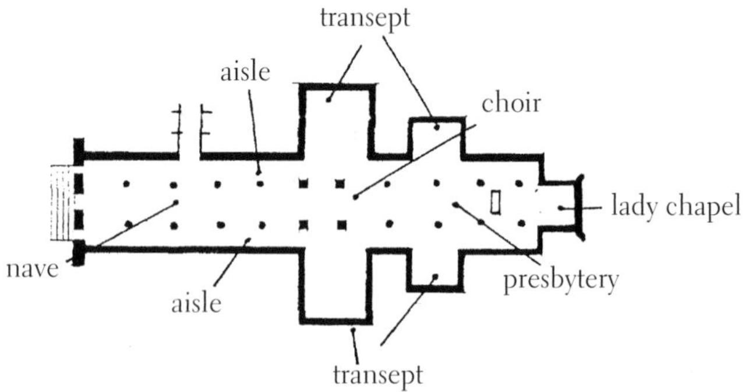

68. Cathedral layouts

and the presbyters (senior clergy), with exceptions made for minor clerics and the acolytes permitted to attend the choir. Following the Reformation the area was opened to the laity and the space in parish churches became more generally known as the chancel.

It was not until the fifteenth century that lay singers began to augment the choir, and the original location was gradually altered. In the twelfth century the retro-choir appeared between the apse and the high altar; this was a particular characteristic of the Cistercian Order although not exclusively so. In churches in which the remains of a venerated saint rested, the area might also hold a feretory (*feretrum* – a tomb or shrine), an elaborately worked and elevated shrine placed behind the high altar. It was often separated from the presbytery by a decorative screen. An ambulatory created a walkway around the apse and behind the sanctuary altar, sometimes with a chapel or a series of small radiating side chapels. This arrangement is known as the chevet and is a feature which came from the Romanesque cathedrals of continental Europe; one of the rare examples found in Britain is in Norwich Cathedral. This change enabled those selected to participate in processions to witness at close hand the splendour of the high altar and the shrine of a patron saint. Up to the beginning of the thirteenth century it had been regular practice to terminate the eastern end of the church with an apse. This was later dropped in favour of a rearrangement which led to the transepts being extended to accommodate side chapels and some supplemental activities.

The side chapels in particular were needed for those lower-ranking members of the clergy who had not been authorised to conduct services from the high altar. The apsidal (rounded or polygonal) ends at many of the early cathedrals were, however, never changed and have remained unaltered to the present day. Shrines commemorating or containing the remains of patron saints were often substantial in size and had lavish ornamentation, but only a few survived the large-scale destruction of the Reformation. Reliquaries (receptacles) containing relics of importance or value were similarly treated, with some made from a precious metal, and a large number are known to have been in lead with rich oil gilding.

A special feature of the great churches concerned the chapter houses and cloisters. A chapter house (*capitulum*) is a building linked to the church, used for the daily meetings of the monastic chapter. These buildings are often polygonal in shape and in later times the secular cathedrals also had a chapter house for similar purposes; most were built between the thirteenth and fifteenth centuries. A cloister is a rectangular court surrounded by a covered and colonnaded passageway on all sides. The cloisters were used

69. The cloisters at Gloucester Cathedral

by the monks for study and as places of recreation. They also served as passages and communication links between the church and the monastery, and occasionally they were provided with cells or stalls (*carrels*) for solace and privacy. Although this was an item of secondary importance this seldom meant that it had poorer quality masonry – a good example is the cloisters at Gloucester Cathedral (Fig. 69).

Geometry was used by the medieval masons as the basis for church design, just as it was also employed for the making of mouldings, tracery and various other architectural features. With floor layouts everything was taken from the square, which was applied in modules to create bays identifiable by the spacing of columns and pillars. It is a method which remained a constant determinant of church design throughout the middle ages, the involvement of geometric applications resulting in the widespread use of circles, triangles, rectangles, octagons and diagonals. Work was always carried out in accordance with time-honoured rules in which formative decisions conformed to a mathematical system of measurement, each being able to relate to the other through a series of ratios. It involved a methodology of proportion using one to the square root of two, one to the square root of three and so forth.

Some of the basic processes were made simpler for craftsmen by earlier discoveries such as the deduction by the Ancient Greek astronomer Thales of Miletus, who proved that triangles drawn on the diameter of a circle and touching the circumference are always right angled. Also used to good effect was a geometrical sequence whereby a larger square could be precisely formed around a smaller one and a smaller square could be accurately created within a larger square. This was achieved by drawing a circle and then creating a square as shown by the solid line in Figure 70a; a second and larger square could then be formed by setting a diagonal plane AB, and then it was possible to complete the square along the lines BC, CD and DA. The rules of proportion ensured the sides of the larger square were always equal to the diagonal of the smaller one. Conversely the system could be applied to form a smaller square from a larger one – the sides of the smaller square would always be half the diagonal of the larger square.

The ancient concept of divine proportion was regarded as being fundamental to arrangement and shape and is based on the mathematical relationships in the growth patterns found in nature. From this came the 'golden rectangle', which occurs with regularity in medieval design. It was taken from a square as shown in Figure 69b as ABDC. A line EF then bisected the square and, with the compass set at the distance FB the arc BH could be drawn. By extending the lines AB and CD a vertical line from H set at 90 degrees forms the rectangle AGHC. This can then be subdivided with an additional square being drawn within BGHD, from which another and smaller golden rectangle can be created, as shown at BGYX in figure 70c. It is a process which can be repeated as required.

Simple rules such as these enabled size and proportion to be obtained by expanding or reversing the various sequences. It was straightforward and understandable techniques of this type that allowed the master masons to work with ease and accuracy without the need for advanced mathematical knowledge. The reliable 3–4–5 triangle made by forming a triangle using a selected measurement in this sequence was much used in the fixing of right angles; its application dates back to the building of the pyramids. The important factor of height was also set through geometrics, using either the square from the square root of two (*ad quadratum*) system or the equilateral triangle (*ad triangulum*) system. Through the way the module was applied the square gave the greater height – a feature much used in Gothic church building in England. Use of the equilateral triangle made for churches of a lower height when determined by the square root of three (Fig. 71).

In medieval Gothic architecture the basic ratio was 1:1, which is the square, the next was 1:2, and the rectangles 2:3 and 3:4 were also in regular use. These four ratios were dominant throughout the English Gothic period and in combination can be found in a wide range of church designs in relation to length, width and height. The stability of the Gothic design depended upon a balance between thrust and counter-thrust in the use of these ratios. The downward pressure of the main walling, overhead vaulting and roofing was counteracted by techniques such as carefully contrived arching and deep projecting buttresses suitably weighted with pinnacles.

Historians frequently comment that no plans (*platte*) are discovered with the original contract documents for church building. The master masons drew plans on expensive parchment, and it is likely this was cleaned for further use if it survived the rigours of handling onsite. One reason why the dating of churches has to rely so heavily on examining surviving elements is that there is very little documentation from the time of construction. Throughout the various phases in church building the shape and size of the windows can be a good indicator of the period of origin, providing an earlier style has not been replicated by later work. In strict Classical architecture windows vary in proportion according to the location in the elevation and are almost a language of interpretation, having been determined as an outcome of the main rules of symmetry, proportion and progression in the overall design. The various Gothic forms are covered in the section on windows (page 176); particular attention needs to be given

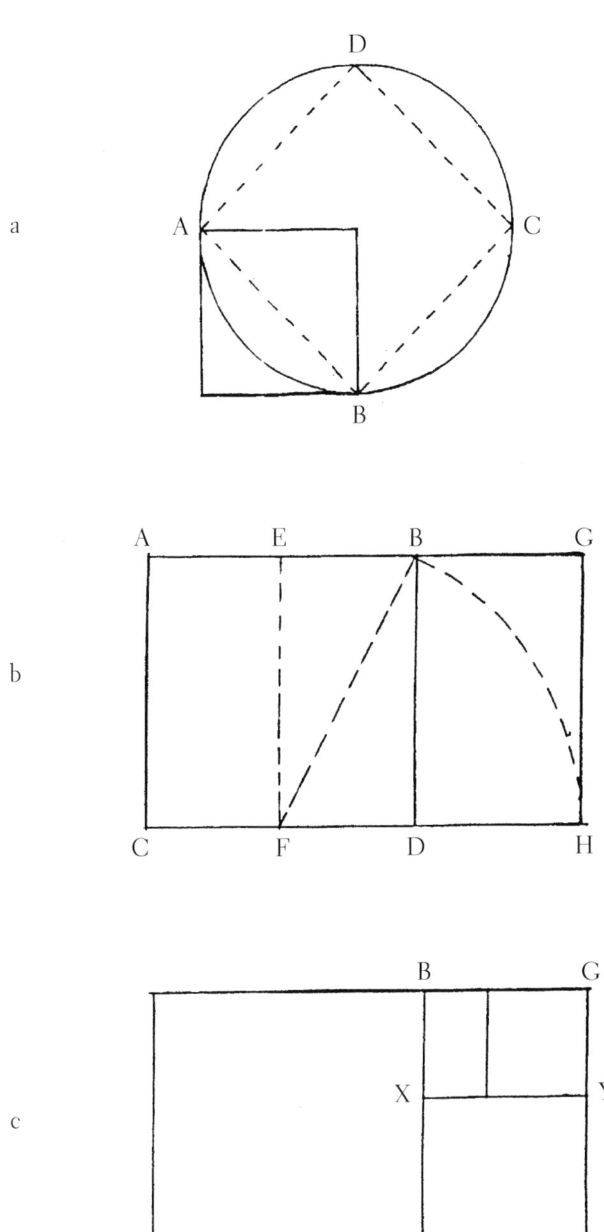

70. Geometrics

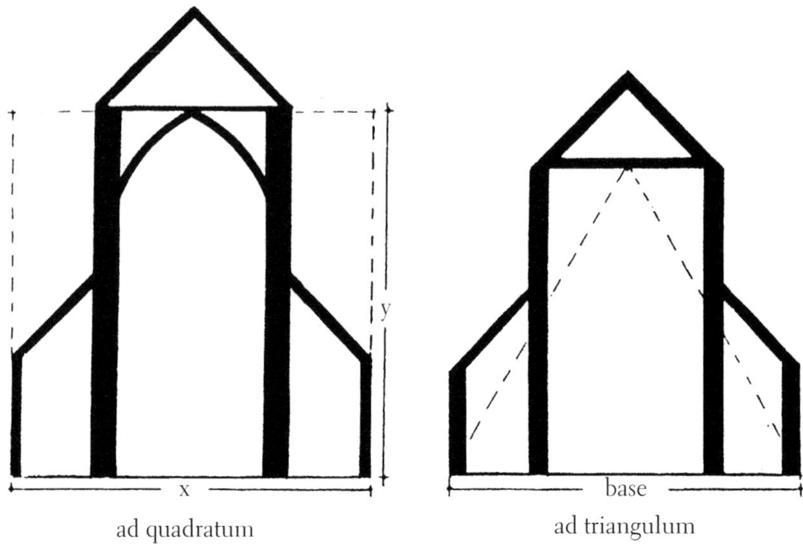

71. Church height-to-base proportions calculated through geometrics. The measurements x and y are equal and form a square.

to the individual styles between the three Gothic phases. Mouldings that form a band or contour around various parts and elements of a church can also be a useful source of guidance. In addition, mouldings and decorative features on capitals, bases, cornices and similar items can be highly revealing in the dating process. In true Classical architecture the types of moulding do not alter because they are made to set rules and are not influenced by fashion or phases over the course of time.

At the beginning of the middle ages women were prevented from entering the main body of a cathedral or a church belonging to one of the monastic foundations. In practice this proved to be highly restrictive and precluded them from going beyond a small designated area at the extreme west end of a church. This area was termed a gallilee and was defined by a screen or a line in the floor. Evidence indicating this can still to be found on occasions but many churches catered for women by constructing a separate chapel or by reserving a vestibule or porch for their sole use. Most were located at the west end but variations are to be found, such as the one at Lincoln Cathedral, which is in the form of a porch on the west side of the south transept. At Durham Cathedral the same provision is at the west end of the nave, while others sometimes occur in most unexpected places. Also at Durham is a black marble line placed immediately in front of the font which marks the point beyond which women should not go. Eventually the use of the gallilee altered and as it was considered to be a much less sacred part of a church it became a reservation for penitents.

Smaller Churches and Chapels

Most of the smaller churches and chapels which date from earlier times have been built to one of four basic plan types and are either one cell or cruciform in shape, or have two or three linked but differently proportioned cells. The original form may not always be immediately apparent because of later alterations and additions but there are few deviations. During the medieval period the nave was often used for social and other secular activities but the Lateran Council considered that this would debase the sanctity of the altar, and in 1215 issued a decree requiring the sanctuary to be isolated from the nave by an intervening space we now know as the chancel. As a result more three-cell churches were built after that date, but the ruling was not fully observed.

Notable exceptions are the few circular churches which appeared just before or during the twelfth century. They were designed to serve the needs of the Knights Templar and the Knights Hospitallers; the Templars were later disbanded and banished by order of the Pope. In the middle ages the term 'hospital' had a much wider meaning than it has today. It was a place of refuge for the sick, the elderly and the needy, orphans, pilgrims and travellers. The circular plan was based on the design of the Church of the Holy Sepulchre in Jerusalem and in England few of these churches have survived. The only remaining examples are St Sepulchre, Northampton, Temple Church, London, Holy Sepulchre, Cambridge, Little Maplescombe, Essex, and the chapel at Ludlow Castle, Shropshire.

All but a few ancient churches have the chancel pointing eastwards and, although the reason is not fully understood it is thought that this may symbolise the direction of the route to Jerusalem. Many alternative theories have been put forward, but none can be proved. Few exceptions to an eastern orientation are found but the notion may also have had a practical reason as this gave the maximum amount of available natural light for the dawn mass. The practice became a long-established tradition and is still generally observed. In many medieval churches the chancel is frequently found to be slightly out of alignment with the nave. This occurs with regularity and again the reason is not known, although it is clearly not accidental.

The original northern entrances in some ancient churches are often discovered blocked up. This arose through the emergence of a superstition that evil came from the north. At one stage the feeling became so strong that in a number of churches all window and door openings on the northern side can be seen filled, typical examples being St Michael's Church, Duntisbourne Rouse, Gloucestershire, and St Mary's, Breamore, Hampshire. Before this the north door was in constant use for processions, funerals and christenings. Known as the devil's door, it was always left open during a baptism so that any evil spirits in the child could be exorcised by way of the north door. This superstition is also the reason why the priest's door is more often found on the southern side of the chancel.

By the fifteenth century many churches had a chantry chapel (see page 213). Some took the form of a small extension in the north or south wall, but most were within the nave enclosed by a parclose (an open panelled screen). In 1547 chantries were dissolved by decree and the space was adapted for other church use. If a parish church has a crypt it is an indication that it enjoyed wealthy patronage sometime in the past.

The layout of some local churches is similar to those seen in the cathedrals and completely unlike the conventional arrangement in the usual parish church. These are the collegiate churches which were served and administered by a college of secular priests or canons although they were not the seat of a bishop. The colleges were formed by non-monastic clergy who held services in churches receiving special funds for the maintenance of a life of prayer. In medieval times a main requirement when a foundation was created was an obligation to pray for the souls of the providers. In an adjusted form this practice also extended into some of the monastic cathedrals which had collegiate chapters. Most collegiate churches enjoyed the benefit of a superior finish and had better-quality fittings and furnishings, more particularly the stalls and the misericords (Fig. 119). An uncommon feature was the setting of the pews at right angles, which resulted in either side overlooking the other across the central aisle. At one time the laity had no rights to the building and had no responsibilities for its maintenance and upkeep. Normally the canons used the choir for services, keeping the nave for processions to which lay people could be invited. In the course of time most collegiate foundations became local parish churches and some have remained unaltered. Among the surviving examples are the Church of St Michael, Ledbury, Herefordshire; St Peter's, Tiverton, Devon; St Boniface's, Bunbury, Cheshire; and St Andrew's, Wingfield, Suffolk.

Ossuaries or charnel houses are places where the bones of the dead were kept. In the past a shortage of burial space sometimes meant that older graves had to be reclaimed for further use. The bones of the original occupants were placed in a building attached to the outside of the church or in a freestanding structure within the graveyard. A few were vaulted underground chambers. During the nineteenth century ossuaries were gradually cleared and their entrances permanently blocked up. Later most were demolished but a few have survived as a feature of the past, a rare example being one in the crypt in St Leonard's Church, Hythe, Kent. Many churches still have a stone platform with steps located either near the entrance or the main access to the churchyard. This is a legacy from the time when horses provided the only means of travel. Known as upping stocks they were used for mounting.

Saxon Churches (c. 600–1066)

Throughout the Northumbrian region the early Saxon parish churches followed the simple Celtic design, with the walls high in relation to the size and width of the nave, and the length three times the width. They were also aisleless and had a small rectangular chancel accessed through a narrow-arched opening. In southern England different proportions applied, with the length being twice the width, and many had an apsed sanctuary the same width as the nave. Sometimes these churches had shallow transepts on either side or a recess known as a porticus, a feature that reflected the Roman basilica style (Fig. 72). A porticus is a chamber or recess entered from the nave or crossing through a narrow opening. The transept evolved out of the porticus, the difference being that the transept is open to the nave and is part of the main body of the church. A porch or narthex at the western end gave the congregation access to the church (see also page 167, Porches). After the Synod of Whitby in AD 664 church design in the northern region began to follow the southern style. Some of the larger churches built to the basilican pattern have a small crypt (*confessio*) immediately beneath the altar, housing the remains of saints or important church relics. Most were accessed by stone steps from the nave but there is evidence to indicate that a limited number were entered in a similar way from a porticus.

The method of shaping the quoins known as long and short work is a particular feature of Saxon architecture (Fig. 25). It was regular practice to use rubble stone for the walls except for the quoins and door and window openings. Much of the rubble facework was plastered and divided into panels by protruding horizontal bands and matching lesene strips worked in ashlar form (a lesene is a pilaster strip without any form of capital or

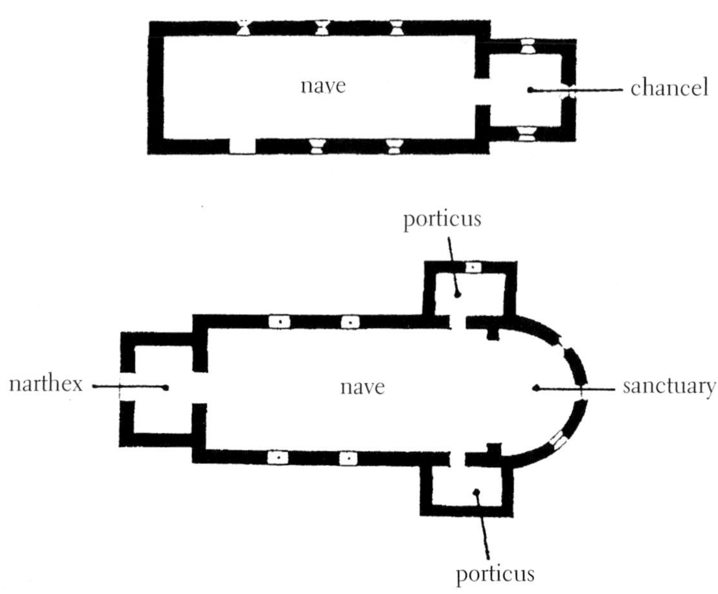

72. Saxon church layouts – *top*: the Celtic style; *bottom*: the Roman style

base) (Fig. 25). Saxon door and window openings were narrow and had an emphasis on height, with the windows placed at a high level to enable the overhanging eaves to provide better cover from the weather. Window openings were widely splayed with the aim of bringing in more light and ventilation; sometimes the splays run both internally and externally but they can also be found splayed internally with a chamfered jamb externally (Fig. 91). Doorways have narrow openings with heavy triangular or round arches supported on large square imposts. Buttressing was seldom used and few of the smaller churches had a tower. Towards the end of the Saxon period Romanesque features also began to appear alongside traditional Saxon designs. The shape of the pillars, columns and piers together with the design of the shafts, capitals and bases are distinctive features (see Pillars, Piers and Columns, pages 76–84). An exceptional example of an unaltered Saxon church is the Church of St Lawrence, Bradford-on-Avon, Wiltshire (Fig. 73). Also noteworthy are St Mary's, Breamore, Hampshire, St John's Escomb, Durham, and the churches at Corhampton in Hampshire, Bradwell-on-Sea in Essex and Wareham in Dorset.

73. Early Saxon church, Bradford-on-Avon, Wiltshire

~

Key Indicators for Saxon Churches

Arches	Half-round
Windows	Window heads half-round or triangular. Most single windows had either semicircular arched heads or long stones placed on end to form a triangular opening. Larger windows usually featured two lights with a central baluster and long and short work at the jambs.
Buttresses	Appear more like pilasters and have shallow projections.
Masonry	Rough masonry is a particular characteristic of the period especially in the north of England. Sometimes

	more refined work found in the south. Long and short work a distinctive feature.
Capitals	Capitals mostly square or in shallow cushion form. Generally plain but occasionally more decorative.
Bases	Generally lack depth and are often extremely shallow.
Columns, pillars and piers	Spiral shape occurs from time to time. More generally plain. Occasionally ornamented.
Ornament	Surviving examples are carved figures, spirals, angles and strange creatures.
Mouldings	Few and plain.

~

Norman Churches (c. 1066–1199)

The Norman Conquest resulted in an enormous cultural change which affected both architectural design and methods of construction. Once established, the Normans embarked on an expansive building programme which included remodelling or rebuilding many of the Saxon churches and abbeys, especially the larger ones. They built two-cell and three-cell churches with the nave wider than the chancel, some with an apse which was superseded later by the square-ended chancel. The more prestigious churches were usually three cell, with wide-arched openings to the north and south transepts and much narrower arches dividing the chancel from the nave and the chancel from the sanctuary. After the Norman period, this began to change in the fourteenth century with the arch between the nave and the chancel being enlarged and the division marked by a rood screen. Chancels also began to be increased in length to meet the needs of growing and more intricate ceremonies. The cruciform plan with a central tower was more regularly used in the larger churches and side aisles appeared in some for the first time, usually narrower than those constructed later (Fig. 74).

The side aisle (*aile* – a wing) is a lasting legacy from the Normans. The elevation is characterised by walls of extreme thickness and small round-headed windows with deep splays, with some being two light with a small pillar between (*fenestra columpnata*). In the early stages of the period the ornamentation around openings was somewhat restricted, with most having a shallow recess externally and a hood mould over. As time went on the mouldings to the arches and the jambs became far richer and more ornamental. Two-light windows steadily became larger, especially towards

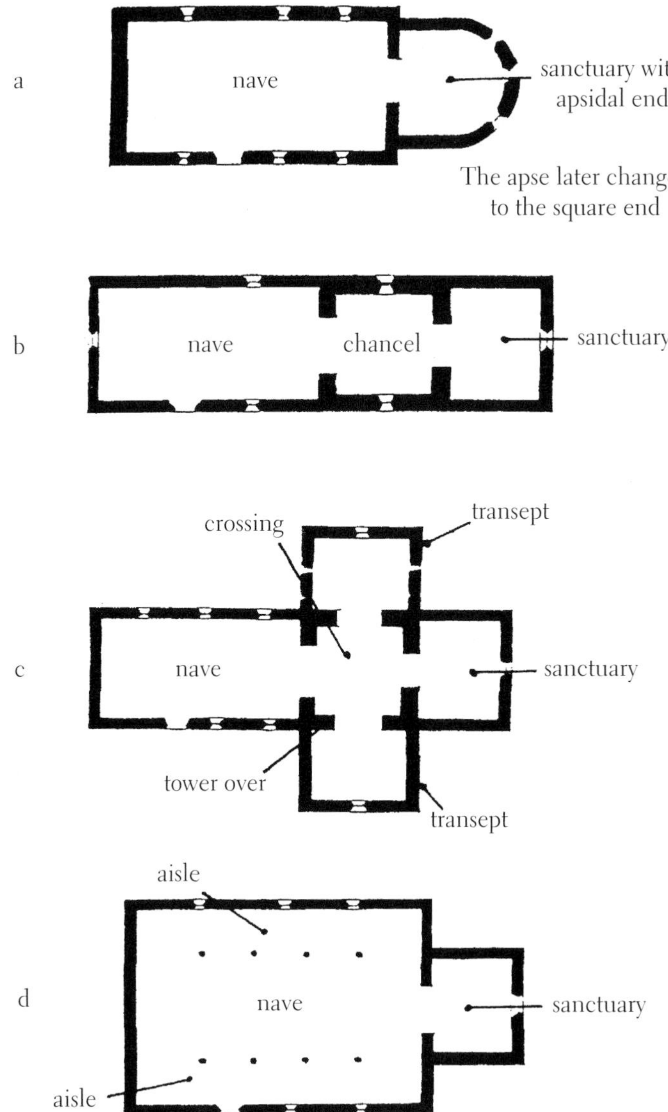

74. Norman church layouts – (a) two cell; (b) three cell, (c) cruciform; (d) aisled

the latter part of the period, and some had much shallower recesses with arched heads that embraced the whole opening. It was the custom of the time to feature heavily enriched carvings on the chancel arch and the entrance doorway, the ornamentation to the doorways was plainer in the early stages of the period. Enrichments were various and generally bold and the weather mouldings usually terminated with carved corbels. Sculpture was seldom used before the twelfth century but was frequently introduced into the earlier churches later in the period. The shafts used in the jambs were mainly circular but occasionally octagonal. The ornamentation was mostly zig-zag or spiral moulding enriched with foliage. Grotesque heads set in hollow mouldings and the signs of the zodiac sometimes appeared.

The Norman style began soon after the Conquest in 1066 and continued with little change until about 1159 (Fig. 75). After this the gradual transition to Gothic started to take hold. The Norman cathedrals and a large number of churches had three levels, with an arcade on the ground floor and a triforium above, over which was the clerestory that provided most of the natural daylight (Fig. 76). Another regular feature was the provision of a crypt under the main floor, sometimes used to house relics or the remains of a saint, and the arrangement of passageways so that pilgrims could pass through in continuous file. A particular characteristic found in the later part

75. Norman church

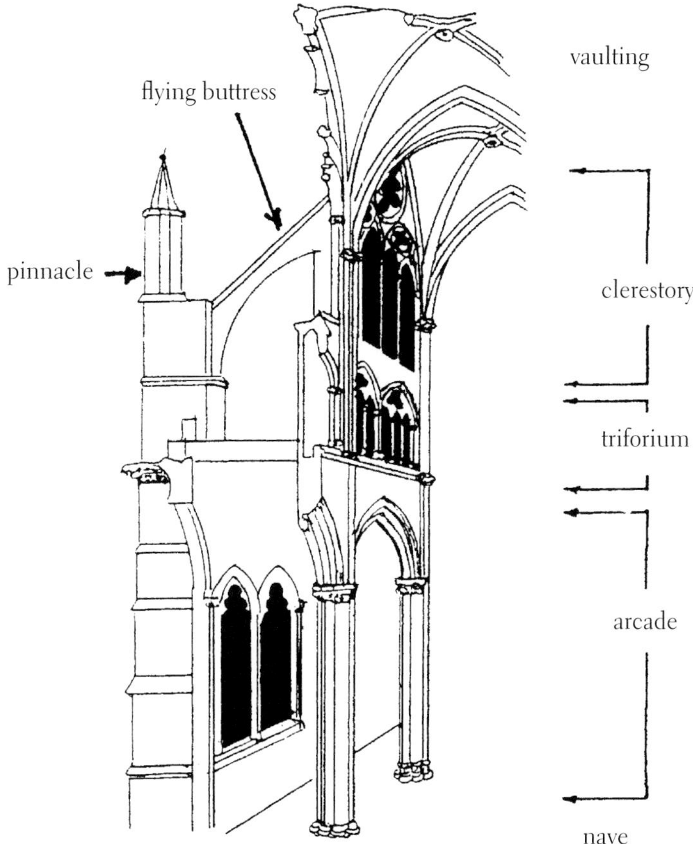

76. Norman church features

of the period is blind arcading (see also Arcading, page 168), which is a form of decorative embellishment worked on the face of a wall, depicting a series of protruding interlocked arches (Fig. 77). Arcading of an exceptionally high standard can be seen at the Priory Church, Christchurch in Dorset and at Much Wenlock Abbey in Shropshire. Towards the end of the period masonry became more finely jointed, which is a factor that needs to be taken into consideration when dating original work. Norman churches of interest are St Michael's, Stewkley, Buckinghamshire, the Church of St Mark and St Luke, Avington, Berkshire, the Church of St Nicholas, Old Shoreham, West Sussex, and the Church of St Mary and St David, Kilpeck, Herefordshire.

77. Blind arcading

~

Key Indicators for Norman Churches

Arches Half-round.

Windows Round headed. Circular windows also found.

Buttresses Generous breadth with small projection.

Masonry Extremely thick walls using small stones.

Capitals Cushion-type common, more regularly seen on circular shafts in small churches – an adaptation cut the under part to rounded mouldings. Late styles ornamented with heavy foliage. Foliage and decoration eventually becoming lighter in style. Towards the end of the period some capitals scalloped.

Bases A considerable variety of styles produced. In the early part of the period few mouldings. Bases are often large and square. Many also have a rounded sub-base upon which stands the shaft with later examples having decorative foliage or small creatures carved into the corners.

Columns, pillars and piers: Norman piers are generally massive and are mostly cylindrical or polygonal. Some were ornamented with flutes but the earlier dimensions tended to be reduced in size towards the end of the period. Later fluted, spiral and zig-zag decoration frequently occurred with the fluting sometimes in the diagonal. Square or rectangular pillars sometimes found. Clustered or compound pillars can be discovered with square recesses cut at the corners. Polygonal pillars may also be found clustered.

Ornament: Mainly billet, nail-head, chevron, beaked, cable, scalloped, and cone designs found along with others.

Mouldings: Usually plain, sometimes with rounds, square and hollows.

~

The Transition to Gothic Style

The strong influence of the Norman or Romanesque style began to falter more noticeably at around the end of the twelfth century, but a full transition to Gothic was at first slow and somewhat hesitant. It was the influence of the Gothic cathedrals around Paris and later the Cistercian abbeys of Burgundy that motivated an interest in the Gothic form in England. Half-round and pointed arches started to appear in the same elevation and towers became slender and less overbearing. A good example is Boxgrove Priory in West Sussex. Mouldings and ornamentation also altered to become bolder and deeper, and more sculptured decoration gradually appeared. The essential factors which distinguish Gothic designs from the Saxon and Norman styles are pointed arches, ribbed pointed vaulting, a divergence from the square-bay module and an emphasis on height through the extended spire.

Whereas Norman churches gave a visual expression of substance and strength the Gothic form steadily became more subtle and artistic. In the larger churches masons aimed at creating a sense of grandeur and delight through balance and proportion. The size of masonry blocks, for example, were chosen to ensure they achieved a harmony with the volume and size of the structure. As the delicacy of the style developed, the decoration and ornament were more frequently worked in a way that gave alternative perceptions and an added interest to the eye. The various forms of relief in the carvings were designed to establish a range of contrasts between light and shadow which changed constantly according to the intensity of the sun. All this made for a vibrancy that was at variance with the plainer images that had gone before. Once the style was established the change became vigorous, and over the course of the thirteenth century most parish churches had acquired many aspects of the Gothic style.

While Gothic architecture is mainly characterised by the pointed arch, traceried windows and slender piers, the advancements in vaulting and buttressing were the decisive innovations that moved the style forwards. They resulted in the walls of churches gradually becoming taller and thinner with more window space, and in designs becoming complex and eventually more skeletal in structure. The increase in natural light nurtured a growing view among the clergy that this, and the magnificence it revealed, enabled people to be drawn closer to God through the creation of 'a piece of heaven on earth'.

The English Gothic period passed through four distinct phases of change which Thomas Rickman (1776–1841) grouped in his book *An Attempt to Discriminate the Styles of English Architecture from the Conquest to the Reformation* (1817) into classifications he termed Norman (the transitional stage, sometimes described as English Romanesque), Early English (1202–1300), Decorated (1301–1400) and Perpendicular (1400–1500). The clearest distinguishing features between these stages are best found in the cathedrals and larger churches. The English interpretation often differed from that of continental Europe: while in overall terms the building was to a high standard and rich in quality, it was nevertheless generally more restrained and less flamboyant than that seen in mainland Europe. Before each phase reached maturity there were long transitional stages which became mixed and interrelated, especially in the early cathedrals, many of which had previously been built as abbey churches to monasteries.

Great English Cathedrals

The twelfth century was a period of rapid growth, and the great advance in the Norman style mostly took place during the reigns of William Rufus and Henry I. The acceptance of the pointed arch began in Britain with the rebuilding of the choir at Canterbury Cathedral, where the majority of the work was undertaken by a French stone mason known as William of Sens; the main period of transition then took place in the latter part of the long reign of Henry II. Much new church building was done in the final decade of the twelfth century, together with alterations and extensions on many of the older churches.

Canterbury Cathedral (Fig. 78) was founded by a mission from Rome in 597 and was built in the basilica style. It was subsequently destroyed by fire in 1067 and again in 1170. The present structure mainly displays the transition from Norman to Early English Gothic and the later Perpendicular style, especially in the major part of the nave, which was constructed between 1380 and 1411. Canterbury is probably the only church in England to have a true corona – a circular projection leading from the apse and entered from the ambulatory.

The earliest complete example of an Anglo-Norman cathedral is Durham; the more notable features are the coupled arches resting upon Cyclopean columns of stone some 23 feet (7 m) in girth, which are deeply channelled with furrows, vertical lines, zig-zags and reticulated designs.

78. Canterbury Cathedral

The square bases to the columns measure 12 feet (3.6 m), and the transverse arches to the vaulting extend in area to 225 square feet (20.9 sq m). The two west towers are massive: each is 144 feet (44 m) high. The whole arrangement gives an imposing message of power and strength.

York Minster has a special place in our history and stands on the site where Constantine I was declared emperor of Rome. Not only is it the largest cathedral in Britain, covering more ground than any other (84,860 square feet – 7,884 sq m), it also has the longest roof. The three great towers are another notable feature. The nave and the chapter house are in the Decorated style with the transepts in the Early English and the choir mainly in the Perpendicular phase (Fig. 79).

Salisbury Cathedral dates from 1220 and is entirely Early English Gothic apart from the cloisters and spire, which are in the Decorated style. The plan is in the form of a Latin cross – the double transepts being a favourite feature with masons at around that time. The fenestration is in the lancet style throughout except at the west ends of the nave aisles, while much of the stonework in the cloisters and chapter house exhibit the transitory state between Early English and Decorated.

Winchester Cathedral dates from 1079 and stands on the site of an earlier Saxon church. The present structure is Norman in origin, and the rebuilt tower has piers of undue bulkiness which are the largest in England in proportion to the span of the arches that rest upon them. The remodelled west front, which includes the great west window, is in the Perpendicular style. There are also four celebrated chantry chapels, including one to Bishop William of Wykeham (Fig. 80) and a shrine dedicated to St Swithin. Swithin was a much-revered bishop who held the episcopacy at Winchester from AD 838 to 862.

English Church architecture is mainly the outcome of the influence and religious customs that came from the Celts, the Saxons and the Normans and the direction that the continental European Gothic form took in Britain. All English cathedrals nevertheless possess a particular individuality and, among others, this is evident at Southwell Minster in Nottinghamshire, Chester Cathedral, Gloucester Cathedral and Bristol Cathedral. At Southwell (Fig. 81) most of the structure is thirteenth century but the tall lead-covered pyramidal roofs to the towers have an overbearing effect not found elsewhere in England. The nave of Chester Cathedral (Fig. 82) houses an old consistory court – the only surviving example in Britain. The court dealt with matters of probate, slander, libel, non-attendance at church and the enforcement of church discipline on the clergy.

79. York Minster, showing *bottom:* detail of the sculptural ornament to the west front

80. Winchester Cathedral, showing *bottom:* the tomb of Bishop William of Wykeham in one of the chantry chapels.

81. Southwell Minster

82. Chester Cathedral

Gloucester Cathedral (Fig. 83) is an exceptionally fine illustration of church building and is on the site of a Saxon abbey founded in AD 681. The existing structure was built by the Normans in 1089 and still has the scriptorium where each monk had a cell for private study. Bristol Cathedral (Fig. 84) began as part of an Augustinian Order in 1140 and is the only cathedral in Britain where the choir, nave and aisles are the same height. When compared to other cathedrals this gives the feeling of a different environment and creates a strong sense of freedom and space.

The origins of Wells Cathedral (Fig. 85) date from 1180, but in the fourteenth century the building went through a number of major changes, mostly in the Decorated form but much of the concluding work is clearly Perpendicular. The thirteenth-century chapter house is polygonal, which was an English innovation, and fronting the clerestory is one of the earliest examples of a stone minstrel gallery.

Ely became a cathedral in 1109 and is a superb example of medieval workmanship. It is entered through an impressive gallilee porch in the

83. Gloucester Cathedral

84. Bristol Cathedral
85. Wells Cathedral

Early English style and the lady chapel has one of the widest medieval vaults in England. The wood ceiling to the nave has been exquisitely worked and painted. The timber lantern, including the octagon – which is mostly in timber – is a feature unique among English churches. The misericords in the fourteenth-century choir stalls are also particularly noteworthy.

The present cathedral at Lincoln dates from 1072 and is essentially an Early English structure although the three periods of Gothic are present in the western facade (Fig. 86). The main core of the building is Norman, along with the lower stages of the tower. It also has one of the few remaining cathedral rood lofts.

The original church at St Alban's was Saxon (AD 793), but the present church was not granted the status of a cathedral until 1877. The Norman tower of 1080 is the oldest cathedral tower in England with Roman bricks and tiles used in the walling. The main structure represents every phase of English architecture, ranging from Saxon to Perpendicular. Externally the nave is 292 feet (89 m) in length and is claimed to be the longest in the Gothic style in the world. The shrine of St Alban is an important focal point and the thirteenth- and fourteenth-century wall paintings are some of the finest in England. There is also an interesting high altar reredos which has been dated to the year 1448.

86. Lincoln Cathedral

Lichfield Cathedral was built in the Early English style and later enlarged in the Decorated form. The chapter house was built in 1249 and has unusual rib vaulting which springs from a single central pillar. As a result of progressive changes, the body of the church provides an unbroken sequence of works, each illustrating a particular phase. The lower part of the west end, the choir, the crossing and a large part of the transepts and chapter house are Early English. The nave is transitional between Early English and Decorated and the lady chapel and the remaining part of the choir are also Decorated. Works of the Perpendicular period are chiefly the vaulting in the transepts and in the insertion of the larger windows.

Although not in England, certain features of St David's Cathedral are of special interest and warrant a mention. It has a rare thirteenth-century stone shrine, an exceptionally fine fourteenth-century pulpitum (see page 215) and a carved timber roof which is a noteworthy example of the Perpendicular period. The ceiling to the tower is also unusual and has the coats of arms of the various bishops involved in the construction of the cathedral painted in heraldic colours.

The earliest known record of a church on the site where Ripon Cathedral (Fig. 87) now stands is AD 671. Built by Wilfrid, then bishop of York, the only surviving part is a rather curious and interesting crypt. The existing

87. Ripon Cathedral

88. Norwich Cathedral

building was begun in 1154 with extensive alterations and additions being made during the three Gothic phases.

Exeter Cathedral has origins going back to 1050, and foremost among the distinguishing features are the imposing transeptal towers, together with the long unbroken line of the ridge-crested roof. A remarkable aspect of the layout is the equal length of the nave and choir and in the equal number of bays they possess. This is a most unusual feature in a cathedral or any other medieval church. The rest of the building has been remodelled mostly in the Decorated style; a notable feature is the wooden ceiling to the chapter house, which has been painted to imitate fan vaulting.

Norwich Cathedral (Fig. 88) dates from 1069 and has the oldest cathedra in England. The spire is the next highest after Salisbury and replaced an earlier structure destroyed by a hurricane in 1362. In the fifteenth century significant alterations took place, including the replacement of the timber ceiling in the nave with stone vaulting.

The Classical style of St Paul's Cathedral remains a dominant feature of the London skyline and has a special place in the architectural heritage of the nation (Fig. 115). The first church on the site is said to have been founded by King Ethelbert in AD 597. The Collegiate Church of St Peter, Westminster, more commonly known as Westminster Abbey, is a royal peculiar, which means it is under the direct control of the Crown and is not connected to any diocese. History refers to a church being on the site as far back as the reign of Serbert King of the East Saxons, but the earliest evidence of a church in the same location goes back no further than AD 909.

Early English Churches (c. 1200–72)
The Development of the Gothic Style

As it marked the beginning of a new era, the first phase of the Early English style involved the need for extensive adjustments to be made in both concept and building practice. The style is rather more austere than the later periods and is characterised by an air of simplicity. Tall, narrow window proportions with or without plate tracery are a particular feature and, while the lancet arch is predominant, pointed obtuse, segmental and equilateral arches were occasionally featured. Plate tracery began in a plain and simple fashion during the late Norman period but developed to become the distinguishing feature of the Early English phase. At this stage tracery involved no more than the cutting of decorative openings into the tympanum of an arch. The Early English style also had a distinct vertical emphasis which in the larger churches was underlined by more slender towers and spires, and in windows frequently displaying shafts in the reveals with decorative moulding. A feature of the thirteenth-century Gothic style is the difference in the shape of many pointed arches on the internal face. As mentioned earlier, these were known as rere-arches and remained much in use until the Perpendicular period. Mouldings were plain, with alternate rounds and deeply cut hollows, and many had trefoils and cinquefoils. Diaper patterns also became a favoured form of decoration, made up of carved patterns of small square or lozenge shapes.

Generally, capitals are plain moulded or have sculpted foliage. The abacus is usually round, but occasionally toothed ornament or some other form of enrichment was added. In overall terms there was a lack of variation or diversification, but string courses became more prolific and prominent. Other notable features are plain hood moulds and dog-toothed or zig-zag carvings. Projecting buttresses became prominent, and flying buttresses appeared for the first time. Door jambs were often recessed to receive up to three shafts on each side, but in small openings this was reduced to one shaft on each side. Capitals to the shafts were often generously enriched with carved foliage, the archivolt and the space between the shafts having toothed ornament. Door openings were sometimes split to provide two doors divided by a slender central pier, called a trumeau.

Most external arches have a hood mould over the extrados and occasionally feature a trefoil or cinquefoil outline together with dog-tooth ornament. The end of the phase also saw the introduction of crockets. By the later stages many churches had a tower and a porch, the size and quality of the porch becoming a parish declaration of pride, commitment and means. The cost was usually met by a benefactor, a bequest or the local gentry. Among the many good examples of this period are the Church of St Mary and St Nicholas, Chetwode in Buckinghamshire, St Oswald's, Ashbourne in Derbyshire, the Church of St Lawrence, Affpuddle in Dorset and the church at Breedon-on-the-Hill, Leicestershire.

~

Key Indicators of the Early English Period

Arches	Lancet arch dominant but obtuse and segmental also used.
Windows	Window proportions vary and can be found as single elements or in combinations of two, three, five or seven, and are often surmounted by a large arch embracing the whole group.
Buttresses	Have narrow breadth and deep projections. Sometimes taken to the full wall height without any diminution but are more often broken at various stages with successive reductions in the projections.
Capitals	Many are plain and have deeply undercut mouldings, some with carved foliage. Occasionally toothed ornament used. Foliage sometimes worked around the bell of the capital. Leaves generally given stiff stems and stand well proud and bold. In later work animals appeared with foliage.
Bases	Bases tended to differ little from the Norman period, with the square form being mostly retained but some bases have a double plinth. Later they increased in height to become in effect a pedestal. Later in this stage they had attic mouldings (one above the other).
Columns, Pillars and piers	Plain, compound, cylindrical or octagonal, often surrounded by detached shafts. A common feature is a series of small shafts arranged around a large central pillar. A change in style resulted in the appearance of square pillars with small projecting shafts in the middle

of each face. Sometimes shafts take the form of four half-round circles joined together.

Ornament Dog-tooth prominent. Single leaf and flowers common, together with various foliage patterns. Much stiff foliage.

Mouldings Mouldings plain but more boldly cut. Mostly a series of alternating rounds and hollows. Ornament not much used.

~

Decorated-Style Churches (c. 1272–1349)

The Decorated period is considered to be the stage at which the Gothic style reached maturity. It hosted a period of much enrichment and gave opportunities to innovate, extemporise and be expressive. The most prominent characteristic is the bar tracery, which is either geometric or worked in delicate and easy flowing lines. Bar tracery is the piercing of stone into a fret-like form to create interlaced patterns and designs. During this stage it steadily became more elaborate, elegant and graceful. In the larger churches the designs were often more intricate, with liberal use being made of the ball-flower design (see Fig. 95p). Hood moulds over the heads of windows and doors were generally supported by corbel heads with bosses decorated in foliage designs. Larger windows were divided by mullions with separate lights, the most prominent arch in windows being the two-centred type. Capitals for the most part were plain or enriched with foliage.

Mouldings around the capitals were round, ogee or hollows – not so deeply cut as in the Early English phase. Niches appeared as a feature and the building of porches became more extensive, with many being rebuilt. Mouldings generally became broader and more shallowly formed, mostly from rounds and hollows separated by small fillets. The hollows were sometimes enriched with carved foliage, especially the ball-flower design. A flower of four leaves succeeded the dog-tooth ornament of the Early English style. Arches became much less pointed, with some being ogee shaped. Windows were larger, with decorative heads, and there was a greater complexity in vaulting. Crocket shapes changed to curve inwards. Doorways were not so deeply recessed and had plain arches which were rarely moulded. Some doorways had shafts to the jambs with ogee arches over, a feature that gradually became more prominent. Mouldings to arches often continued down to plinth level. Shouldered arches were occasionally used and jambs started to have lighter proportions, while plain mouldings with enrichments were less popular, except for the ball-flower design.

At this time buttresses tended to be continued upwards, above the parapets, and terminated as pinnacles. While the Decorated phase is considered to have been the high point of Gothic architecture, few churches were built completely in the style, an exception being the Church of St John, Shottesbrooke, Berkshire, which dates from 1337. A number, however, are predominantly in the Decorated theme; some good examples are the churches at Stebbing and Great Bardfield in Essex and the Church of St Mary and St Michael at Trumpington in Cambridgeshire. All phases of the Decorated form can be seen at St Botloph's in Boston, Lincolnshire.

~

Key Indicators of the Decorated Period

Arches	Equilateral, obtuse and symmetrical arches mostly used.
Windows	Became more enlarged, many being divided by mullions to form separate lights within the same frame. Tracery became more delicate, including the geometrical, intersecting and reticulated forms. Two central arches became more prevalent. Square window heads found from time to time.
Buttresses	Usually worked in stages and often ornamented with niches and crockets. Frequently capped with pinnacles. Buttresses began to be set diagonally. Crockets curve inwards.
Capitals	More often circular, with moulding less deeply cut than before. Mouldings generally plain but sometimes have the ball-flower design. Varying forms of foliage also used. Rounds and hollows not so deeply cut. Later foliage took a more natural form.
Bases	Much variety occurs at this stage. Fewer mouldings, and shape often similar to the shaft. Plinths are often double and of considerable height. Circular mouldings often overhang the base.
Column, pillars and piers	Pillars which have clustered shafts are sometimes lozenge shaped but are more regularly plain, circular or octagonal. If square, pillars are usually set at the

diagonal. Another style took the form of four half-circles joined to a small central shaft. They can also be diamond shaped surrounded by engaged shafts.

Ornament Ball-flower design much used. Foliage tended to be in a true natural form. Diaper work. Four-leafed flower.

Mouldings Filleted style favoured. Generally less deeply cut. More diversified. Hollows became broader and shallower.

~

Perpendicular-Style Churches (c. 1350–1539)

A particular characteristic of this style is the wide proportions given to window openings and the application of finer and exceptionally delicate tracery, accompanied by arches being much less pointed. A strong emphasis was placed on vertical lines, and a notable feature is the regular use of transoms that cross at right angles to the mullions, an item often repeated several times within the same frame. Many larger windows contain numerous small rectangular lights and a greater variety of designs were used in tracery. Mouldings differed little from the previous phase. The square arrangements over arched doorways have distinctive ornamentation in the spandrels (in this context a spandrel is the space between an arch and the top of a window head, doorway or similar; the word can also be applied to the quasi-triangular space between two arches). In the early stages of the period, arches are two- or four-centred, but became considerably flatter later. Small openings are frequently in ogee arch form. Clerestories became larger and more of a feature in the smaller churches, with a triforium being included in some. The Church of St Mary at Melton Mowbray in Leicestershire has a much-acclaimed clerestory which is continuous and a dominant feature externally. Towards the end of the period ornamentation became shallower and of poorer quality. The jambs of doorways sometimes have niches and are more usually moulded. They also frequently have a small shaft (or a series of shafts) with round mouldings with a base but no capital. There is often an abundance of stone panelling in the walls, and flying buttresses became more decorative.

Mouldings became shallower and more angular and are sometimes carried around an arch before going down to ground level. Double ogee mouldings became popular. Many of the carvings in the walls and buttresses reproduced the designs in the window tracery, and piers became more slender and fluted. Towards the middle part of the sixteenth century the Tudor rose became the favoured ornament, which – along with various other changes – resulted in the concluding phase being dubbed Tudor Gothic. A popular design for pillars was the plain octagon with the faces sometimes slightly hollowed. Compound pillars had a large circular central shaft with a series of small attached shafts which are sometimes filleted or hollowed. Another type features a square with recessed concave corners and small projecting shafts to each face. The capitals to columns are mostly large and plain but some are ornamented with foliage, especially in the larger churches. Sometimes the abacus is octagonal with a rounded necking. Ogees, beads and hollows prevailed in the moulding, much of it in lower relief. Battlements became more of a feature. Churches of this period worthy of special mention are St Nicholas' at Newbury in Berkshire, St Mary's at Burwell in Cambridgeshire, St Oswald's at Malpas in Cheshire, All Saints' at Odell in Bedfordshire and Holy Trinity Church at Long Melford in Suffolk.

~

Key Indicators of the Perpendicular Period

Arches	Obtuse and equilateral arches favoured in the early stages, later replaced by the four-centred arch. Intrados often trefoil in outline.
Windows	Wider and more expansive windows with flatter arched heads. Considerable use of mullions and transoms. Panel tracery.
Buttresses	Similar to Decorated and usually go to the full height of the wall in stages. Much more panelling than before.
Capitals	Large and generally plain and may display the ball-flower, but many are also polygonal and have less-pronounced moulding. Foliage occasionally featured. Upper parts sometimes octagonal. Decoration often shallow in form. Leaf designs are less natural.
Bases	Generally high and invariably octagonal and large. Shape often the same as the shaft. Reverse ogee common, sometimes in double form, where it might be divided by a bead. If a sub-base has been provided it is almost standard for this to be circular, with the lower base underneath sometimes octagonal.
Columns, pillars and piers	Plain octagonal form much used. Sides sometimes hollowed. Small shafts attached to the main pillar usually plain but sometimes filleted. Piers became more

	slender and often oblong in shape. Casement moulding fairly common. Clustered shafts often have different levels to each element.
Ornament	Fillets frequently found. Patterns of foliage and flowers a feature. Individual leaves also found. Heads of animals, heraldic shields and grotesque images regularly found. Tudor flower. Running patterns of foliage.
Mouldings	Mostly flatter than before. Hollows larger and shallow. Ogee shape popular.

~

Features of the Buildings which Aid Analysis

Porches and Vestibules

In comparative terms porches built in the Saxon or the early Norman periods are plain in appearance; it was not until the Gothic phase that more attention was given to style and ornamentation. Most porches cover the main church entrance on the south side and if positioned elsewhere they are likely to be smaller and less prominent. Those seen in the larger churches are in stone and some have a vaulted ceiling, and at parish level the provision of a porch became increasingly regarded as a necessity, with many being built of timber because of limited funds. A limited number appeared during the first part of Early English phase but from the Decorated stage onwards they became more of a general feature in the parishes. In the more affluent parts of England the size and quality of the porch was often a competitive issue between the parishes, who vied with each other for the best edifice. Sometimes these structures included overhead accommodation; in this form it is known as a parvis and at times provided accommodation for an extra priest, a small chapel, a library or an office for the parish clerk. Particularly fine examples occur in the fifteenth-century porch at the Church of St Margaret, Cley-next-the-Sea in Norfolk and at the Church of St Peter and St Paul, Northleach, Gloucestershire, where the two-storeyed porch has a built-in fireplace in the overhead room. A further example can be found in the oversailing timber-framed porch at the Church of St Mary, Radwinter, Essex. Most later porch additions are date marked, and a few still have a stoup (*stope* or *aspesorium*) for holy water. A number have a niche for the patron saint and in some cases the original stone benches remain.

Apart from being used for business meetings, public declarations, announcements and other secular activities, the porch had an important function in the working of the church. At one stage it was used in the first part of the marriage ceremony, and at funerals, in addition to being a place where wrongdoers could undergo penance. Vows were commemorated by scratching a small rudimentary cross known as a votive cross into a wall or door of the porch – but these crosses can also be found in various places around other outside parts of a church. Some churches are entered through a narthex, which is an access area extending across the main entrance. It was generally placed at the west end and most were separated from the nave by a wall, although in a few isolated cases the division was made with a screen. In England it is a feature which originated in pre-Conquest churches, with the entrance occasionally approached through a small ante-chamber called an exonarthex. The porch was never considered a liturgical part of the church and is the reason why penitents were restricted to it. In church architecture a vestibule is normally an ante-chamber or a lobby which provides access to an outer door of a monastic building or a chapter house.

Arcading

The term arcading is used for the open arched divisions between the nave and aisles of a church (Fig. 76). In the Norman period arches were semicircular and in the later phase often intersect with each other. During the Gothic phase pointed arches became excessively ornamented as the style progressed. Blind arcading refers to a series of decorative arches seated on columns, piers or pilasters, with the areas beneath the arches solid stone or brickwork (Fig. 77).

An Anchorite Cell or Evidence of One's Existence

Most anchorite cells have been removed or altered for a different use, but a limited number have survived much in their original form. They provided privacy and shelter for people who dedicated themselves to lives of solitude, prayer and mortification. In order to be resident in a church an anchorite (*reclusiorum* or an anchoret) needed the consent of the bishop, who had to be satisfied that the applicant was worthy and suited for the way of life. Anchorites should not be confused with coenobites, who undertook a similar role but within the confines of a monastery or convent. More usually sited on the north side of the church, the cell was either let into the walling of the church or built out as a lean-to. After dedication, the participant entered the doorway, which was then fixed or built up, leaving only a small window through which food and water could be passed. Most also had a small opening known as a squint going through to the interior of the church to enable the occupant to celebrate mass. Anchorites often relied on local parishioners for sustenance but some were able to live by way of an endowment. The surviving parts of an anchorite cell can be viewed at the Church of St James, Shere, Surrey, and at the nearby Church of St Nicholas, Compton, where there is a small window in the sanctuary which originally gave an anchorite a line of sight to the altar. At St Botolph's Church, Hardham, West Sussex, a squint can be seen in an external wall of the chancel, which would have originally been enclosed by an anchorite cell long since demolished (Fig. 89). The church was built during the Saxon period in around AD 1050, and records show that Prior Richard occupied the cell in 1285.

Columns, Pillars and Piers, Capitals and Bases

See pages 79–84 for the key indicators for the different architectural styles. While the various designs and styles can be an essential guide in identification, considerable care is necessary before reaching a final conclusion concerning the period or periods involved. The length of time taken to progress from one style to another varied considerably between the regions, and many of the transitional stages were prolonged. Any analysis should also take into account the possibility that items may be later replicas or reused from elsewhere.

Doorways

Saxon doorways are very different to the designs which followed, the openings being narrower and taller with square jambs. Little or no moulding is found, and a particular feature is the enlarged size of the impost block, the dimensions eventually being somewhat reduced later in the period. Many of the original doors can be seen hung on the inner wall face, but gradually this altered to the middle part of the wall. Norman doorways began in a modest form but gradually developed into a highly ornamented and elaborate feature, with some being heavily recessed. At this stage it was usual for parish churches to provide a north and south entrance, often placed towards the west end of the nave, although in some churches an additional door was also inserted in the western elevation. Many chancels

89. St Botoloph's Church, Hardham, Sussex. In the top photograph, the arrow indicates the squint to the left of the chancel window; the bottom photograph is an enlarged view of the squint. The cell has long been demolished, and the existing window is a later replacement.

had a priest's door at the western end of the south wall; any deviation from this is most rare. It was the practice to make the outer half of door openings slightly narrower than the inner part, thereby creating a recess or rebate into which a door could be hung.

Decorative concentric rings seen around the arches tend to be individualistic – some are left plain while others have carvings or hollows with the zig-zag design very popular. In the early Norman stages the mouldings were predominantly plain, but as the style advanced they began to acquire an increasing abundance of enrichment. Moreover, the concentric mouldings around arched Norman doorways steadily expanded to a point where they almost equalled the width of the door opening. It was not always the practice to build semicircular arches; although this was the heavily predominant style, segmental and horseshoe forms were also made. Carved circular shafts are often featured in the jambs, some examples are octagonal. Capitals in the later part of the period are always highly ornamented with carved figures or foliage; the moulding on the impost frequently continued along the wall as a string.

Most Early English doorways have pointed arches but occasionally the heads are flat or semicircular. The principle of constructing arches with several receding rims and borders is very much a feature of the Gothic period. Known as receding orders, this style is found in both early and later work. Mouldings are often numerous and in the larger churches the jambs are inclined to replicate the earlier Norman fashion, which includes the shafts. Sometimes these were detached and in later work often stand well clear of the pier or column. Capitals may be foliaged and are more likely to be moulded. With the exception of the great churches the extraordinary level of enrichment used by the Normans was discontinued in the parishes. As a result, many of the smaller churches have plain doorways with simple dripstones or hood moulds over. The dog-tooth was typical of the enrichment generally seen at around this time (see also Mouldings, page 177). As the Gothic period progressed, the shape and proportion of the arch gradually became flatter and wider. By the Decorated phase doorways were not so deeply recessed and were generally much plainer.

The shafts in the jambs became smaller and the fashion then changed more towards splayed openings to the exclusion of recesses in series. A feature of note is the moulding around the arch, which was more often ovolo and continued on either side down to the plinth An ovolo is a convex moulding in the form of a quarter-circle, often decorated with motifs or similar. The arches to small side doors are invariably ogee and the dripstone or hood mould is usually scrolled. The more prominent forms of

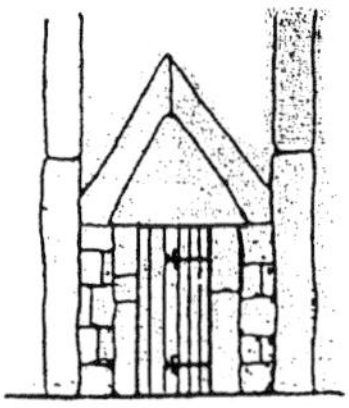

a  b  c

d  e  f

g 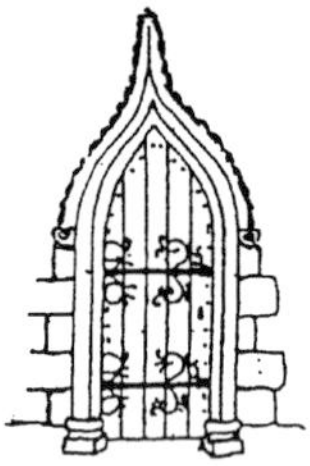 h 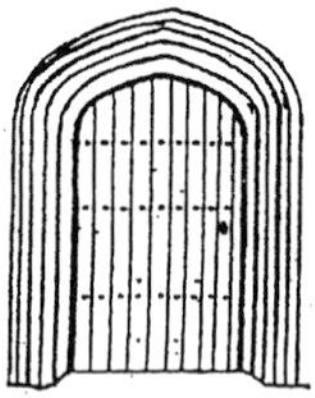 i

j

k

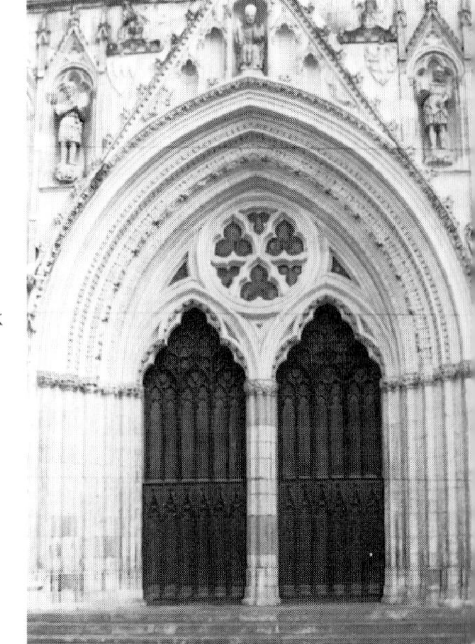

90. Doorways – (a) Saxon; (b) Saxon; (c) Norman; (d) Norman; (e) Early English; (f) Early English; (g) Decorated; (h) Decorated; (i) Perpendicular; (j) Perpendicular; (k) photograph showing a trumeau

ornament are the ball-flower and the four-leafed flower, while the shoulder arch came into more general use.

In the Perpendicular period a considerable change took place in the appearance of doorways. The arch became four centred but not to the exclusion of the two-centred arch. The most characteristic feature is the framing of a rectangle around the arch over the smaller doorways, which often have carving in relief or blind tracery in the spandrels. A few elliptical arches began to appear at this stage. In the larger churches the jambs invariably have large hollows which are sometimes filled with niches for statues, but were more often left plain. In other churches small shafts did occasionally appear in the jambs but this is not a general feature. Various doorway designs covering the Saxon, Norman and Gothic periods are shown in Figure 90. Wide church entrances sometimes have doors on either side of a vertical stone member supporting the tympanum over the doorway called a trumeau (Fig. 90k).

Windows

The narrowness of window openings is a distinctive feature of Saxon churches, and to maximise the penetration of light they were sometimes double splayed both inwards and outwards (Fig. 91i). Windows in the earlier examples have more generally been set in the centre of the wall, but in later work they are mostly placed near the outer face with the splays running inwards. An occasional variation is the provision of internal splays with angled and chamfered external jambs. In Saxon churches the stonework around both window and door openings is never found recessed. In locations such as a church tower, where protection from the weather was not a primary concern, windows usually have larger openings divided by small pillars (Figs 91c–f). Window heads are nearly always semicircular or triangular (Figs 91a–e), although on occasions flat stone lintels were used, mostly cut to a curve on the underside to give the impression of a half-round arch; a good example of this can be seen in a window at the Church of St John, Escombe, County Durham. It was also a regular practice at the time to cut rounded arches from a single piece of stone.

Apart from a few exceptions, windows in the early Norman period continued to have small proportions but later they became bigger, with some being a considerable size (Fig. 92). A particular feature of the early Norman phase is a regular scarcity of ornament, although many openings have small shafts in the external recesses and a label mould over the head. Later work had both mouldings and ornamentation in the arches,

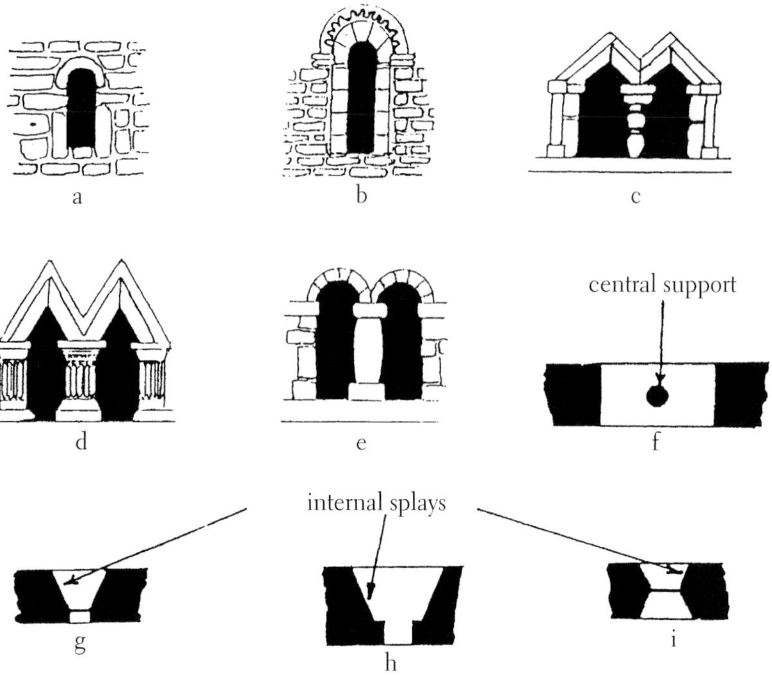

a b c

central support

d e f

internal splays

g h i

91. Saxon Windows

92. Norman windows

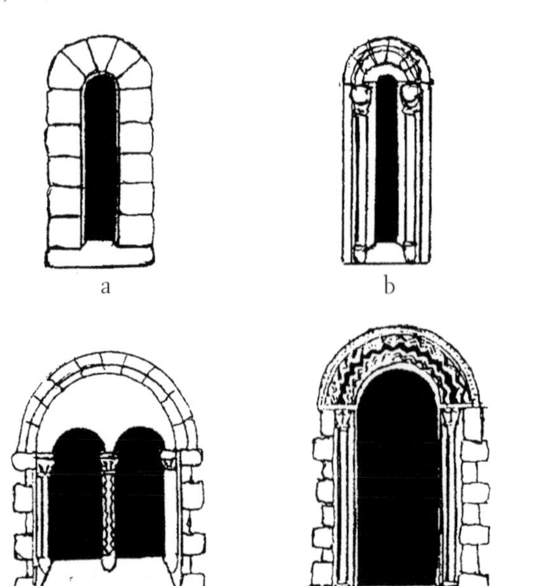

a b c

d e f

sometimes extending into the jambs. Surviving larger windows are most likely to feature two lights divided by a central shaft or pier (Fig. 92d). In the later part of the period circular windows began to be featured – some of them large and prominent – and although generally plain, a limited number had radiating decorative mullions similar to the spokes of a wheel.

In the Early English style window proportions can vary considerably, but in the main they are tall and narrow. This was the time which began the long dominance of pointed-arch window heads. Windows in this style were mostly used either singularly or in the form of small lights combined into groups of two, three, five or seven, often with an all-embracing arch over (Fig. 93). A feature of particular note is the difference in the arrangement and ornament between many of the external and interior openings. In overall terms the interior is likely to be more ornamented than the exterior. Moreover the jambs are always well splayed on the inside and usually have a rere-arch over (see also Arches, page 75). As a subordinate part of the fenestration small triangular windows can occasionally be traced from this time.

During the Decorated style which followed, windows became further enlarged, with many divided by mullions to form separate lights and the heads over filled with tracery (see also Tracery, page 181). This is a feature which in early records is occasionally termed *couronnement* but this only applies where a window opening gives the appearance of a large bay. Two-centred arches became prevalent although segmental and ogee arches were also used. Square window heads appeared infrequently and usually in minor locations. In the smaller churches window mullions were often splayed and had mouldings in a rather plain or simple style, unlike what was often being found in the larger churches. The ball-flower design was much used in mouldings and in some cases even extended into the mullions and tracery. Most circular windows at this time took one of two forms and normally occurred in either the gable ends of the nave or chancel, or in the gables of the transepts.

The rose window has a complex traceried design similar in arrangement to the petals of a rose, whereas the alternative wheel window (Fig. 93) has tracery that radiates out from a central hub, replicating the spokes of a wheel. This style commemorates St Catherine of Alexandria, who was martyred and sentenced to death by being run over by a chariot with knives fixed to the wheels. By way of contrast a smaller round or oval window is known as an oculus, but this feature never became prominent during any of the medieval periods. An oeil-de-boeuf (a bull's eye window) refers to a particularly small round or oval window, often with glazing bars radiating

93. Windows – (a) lancet; (b) group lancet; (c) plate tracery; (d) Y tracery; (e) intersecting; (f) geometric; (g) geometric; (h) reticulated; (i) reticulated; (j) ogee; (k) curvilinear; (l) early Perpendicular; (m) Perpendicular; (n) Perpendicular; (o) late fourteenth century; (p) late fifteenth century; the photograph shows a wheel window

out in the same style as the wheel window. An eye window is a small window set within a pediment.

The purpose of some low-placed windows can be difficult to determine and many have long perplexed the experts. Now normally known as low-side windows they were at first thought to be leper windows, but more recent analysis has generally moved away from this assumption. Placed at a level below other windows but at a convenient height from the ground they are more commonly seen on the south side of the chancel, but a few have been found located in the nave close to the entrance to the chancel. They never occur in an east wall but occasionally can be seen on the north side of a church with none of the known examples pre-dating the Early English period. When discovered in Saxon and Norman churches the evidence indicates they are always later installations. Many still have the original fixing points for shutters or a grille and most provided a distant view of the altar, which was probably the main purpose. At the time only the clergy and nominated acolytes were allowed access to the presbytery and lay-folk could only get a glimpse of the host from a vantage point of this type. These windows should not however be mistaken for a small shuttered opening immediately beneath a window in the south wall of the presbytery. This was used to admit fresh air as the length of the mass often meant that there was a heavy accumulation of candle smoke and strong vapours from the burning of incense. Sometimes a similar opening occurs on the north side to give cross-ventilation.

The basic difference between the Decorated and Perpendicular styles is mainly in the altered arrangement of the tracery and in the arching. The latter involved the wide use of four-centred arches and the introduction of transoms, which significantly altered the appearance of the Gothic form. The flowing lines in the windows of the Decorated period were replaced by vertical and horizontal ones, creating more of a geometrical or gridiron effect. This was also accompanied by the provision of wider and more expansive openings and window heads gradually became flatter. The use of additional mullions produced a proliferation of small rectangular window lights, while the ogee arch so frequently used during the Decorated period was all but abandoned for window designs.

Mouldings and Ornament

Moulding is the term applied to all varieties of outlining or contouring of various parts or features of a church; the diversities in design and arrangement are considerable throughout the medieval period. Mouldings can be formed from extended, projecting, or recessed bands in a plain or enriched style, whereas ornamentation can be a motif, a decorative feature or a series of decorative features (Figs 94 and 95). The wholesale removal by the Normans of Saxon adornment in churches has left limited physical evidence of that period. Nevertheless, enough has survived to indicate that Saxon mouldings were few and plain, the most used being strip-work (narrow lines of stonework usually around door and window openings). While Saxon ornamentation was not a particular feature, when it is found it is (especially on tombstones) an unusually odd mixture of strange creatures, angels and spirals.

The development of moulding was a particular feature of the Normans, beginning in a modest way but then advancing into regular sequences with prominent displays and much varied detail. The Normans seldom used sculpted decoration and preferred geometric ornamentation in the form of squares, rounds and hollows, often found combined variously with splays and fillets. The richer mouldings mostly have a generous assortment of zigzag, chevron, billet, lozenge, nail-head, pellet, bowtell and cable forms, plus the generally abundant beak-head.

Many of the mouldings in the Early English Gothic period took the form of rounds and hollows with the hollows deeply cut, often with fillets (*felet* or *filum*). Also seen are flat, narrow bands used to separate mouldings or to terminate a series of mouldings, (which are occasionally termed *listels*). Small and large rounded mouldings were often worked together. The keel moulding and the dog-tooth ornament are very much a feature of the period, the latter often being found in the rounds of hollows.

During the Decorated phase, mouldings became more diversified and while at the beginning hollows continued to be deeply cut, this later changed to them being much shallower and broader, and sometimes worked to a diagonal plane. The most common feature of the time was the ball-flower, and crockets gradually became more heavily carved – usually with vine motifs. Enrichment generally appeared in the form of foliage, with ogee and scroll mouldings much in favour and to a lesser extent the ovolo. Base mouldings to walls became more strongly defined.

The Perpendicular phase produced a distinct change in style, with mouldings becoming much flatter and less dominant overall. Crockets were more finely carved, using human and animal figures as well as foliage. Small bead-like rounds were also abundant and the casement moulding became a regular feature. Large hollow mouldings also appeared in the jambs to door and window openings and heraldry became a decorative

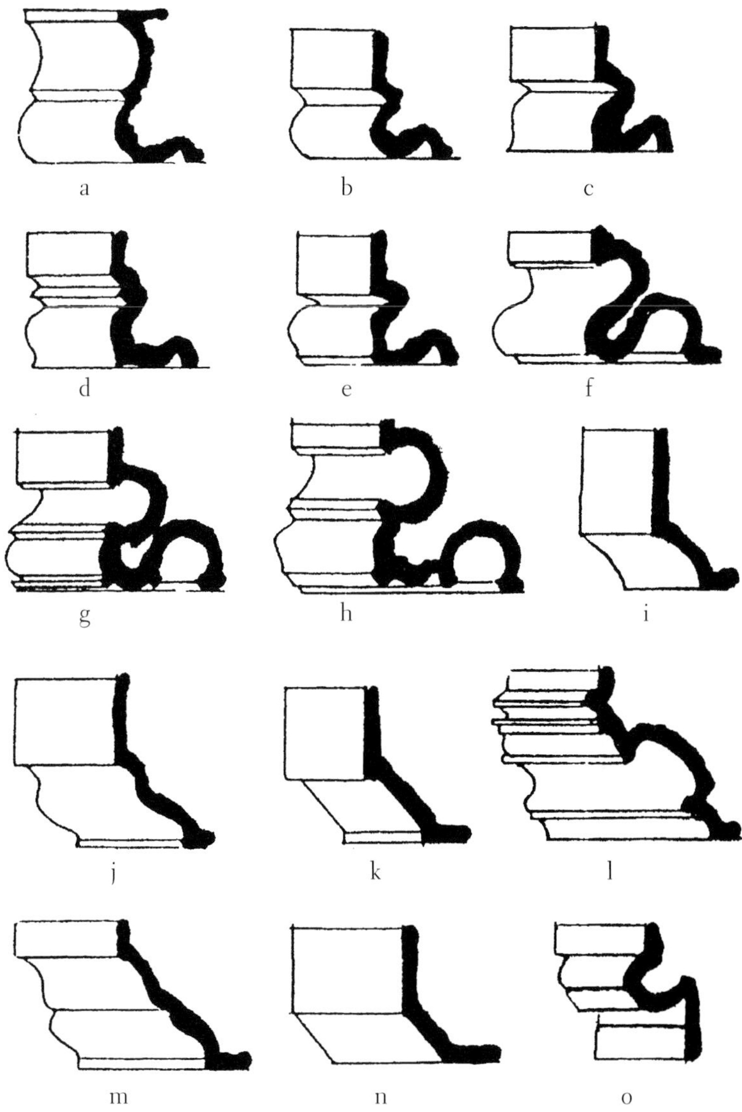

94. Mouldings – (a) roll and shallow hollow; (b) bowtell; (c) pointed bowtell; (d) keel; (e) roll and fillet; (f) scroll; (g) roll and triple fillet; (h) decorated fillet; (i) hollow chamfer; (j) wave; (k) sunk chamfer; (l) casement; (m) double ogee; (n) plain chamfer; (o) chamfered bowtell

95. Ornament – (a) Saxon; (b) Saxon; (c) Saxon; (d) Saxon; (e) indented; (f) zig-zag; (g) billet; (h) double cone; (i) pellet; (j) lozenge; (k) cable; (l) star; (m) beak-head; (n) nail-head; (o) embattled; (p) ball-flower; (q) bay-leaf; (r) bifurcated; (s) brattishing; (t) chevron; (u) dentil; (v) channelling; (w) ovolo; (x) patera; (y) pear-drop; (z) reeding; (aa) rosette; (bb) scalloped; (cc) strapwork; (dd) Tudor rose; (ee) vine; (ff) scroll; (gg) waterleaf; (hh) dog-tooth

element, with tablet flowers and flowing vines often being introduced as additional enrichment.

The projecting mouldings around arches, doorways and windows are especially associated with Gothic architecture. Known as hood moulds (sometimes termed dripstones), they were designed to throw off rainwater and so generally lack decoration to avoid impeding their primary function. With the exception of the ogee style they also follow the contour of the openings they have been designed to protect, while the label stops or corbels upon which they are usually seated are often found worked in the shape of a human head. When forming a rectangular outline over door and window heads they are more correctly termed label moulds.

Grotesques are a form of decoration featuring either fanciful human or animal images and are sometimes enhanced with designs such as foliage, flowers or similar. In churches they are invariably seen as distorted human figures, often linked to mysterious animals or mythical creatures, and at times can be found in sequences which portray all the human emotions. Sometimes they were placed near or around church eaves in the belief that they gave protection from the influence of evil. A church noted for a spectacular display of grotesques and monsters is St John's Church in Thaxted, Essex.

Tracery (Formas) and Foils (Folium)

Tracery is essentially a feature of the Gothic periods and appears in two main forms. The earliest is plate tracery, which, as previously mentioned, consists of thin slabs of stone into which have been cut decorative openings. This is mostly applied in the heads of lancet arches. The later bar tracery is far more elaborate and has slender and different-shaped shafts which branch out from the mullions to form ornamentation in the window heads and lights. All tracery designs are geometric and are mainly derived from a series of circles and arcs. As the style developed, much of this work became exceptionally delicate and sometimes gives the impression of being a freehand creation (Fig. 96).

Plate tracery began in the late Norman period with small circular openings usually made through the spandrel between two round-headed arches, usually under a large circumscribing arch. The concept became fully established in the Early English period and by the later stages some Y or geometric tracery had appeared. More complete bar tracery began in the Decorated stage and at first consisted of foliated circles. This was quickly extended and enhanced by designs featuring trefoils and quatrefoils, which

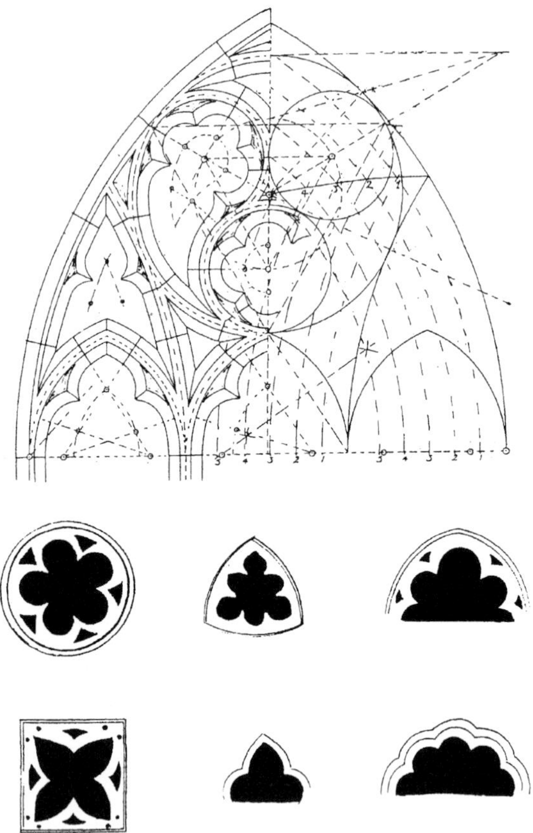

96. *Top:* the application of geometry in tracery designs; *bottom:* foils

steadily became more complicated and elaborate in design. One of the earliest indications of a conversion to Perpendicular Gothic was the sudden introduction of straight lines into tracery patterns. As they became more vertical the Perpendicular phase became more firmly established. In large expansive windows it resulted in transoms being introduced in series, thereby creating small individual lights within the framework of a single window, each light sometimes being given slight arching at the head (see Fig. 93). A particular change is in the appearance of uninterrupted mullions which extend from the sill to the window head. In all tracery work the cutting and setting of each individual piece had to be extremely accurate to ensure the various elements connected and fitted properly, otherwise strength and durability would be diminished.

The use of foils (*folia*) grew to become a quintessential element of Gothic architecture; they were applied as a variety and range of different cusps worked or arranged into an artistic design. Cusps are the projections and the foils the spaces between them. Foliation began to be a strong feature in the later stages of the Early English period and continued to develop and change until the Classical era. The different forms of foliation are numerous and mostly occur as trefoils, quatrefoils or cinquefoils. Once established, the different designs became a standard element in tracery and in other Gothic ornamentation (Fig. 96). In the Early English style cusps were sometimes given a small leaf design at the ends, and in the Decorated and Perpendicular phases they were occasionally ornamented with miniature representations of heads, leaves or flowers and sometimes with creatures or animals.

Parapets (Egeoves)

Parapets may be plain, battlemented, pierced or carved; the component parts are the parapet wall, cornice and coping, and some have string courses underneath whilst others are set on corbelling. Parapets are features which need to be dated with caution as many have been rebuilt in more recent times – especially in the nineteenth century, when the fashion returned to the earlier battlemented form. The Normans kept to a plain style but occasionally provided narrow embrasures between the parapets spaced widely apart (embrasures are openings). The Early English phase began by continuing the plain style with an uninterrupted horizontal line along the coping, but gradually this altered more towards inset panelling and occasionally pierced work featuring trefoils, quatrefoils and some ornament.

At the Decorated phase a few simple battlements appeared, but in the larger churches there was more of a preference for straight coping with carved panelling and tracery. Where battlements were provided, panelling and ornament were also featured. In the Perpendicular period plain battlemented parapets returned, but there are a few notable exceptions which also have inset panelling and pierced work. A good example is the pierced work to the parapets on the fifteenth-century tower at St James' Church, Winscombe, Avon. Box gutters immediately behind parapets were originally known as alurs (*alours*), which also referred to a walkway behind. An overlying course of stone known as a blocking course is regularly placed as a top concluding course to give bonding and stability, best practice requiring this to be slate dowelled into the stonework underneath. To ensure complete unity and to prevent any thermal movement the blocking course stones were cramp jointed, with the top surfaces provided with a slight incline for weathering.

Cornice

A cornice is a horizontal projection encircling the top of a wall or the component parts of a building. In Classical architecture a cornice (*corona*) is the uppermost part of an entablature. Cornices were not much of a feature in Saxon times; when they do occur they are likely to be plain and purely functional. Early Norman cornices differed little from the Saxon but later became decorative and more intricate. In the Early English period they became more ornamented than before and frequently have trefoils, together with additional carvings in various designs. During the Decorated phase cornices changed to become more regular and precise and usually have flower and leaf patterns spaced equidistantly. A different trend began from the start of the Perpendicular period and designs altered to feature a series of small mouldings with shallow hollows, within which are figures, flowers or ugly and distorted animal depictions (Fig. 97).

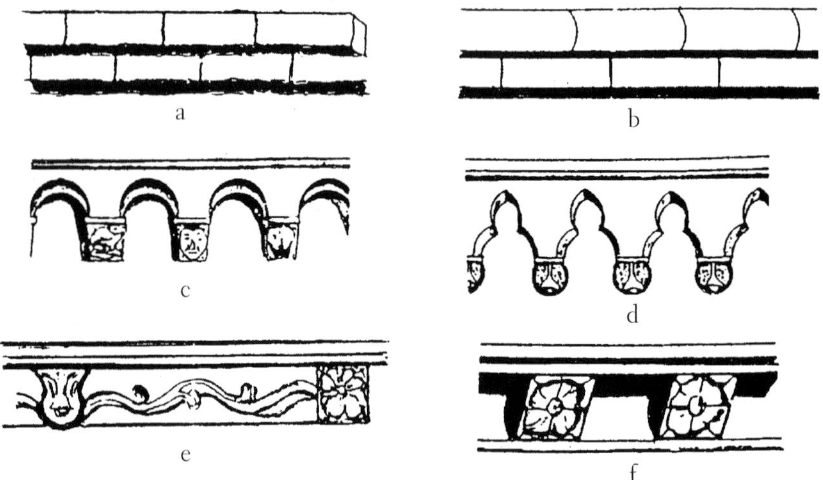

97. Cornices – (a) Saxon; (b) early Norman; (c) later Norman; (d) Early English; (e) Decorated; (f) Perpendicular

Corbel

A corbel (*corbis* – basket) is a projection supporting an arch, a parapet, a beam or anything of a similar nature. Found in numerous forms corbels usually reflect the time when they were carved, and often occur in abundance in Norman churches, where the decorative carvings mostly feature monsters and grotesque animals. From Norman to Perpendicular times the head in some form was constantly used as the main element in the ornamentation. Internally the wall pieces of roof trusses often rest on carved stone corbels. The mask corbel is an interesting feature from the Early English period, carved to resemble a buckle when seen from the front but like a mask when viewed sideways.

Corbel Table

A corbel table is formed from a series of continuous horizontal corbels fixed immediately below a parapet or the eaves of a roof; the projections sometimes having receding profiles which go back to the wall at the base. The ornamental carvings more usually replicate the cornice designs used in the same period. The Norman practice of carrying the eaves of steep-pitched roofs on corbel tables often meant that they were replaced later, with the corbel tables being adapted to take parapets with a lower-pitched roof behind. In cases where this occurs rainwater had to be taken to lead guttering behind the parapets and discharged through projecting lead-lined gargoyles (spouts).

Crockets (Croc – *a Hook*)

Crockets are carved projections which decorate the edges of pinnacles, spires, mouldings and similar. They were sometimes seen as an artistic way of adding extra weight to achieve the full structural equilibrium of elements, especially buttresses and pinnacles. The earliest of the innumerable forms appeared in the later phase of the Early English period. At this stage they are more likely to be found as carvings of leaves either bunched or on long stalks. Fixed well proud of the surrounding surface, the curvings always lean outwards. During the Decorated period the range of different designs widened, with the broad-leaf style being dominant but the curving changed to an inward direction. In the Perpendicular phase leaf work is prevalent, but flatter, with animals and other figures often occurring within the various designs.

The Regional Characteristics of Parish Churches

Many of the regional characteristics are distinctive and are the direct result of the way local materials had to be applied and worked. The first Saxon churches were mainly in timber and have not survived. Apart from porch construction there have been no phases of timber framing in church building since then, although there are a few lone exceptions – one example is the church of St Thomas a Beckett in Fairfield, Kent, which dates back to the thirteenth century. In this case there was clear logic in opting for timber as the church stands on marshland with dubious bearing capacity. Even although it was encased in brick in the eighteenth century the church has remained in remarkably good condition. There is also a delightful fourteenth-century church at Besford in Wiltshire which is timber framed and even has wooden window tracery. Internally it has some notable and finely worked carvings in the furnishings and finishes. The thirteenth-century Church of St Peter in Melverley, Shropshire, is also timber framed, with the limewashed panels filled with wattle and daub. Another distinctive timber-framed church is St Oswald's, Lower Peover, Cheshire, which – apart from the tower – is in the local timbered style.

In many parts of the North, designs were influenced by the use of the local millstone grit; so called because the texture was ideally suited for grinding corn because the stone's grain is exceptionally sharp and angular, in contrast to most other sandstone particles, which are smoother and more rounded. Although it is strong and durable, millstone grit was hard and difficult to work to fine detail. The problem was overcome by using an abundant Yorkshire limestone for decorative purposes, which gave good results. The parish churches in this area tend to be small and uninteresting externally. In the Lake District the local grey-green slate stone was much used, but in some places a seam of red sandstone was also quarried for building use. In overall terms the churches in this area are mainly plain and unpretentious in appearance and have not been much affected by outside influences. During the latter part of the medieval period some fine churches were constructed in the Yorkshire region, the local style generally following a long low form of design with flattened roofs covered in stone slates. Square window frames also became popular, along with battlemented parapets with slim pinnacles. In Cumbria and Northumberland the medieval towers close to the Scottish border give clear indications of having had a defensive use. In Nottinghamshire local churches tend to have sturdy towers that are lower in height than elsewhere in the region.

In Devon and Cornwall the most used building stones are red sandstone and a pale-coloured limestone known as Beerstone, together with some granite, which is far more prevalent in Cornwall. The local red sandstone and granite are both unsuitable for detailed carving but the south Devon Beerstone fulfilled this role and can be tooled to a fine finish. A large number of churches in Devon have simple designs and are without much decoration but there are a few notable exceptions, such as the parish church at Cullompton, which is in the Perpendicular style. In this area many of the towers are rather small but the walls are exceptionally thick and have battlemented parapets, stunted pinnacles and no spire. Stair turrets are often found built into the middle part of a tower wall; clerestories are seldom found in this area. The only ornamentation of note is usually in the woodwork, which is generally to a high standard.

Many of the parish churches in Cornwall are plain and not very engaging, one exception being the church at Launceston, which has carved wall decoration of particular value and interest. The widespread use of granite in parts of Cornwall has resulted in much of the early walling being irregularly coursed with blocks which are larger in size than in other parts of the South-West of England. This feature gradually changed with mechanisation and advances in tool making. In the West Country and Cornwall there are a number of tall fifteenth-century church towers with large octagonal pinnacles. In this region the gable ends often have either three or five small lancet windows clustered together, graduated in height, rising up to the middle lancet.

The stone best suited for working intricate and fine detail is in the limestone belt which runs from Dorset through to the Cotswolds, Northamptonshire, the east Midlands and Lincolnshire. In many of these areas it was not only used for walling but also roofing. The churches of all categories in these regions display masonry of a high quality. In the Cotswolds the village churches are comparatively small and spires are fairly rare. The availability of limestone has produced the fine towers seen throughout Gloucestershire, together with the broad spires of Oxfordshire and the celebrated fifteenth-century Perpendicular churches in the towns of Cirencester, Northleach and Chipping Norton. The sandstone found in a belt just north-west of these large limestone deposits is more difficult to work, and churches in these areas have less carving and ornament and are plainer and more subdued in style.

The variety of available building materials in the Wessex region has resulted in some area differences in application. In the blue-lias parts the harder nature of the stone has resulted in less fine detail, while the grey-toned stone from the Isle of Purbeck and the limestones similar to those found in the Cotswolds are also prevalent. A mixture of different limestones has produced some distinctive localised styles in parts of Somerset, Dorset and parts of Hampshire. Tall slender spires are a feature in parts of the Gloucestershire region, and in Somerset a number of churches have fine well-proportioned towers with parapets and pinnacles. Somerset is also noted for the number of grand Perpendicular-style towers throughout the county. The perforated belfry openings used instead of louvres is a distinctive local feature which can also be found in parts of neighbouring Dorset.

In the west Midlands the local deep-red sandstone was used mostly in rubble form and is dominant throughout, although the effect is not particularly pleasing and can give a subdued and even depressing first impression. The outcome is completely different in the limestone belt of the east Midlands, which has produced churches of high quality and appeal, a special feature being the fine stone spires. In the north Midlands the use of Derbyshire slate for roofing has produced lower pitches, with sturdy broad spires a hallmark of the area. In the south Midlands builders had the benefit of a wider choice of materials, which resulted in no distinctive local style predominating; nevertheless the area is noted for a series of fine towers and spires and window masonry of high quality. The use of clasping buttresses is a particular feature throughout Northamptonshire.

In the downland areas of Sussex, Surrey and parts of Hampshire and Kent the principal material for church building was flint, which is hard and exceptionally durable. It is found in the upper and middle chalk formations. When used in combination with brick or stone it produces a most pleasing and mellow effect, and is also found worked with chalk as a decorative embellishment, occasionally in diaper patterns. In parts of the Sussex downlands, especially the areas around Fittleworth, a darkish brown or red stone known as ironstone has been used, which further east in Surrey reappears as carstone and is much darker in colour. In some parts of the area small fragments of carstone have been successfully used as a form of galleting. To reduce the loading on the flint walling clerestories were not normally used; the aisle roofs were 'catslides', with many becoming a continuation of the slope of the roof over the nave. In this region towers tend to be lower in height, with some churches having a bellcote or a low timber belfry with a flat-cap roof over the west wall; good illustrations of this style are the Church of the Good Shepherd, Lullington, East Sussex, and St Mary's Church, North Marden, West Sussex. Where spires and porches occur, most are constructed in timber – a feature also seen in varying numbers in the counties of Hampshire, Hertfordshire and Dorset.

While some areas of Kent are within the chalk formations, large parts are on a stratum of greensand, resulting in the extensive use of Kentish ragstone. As a building material it is hard and difficult to work, which has encouraged the use of softer stones for trimming window and door openings and decorative work. In the same region, deposits of a soft calcareous sandstone known locally as hassock is also found. Octagonal stair turrets built into the corner of a tower are a regular feature in this area.

Some particularly fine towers and spires occur in Hereford and Shropshire, and many have individualistic timber belfry terminations. In Hertfordshire churches are especially characterised by the well-known Hertfordshire spike, which is a needle spire rising from the top of the tower. In parts of Middlesex church structures occasionally contain puddingstone – a feature that seems to extend west as far as Wokingham in Berkshire, where a church close to the town centre has parts of the walling in puddingstone.

The region of East Anglia has extensive areas of clay and gravel, and – except for some local flint – suffered from a perpetual shortage of suitable building stone. In Essex where flint has been used, round towers are regularly found because this overcame a difficult problem with quoins, whilst in the adjoining counties of Norfolk and Suffolk local differences have resulted in the round towers often being capped with an octagon (Fig. 98). Few churches outside this region have round towers, although there are exceptions such as St Michael's Church in Lewes.

After the reintroduction of brick from continental Europe in the thirteenth century brick increasingly became an alternative choice for the construction of churches in East Anglia. St Mary's Church, Layer Marney, Essex, has already been mentioned as an example and is sixteenth century with purpose-made bricks used for the window arches, the surrounds and the mullions. The exceptional prosperity the area enjoyed during the fifteenth century resulted in the large-scale rebuilding of local churches, a number of them of particular quality and note. Churches in this region generally have clerestories and the walls are often dressed with thin slabs of freestone containing flushwork, while buttresses are mostly found set diagonally. Another characteristic of the area is the high standard of the carpentry and the decorative carving. Throughout the East Anglian region many of the church towers built during the Perpendicular period are of an exceptional height and make ideal landmarks for shipping. Another unusual feature in the same area is the occasional church tower with octagonal buttresses. A range of different church building styles which have been influenced by the use of local materials can be seen in Figures 99 to 114.

98. Two Saxon churches – *top:* Saxon round tower, Norfolk; *bottom:* Church of St Andrew, Didling, West Sussex. Oil lamps and candles are still the only means of artificial lighting in this building, known as the Shepherds' Church. The original rough-hewn Saxon font has survived untouched (*photo: Ken Woodfield*).

99. Clymping Church, West Sussex. This flint-and-stone church is Norman in origin, with some of the windows and the doorway to the tower (*detail*) remaining unaltered. An item of particular interest is the roof – note how the lower part has been tilted with sprockets and covered with stone slates of diminishing size, the remainder is in plain clay tiles. This has been done because of the large surface area of the roof, to reduce the velocity of the rainwater run-off, and thereby reducing the risk of gutters overflowing during peak times.

100. St Mary's Church, Slindon, West Sussex. The rising cluster of lancet windows in the east wall is a feature of the Early English Gothic period. Differences between the flint work in the nave and north aisle show that this has been added at a later date. The various methods used in building the buttresses also indicate that they have been provided at different times *(photo: Peter Bishop)*.

101. Iford parish church, East Sussex. This clearly pre-dates the Gothic period, with three narrow windows in the east wall and a low robust tower between the chancel and the nave. The aisle extension is on the north side, which conforms to the fashion of the time.

102. Piddinghoe parish church, East Sussex. This church is unusual in many ways and is one of the few outside East Anglia to have a round tower. The low height of the clerestory and the small quatrefoil windows only allow limited light to the nave. The combined width of the side extension and the chancel are greater than the nave and side aisle, which is a feature seldom found elsewhere.

103. Parish church in Lancashire, close to the Cumbrian border. The plain elevation is typical of areas where the local stone is hard and difficult to work; this often results in the walls being rendered and limewashed later.

104. Holy Trinity Church, Bosham, Near Chichester, Sussex. The design and layout of this church is familiar in the South-East. Note how the roof extends down over the aisles and the broached spire overhangs the tower. The pointed arch windows are in local stone, and the tracery is geometric, except for the chancel window, which has a shouldered arch with three lancet windows. Differences in the stonework show the north aisle to be a later addition. If additional accommodation was needed it was usually attached to the north side of the nave, a south aisle being built if the first extension proved inadequate *(photo: Peter Bishop)*.

105. Parish Church in mid-Berkshire. This church is Norman in origin, with one window and the entrance to the nave having survived a number of alterations and additions. Note the higher roofs to the chancel and the transept; normally these are lower than the roof to the nave.

106. St Mary's Church, Yapton, West Sussex. A mixture of stone, brick and flint in the walling, and the different ways they have been laid, are clear signs that this church has undergone extensive structural alterations in the past. The style and overhang of the pyramidal roof to the tower indicate that this is a later replacement. The dormer windows are a particularly unfortunate present-day intrusion *(photo: Peter Bishop)*.

107. St George's Church, Eastergate, West Sussex. The timber belfry is a particular feature in parts of the South-East of England. There are indications that the church has very early origins, with the large windows being later installations *(photo: Peter Bishop)*.

108. Cumbrian church. This church is a good example of a clerestory admitting good natural light to the nave. The stone pointed-arch windows, each with rising lancet lights, stand out against the darker random-stone walling.

109. Church Felpham, West Sussex. This church is built of random rubble stonework; differences in the walling indicate that the north aisle is a later extension. Behind the parapets to the tower is a low flat-cap roof (*photo: Peter Bishop*).

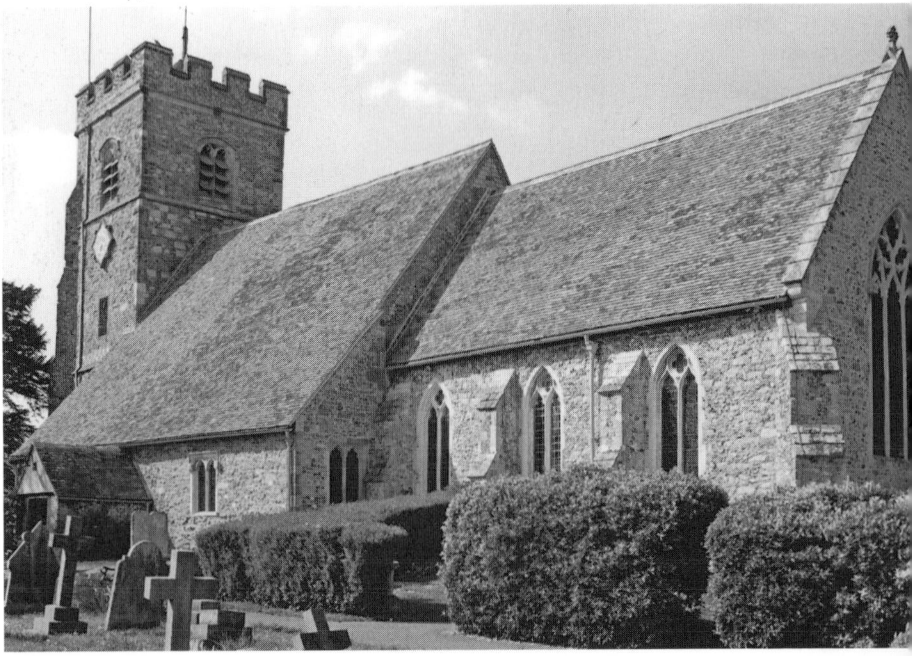

110. Parish church in Headington, Oxford. Most of the walling in this church is in Cotswold rubble stone, but the blockwork to the tower and turret clearly reveal that they are later additions. Note how the turret rises above the parapets to the tower, which is not a regular feature in English churches.

111. Church in Reading, Berkshire. The main feature of this church is the tower, which has intricate chequer work and octagonal buttresses with tall elegant pinnacles ornamented with fine crocketing.

112. Church of St Andrew and St Cuthman, Steyning, West Sussex. Originally a collegiate foundation, and the resting place of St Cuthman, this Norman church replaced an earlier Saxon one. The two larger windows in the north aisle are later installations and the tower at the west end is sixteenth century. The main distinguishing feature is the chequer work, which post-dates the Norman period.

113. Church of St Nicholas, Arundel, West Sussex. Built in the random-rubble style, the walls of this church are an interesting mixture of local stone and flint. The projecting turret to the tower leads to a lead-covered pyramidal roof. *(photo: Peter Bishop)*.

114. Church of St Peter, Hamsey, East Sussex. The church stands on a hillock close to the river Ouse and, although most of the existing structure is Norman, many of the original parts are Saxon. Note the later heavy diagonal buttresses and the geometrical Gothic window at the east end. Both are clear indicators of later alterations.

The Effect of the Renaissance on Church Design

Throughout the Renaissance the Gothic style was never completely forsaken – due in part to the fact that few new churches were needed at the time, the exception being London, which had been catastrophically damaged by the Great Fire. In essence Inigo Jones (1573–1652) can be said to be the first to introduce Classical architecture to Britain, but it was left to Christopher Wren (1632–1723) to establish a clearer direction towards change in regard to church design. In this the task of rebuilding the London churches gave Wren a unique opportunity to advance his ideals, with his best-known commission being St Paul's Cathedral (Fig. 115). The design for the dome is of particular interest and is based on the method used for the baptistery adjacent to Pisa Cathedral in Italy. A peculiarity is the conical structure interposed between the inner and outer domes, which rests on the lower circumference of the former and gives support to the lantern. The ratios used in the leading dimensions are also noteworthy, especially those between the breadth and height of openings, which are 1:2.

The application of science to determine safer loading and more economic construction began at around this time. Robert Hooke undertook a series of experiments on the strength of materials, the structural characteristics of arches and the bending of beams. In the same period Philippe de Lahire also carried out tests on the strength of masonry arches and the ways in which they could be vulnerable to failure. This established a different approach to the design and construction of buildings, much of it arising out of a close working relationship between Robert Hooke and Christopher Wren. The importance of their work is in the construction of St Paul's Cathedral, now recognised as an outstanding pioneering achievement in early structural engineering. The manner in which the heavy loads from the stone lantern have been conveyed down to the foundations is remarkable, and was achieved through a series of calculations that determined the size of the arches, piers and vaults. Of particular interest is the stability of the cone carrying the lantern, which was designed from a theorem produced by Robert Hooke. Another innovation is the way stresses from any outward movement at the base are resisted by wrought-iron tension rings attached to the cone. Mention also needs to be made of a generally unheralded feature of outstanding structural significance concerning – a cleverly devised geometric stairway with each step set as a cantilever with no outer support. Wren's west front at St Paul's Cathedral is probably one of the best-known examples of the Classical form, but other highly acclaimed designs

115. St Paul's Cathedral, London

also appeared in the provinces, in particular the Church of St Philip in Birmingham by Thomas Archer, who was a much-respected architect of the time.

The fundamental differences between Classical and Gothic architecture are in symmetry and balance. Although the Gothic style is based on various geometric shapes and ratios it has no unalterable rules, the outcome being that the churches of the time seldom were the same, due to the masons having been allowed some latitude of expression. Gothic architectural treatments may fall within a similar theme and style, but they are nevertheless not part of a rigidly prescribed sequence. This is in contrast to the true Classical form, in which the various orders have much stricter rules on shape and proportion, along with set designs and features which are directed towards conformity rather than innovation. The main characteristics of true Classicism are centred on set proportions, together with a logical progression of certain elements, within which is a closely defined hierarchy governing symmetry and balance (Fig. 116). English Classical architecture is derived from the styles of the Ancient Greeks and the Romans. The Greek versions emerged through the trabeated form of building – the post-and-lintel method – whereas the Romans used the arcuated system, which is structurally dependent on the arch. This gave scope for much wider architectural expression, especially when used in combination with both the dome and vaulting.

The Baroque style came from Italy, and its influence as an architectural progression in Britain only lasted for around forty years (1690–1730). It is characterised by curvaceous forms and the bold massing of shapes, with much emphasis being made of the variations and effects achieved through light and shade (*chiaroscuro*). English Baroque was never in full accord with the style found in continental Europe – it was more diversified and somewhat more subdued in Britain. It still aimed to be dramatic and to convey an impression of dynamism and flamboyance through the creation of contrasts, but it did not consolidate in England and gave way to the more austere Palladianism.

The change to the Classical style in Britain created a new concept in church internal design, and when it was fully adopted it resulted in one large uninterrupted area of space in a rectangular or basilican form. A basic aim was to bring the preacher closer to the congregation by making the plan wider and in comparative terms shorter in length. When needed, galleries were made much deeper and more steeply tiered, and many churches had a dome to give extra light and a feeling of space. Stairways to galleries were given character and a proper identity and were generally made much easier to negotiate, with half landings and better-designed treads. The Classical colonnade replaced the triforium and clerestory, and large round-headed windows containing clear glass gave increased natural light. Although greatly influenced by the Palladian style, Wren had the ingenuity to combine much of the old with the new in a way which made for outcomes of delight. He did this at St Paul's Cathedral by keeping the cruciform plan, and in other churches he retained the spire and introduced a new composition, giving it a completely different image and an innovative variation in shape. A good example is St Mary-le Bow in

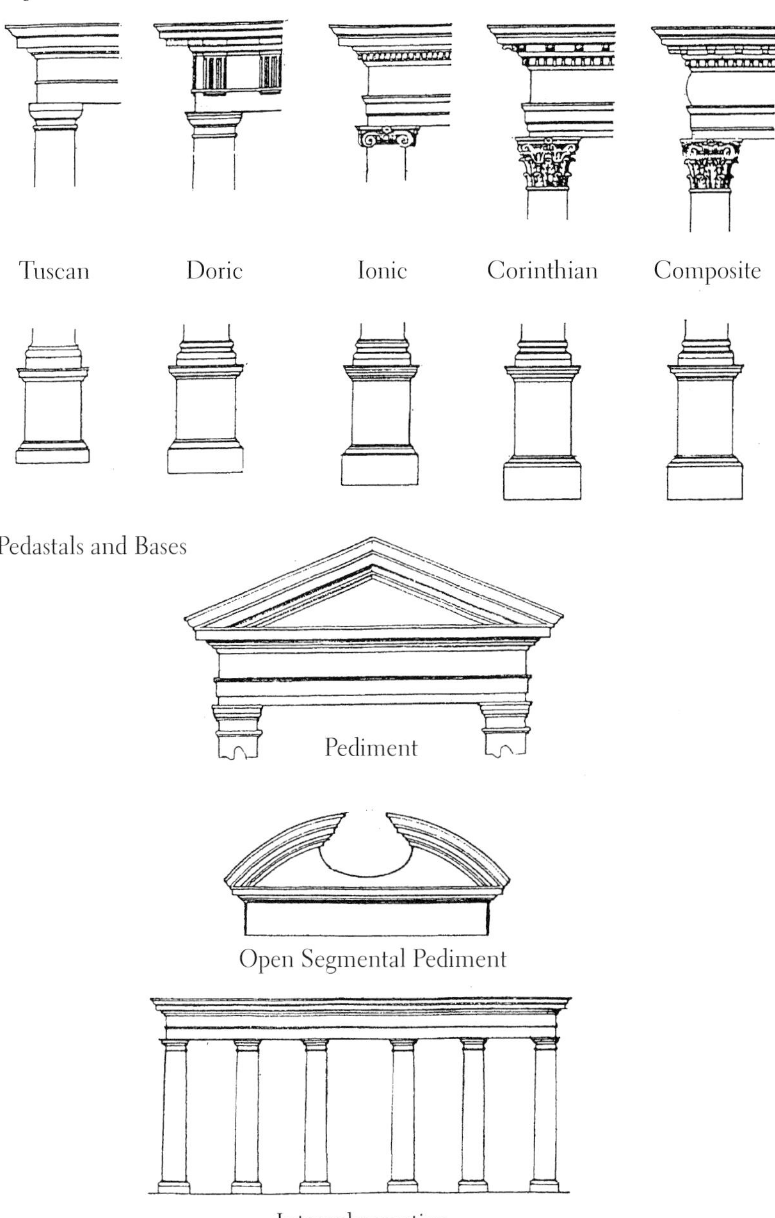

116. Classical features

London, which is in diminishing tiers. Another much-celebrated London church in the Classical form is the one designed by James Gibbs at St Martin-in-the-Field, which resulted in a number of other churches being based on this style. Other churches in London in a Classical style include St Paul's, Covent Garden, St Martin's, Ludgate, St Edmund the King, Lombard Street, and St Andrew's-by-the-Wardrobe. One of the earliest parish churches to have been built in the Palladian style was the Church of St Giles-in the-Fields, designed by Henry Flitcroft.

The impact on church architecture was minimal outside London, but a few churches were built in the provincial towns and country parishes under the Classical influence. One such example is the basilican plan at Nuneham Courtenay, Oxfordshire; another is the parish church at Willen in Buckinghamshire. A number of Gothic churches around this time also acquired undertones of Classicism as a result of alteration works. At parish level some of the churches built in the Classical form were rendered externally with stucco – wet render worked to look like stone, which became a low-cost substitute for stone. The dexterity and articulate skill used in the application made an important contribution towards the resurgence of Classical architecture, the lines, marks and scores being meticulously worked to replicate ashlar stone detail.

Although it had earlier origins, the Gothic Revival received strong support in the first part of the nineteenth century and resulted in matters of design being influenced by the High Church Movement. Its followers believed a church could not be a suitable place of worship unless the architecture was essentially Gothic. As a result, church building passed through a prolific neo-Gothic phase which reached a peak between 1855 and 1885. It was propelled along through the zeal and skill of the leading protagonists of the Gothic form, the best known being A.W.N. Pugin (1815–52), who – along with others – had the knowledge and influence to ensure exceptional standards were achieved.

At parish level, however, the quality of the work was sometimes poor and often lacked vitality, substance and accuracy. A notable exception is the Holy Rood Church, Watford, which is an example of the high standards the Victorians could achieve. Designed by J.F. Bentley, the rather austere nave is prelude to a feast of fine decoration and colour in the chancel and side chapels. A massive, finely carved rood beam enriched with extensive decoration dominates this part of the interior. After falling into disrepair this, the sanctuary ceiling and the north gallery ceiling have more recently been most carefully restored by Howell and Bellion (Fig. 120).

3 Church Interiors

Church Layouts

Old church interiors contain a wealth of antiquity and historical evidence and, while some may not be ornately decorated or extravagantly furnished, they are nevertheless a rich and tangible legacy of the past that can tell us a great deal about our forebears and how they lived. The basic medieval parish church had two clearly defined areas: the nave and the chancel (which includes the sanctuary). The large monastic churches had much expanded accommodation that included an extended chancel, a high altar and a series of side chapels for the celebration of minor masses and other ceremonial. After the Reformation considerable changes occurred, including a ban on the use of the stoup. Before this, every church had a stoup – a small recessed basin filled with consecrated water containing salt – in the porch or at the entrance. On entering the church worshippers were obliged to dip their fingers in the stoup and make the sign of the cross.

Church layouts are planned around a series of structural bays, with the internal floor space sometimes being enlarged by aisles and transepts, over which may be a triforium and clerestory (Fig. 76; the external appearance of a clerestory is shown in Figs 102 and 108). Not every church has all or even some of these elements, and until the fifteenth century few parish churches featured a clerestory and fewer still a triforium. The clerestory is the upper part, in which a series of windows admit natural light to the nave; the triforium (*tribunum*) is a narrow arcaded wall passage placed immediately under the clerestory and above the arcade to the nave. The arcade on the ground floor is formed by a series of piers or columns which support a range of equidistant arched openings between the aisle and the nave. The triforium is a regular feature in many cathedrals and larger churches, but is rarer in medium-sized churches. If a small church has a triforium it usually appears as a particularly narrow corridor space within the thickness of the outer wall; a good example is at the Church of St Mary, Nun Monkton, North Yorkshire.

The ornamental arrangement of the triforium can differ considerably. In the Norman style it is often a single arch within each bay, but a frequent variation is a large encompassing arch within which are small sub-divisions of interlocking arches supported on miniature shafts. In the Early English period most designs were formed from a series of large pointed arches under which smaller pointed equilateral or obtuse arches rest on dwarf pillars. In the subsequent Decorated and Perpendicular styles aisle roofs generally became much flatter, often making the space occupied by the triforium smaller and much less conspicuous.

The larger churches often have a gallery in some form, many of them installed between the eighteenth and nineteenth centuries. In medieval churches they are more likely to occur as a tribune (*tribunus*), which is a broad, open arcaded passageway over the aisle. These can be surprisingly capacious and are generally found in cathedrals and large churches built before the beginning of the fourteenth century. In general terms, a gallery is a floored upper structure, most often with tiered seating, usually accessed from a stairway in the narthex. The growing demand for additional space frequently necessitated a galley being installed in a small church, when they were regularly entered from steps (*asensorium*) attached to the outside

117. External steps to church gallery; more recently the door has been blocked up.

of the church (Fig. 117). In the eighteenth century galleries overlooking the north and south of the nave became popular in the medium-sized churches and were seen as a convenient way of accommodating expanding congregations. In some cases they also extended into the transepts.

Moreover, the building of galleries often overcame seating difficulties in connection with pew renting. At one time families could rent pews for their sole use; the income was collected by the church wardens to cover the cost of church maintenance. This practice often created a demand for additional seating space and the need to provide for those who could not afford the cost of a pew. From the mid-nineteenth century onwards pew renting was gradually phased out.

The area known as the west gallery had a different function. It was located in a space just under the tower but over the nave, and was originally used to accommodate groups of musicians. Exceptions may, however, be found, with some having been built as a private pew for a local dignitary or wealthy landowner.

Mural Art in Churches

Mural art has origins as far back as the cave dwellers; it was used for various purposes by the Ancient Egyptians, the Greeks and the Romans. The early Christian Church also recognised that visual presentation was an ideal way of illustrating bible stories to a largely illiterate populace. This resulted in Pope Gregory issuing a declaration in AD 604 requiring churches to feature the scriptures in pictorial form. Known as the *biblia pauperum* or the bible of the poor, by the thirteenth century this had created a vast array of liturgical scenes on the walls of every church. It made the interiors very different to the sombre appearance usually found today. Internally, churches were full of unrestrained colour and expression, much of it the work of skilled itinerant artists who achieved high standards using a limited range of powdered pigments mixed with water. From these they were able to create different shades and other variations by mixing the base powders with lamp black and white lime putty. Different reds, browns, yellows and purple were obtainable from iron oxides and green from hydrated copper carbonate (malachite). Many of the more suitable malachite deposits were found in Cornwall and ranged in colour from emerald to a dark green. Azurite, which is a basic copper carbonate, gave various shades of blue, much of it probably coming from the seams in Cornwall and Somerset. Various earths, more commonly known to artists as ochre, also provided different red and brown pigments.

In the British Isles most artists worked in secco, which is a process of painting on dry plaster using colours mixed from a water base. High-class work often involved gilding, using solid gold leaf over a thin coat of reddish clay called bole. In continental Europe fresco work was favoured, but it was less suitable for use in Britain because of the damper nature of the climate – the slower rate of drying sometimes resulted in blurring of the images. Rare examples of twelfth-century frescos have survived at St Michael's Church, Copford, Essex, and St Botolph's Church, Hardham, West Sussex. The paintings at Hardham date from 1100 and are probably the finest series in any parish church in England. The style indicates they are the work of the 'Lewes Group', who became highly regarded travelling artists in that period (Fig. 118). The process of fresco painting involved painting over newly applied lime plaster, which allowed the paint to combine with the plaster and dry as a component part of the skim. A base layer of plaster was first applied, followed by a thin plaster skim which became the working surface while still wet. In the larger depictions the skim was applied in stages in conveniently sized patches, which can sometimes be detected by evidence of overlap between each patch. As secco is worked on dry plaster

118. Fresco work in St Botolph's Church, Hardham, West Sussex

this overlapping does not occur, but the process had the disadvantage of the pigments remaining soluble and less durable.

In the late medieval period the secco and fresco techniques were occasionally used in combination. Some interesting wall paintings can also be seen at St John's Church, Clayton, and the chapel at Coombes – both in West Sussex. Mostly in monochrome, fourteenth-century paintings have survived at All Saints' Church, Little Kimble, Buckinghamshire and St Mary's Church at Kempley in Gloucestershire which also has some fine early Romanesque mural work which dates from around 1330.

All church murals had the express aim of not only educating and informing the masses but also creating a climate of fear, devotion and obedience. This was achieved through depictions such as divine judgement, retribution and the joy of salvation. They also featured events such as the last supper, the lives of the saints, scenes from the scriptures and the lives and activities of martyrs and the apostles. Also prominent were the doom pictures, which gave horrifying and gruesome scenes of the effects of evil and the consequences of being sent to hell. During the Reformation and after, church murals were systematically obliterated with whitewash, but this had the effect of preserving many for posterity and has made it possible for some to be carefully restored in recent times. During the Edwardian period a few churches embarked on a programme of re-creating liturgical murals, the origin of the idea being traced back to Georgian times. These re-creations can usually be identified by the extra clarity and in the strength and wider variety of colour used.

In addition to the murals, the remaining wall areas, together with much of the stonework and parts of the woodwork, were often highly coloured with limewash or oil paint and – if funds permitted – this included generous applications of gilding. There was also a fashion to paint lines on the walls in a form that imitated ashlar masonry, with decorative designs sometimes being worked into the centre of each outline. At the Reformation nearly all these depictions were replaced by text. Throughout Victorian times many surviving elements from the past were again lost through a proliferation of extension and refurbishment schemes which sometimes included the removal of the original plaster and exposure of the stonework.

Apart from having had an educational function in the past, stained glass also contributes towards a particular mood or feeling within the confines of a church. Much depends on the intensity and the amount used, but in abundance it can establish infectious emotions ranging from the solemn to the uplifting. Unfortunately, very little twelfth-century glass has survived; the best example is at Canterbury Cathedral, which describes the ancestry of Christ. A Jesse window from this time can also be found at York Minster, which has some exceptional early stained glass. A Jesse window is one showing Christ's genealogy in stained glass (the term also applies if the depictions are found carved only into the mullions or window surrounds). A particularly fine example of a Jesse window can be seen at the Abbey of St Peter and St Paul, Dorchester, Oxfordshire, where the tracery has been worked in the shape of a tree with outstretched branches. At parish level some superb examples of early stained glass are in the Church of St Michael and All Angels, Eaton Bishop, Hereford. In the thirteenth century the fashion seems to have been more towards the depiction of saints and the apostles.

The larger windows which appeared in the fourteenth century gave scope for more flexibility and the coverage of wider topics, and an emphasis appears to have been placed on showing saints with their emblems, with fewer examples of the Jesse window being installed. In the fifteenth century the general expansion of wealth and prosperity provided the means for more highly delicate and intricate designs. At this stage the Jesse window went into sharp decline and the use of heraldic images flourished. As a general trend during the sixteenth century human forms mostly became less celestial and more lifelike, with many background settings being given ordinary images, some featuring everyday landscapes including buildings, vegetation, trees and sometimes animals.

Some of the stained glass produced in the nineteenth and twentieth centuries displays the cipher, initials or signature of the artist. These are glaziers' marks and can be hard to identify or place. To overcome the problem NADFAS (The National Association of Decorative and Fine Art Societies) has published a useful guide on the signs used by different artists. Only a limited amount of medieval stained glass can be distinguished in this way, and most of the work from this period does not give any indication of the artist.

The nave in the parish church was originally pewless, and people simply stood or knelt, although some fixed stone seating was later provided around the inner face of the outer walls for the sick and elderly, a feature which in a few cases has survived unaltered to the present day. At one stage sermons were rarely given and services were short, but in the early part of the thirteenth century a change came with the emergence of itinerant preachers who travelled around the country delivering talks and sermons. The duration of these sermons established the need for seating and resulted in the provision of collapsible benching or trestles, an arrangement which enabled the nave to be retained and cleared for secular activities. At this time the floors were simply beaten earth and it is likely the trestles were three legged, which gave better stability where the floor was uneven. Later, bench seating was provided with low narrow curbing at the back. Next came seating with bench ends that were often elaborately carved. Following the Reformation regular church attendance became obligatory and resulted in a growing need for more and better seating. In the larger churches some of the original seating was replaced with work of exceptional quality, part of the outcome of a decision by Henry VIII to encourage highly skilled foreign craftsmen to settle in England.

After the Reformation the altar was no longer the only focus of attention and the prayer desk and the pulpit also became prominent. At this point subtle differences appeared in seating designs, including the sloping of book rests which had previously been at the horizontal. This change of emphasis encouraged the installation of box pews, many of them taking a highly sophisticated form with lockable doors, upholstered seats and curtains; some even had canopies. This was the time when those with means could rent pews for their exclusive use. During the nineteenth century considerable changes were made to church interiors and box pews fell out of fashion. It resulted in a large number being removed and replaced by benches on slightly raised wooden platforms with low doors at either end to minimise any discomfort from draughts. The Victorians also removed a large number of nave side galleries, especially if they were considered to be a distraction from the architectural character of the church, a factor which often outweighed other considerations.

In the medieval cathedrals and large churches the stalls which lined the chancel on both sides were reserved for the clergy, monks, the choir and the Knights Templar and Knights Hospitaller. If the originals are still in place they are a feature which signals an early connection with a monastic or collegiate foundation. Stalls differ from benches in having arm rests, with those made for the clergy having curved backs with carved projections either side plus hand grips termed elbows. In the cathedrals and large churches they frequently had overhead canopies. Most stall seats were hinged and had on the underside a misericord which, when the seat was tipped up, provided a projection or corbel against which the user could rest when standing. A large number date from the mid-thirteenth century and were provided to help relieve the fatigue caused by long periods of standing (Fig. 119). The craftsmen who made them were allowed a remarkable degree of free expression and depicted in the carvings anything from the ridiculous and the humorous to the macabre. Ely Cathedral is noted for superb misericords, and fine examples are also

119. Clergy stalls with carved misericords. A priest of lower ranking would have occupied the stall set back on the right.

in Ripon Cathedral. At parish level some of very early origin are in the Church of St Mary, Kidlington, Oxfordshire, and others worthy of mention are those in St Mary's Church in Whalley, Lancashire and the Abbey of St Mary in Sherborne, Dorset.

A cathedral contains the throne or seat of the bishop for the diocese. In the monastic cathedrals the throne or cathedra was originally kept in the apse immediately behind the high altar, but was later relocated to the presbytery. In secular cathedrals it has always been located on the south side of the chancel. Thrones vary substantially in shape and form: many are voluminous and exquisitely carved, while others are relatively modest in comparison. An example of extreme ostentation is the throne at Exeter Cathedral, which extends to a height of 67 feet (20 m) and nearly reaches the vaulted ceiling. The oldest cathedra in England is at Norwich, where – in accordance with an early Christian custom – it has been placed at the top of the steps behind the high altar. After the Reformation it became customary to use a chair more akin to domestic design, and a number of those currently in use are of Elizabethan origin. Many parish churches keep a chair for the exclusive use of a visiting bishop.

In the north aisles of the parish churches at Hexham and Beverley Minster are stone frithstools which are believed to be Saxon and were at one time the last sacred refuge for anyone claiming sanctuary, the violation of which incurred the severest punishment. In cases where a bishop has a special relationship with a church foundation such as a school, it has been the practice to provide a permanent seat in the chapel for his exclusive use. This is sometimes described as a faldstool and is an item which is often highly ornate, sometimes with a canopy overhead. The term is, however, somewhat misused and more correctly applies to an upholstered and decorated folding seat.

The choir (*chorus*) was originally a restricted part of the church reserved solely for the choristers and the clergy and at one time was always located within the eastern end immediately west of the presbytery. This is why a section of the chancel often continues to be called the choir even when it is not being used for that purpose. *Chorus cantorum* is the term occasionally given to choir stalls when they are situated in the nave or transepts. In a cruciform church this is more often immediately under a side arch of the central tower.

Chantry chapels date from the thirteenth century, and by the fifteenth century a large number of churches had at least one chantry chapel. These were where a priest had been retained by way of an endowment or benefice to sing daily mass for the soul of the provider and others nominated in his or her will. The word chantry comes from the Latin *cantare* (to sing). Many are adorned with fine sculptures and furnishings, and might contain the tomb of the donor and members of the family.

A large number of tombs were far less extravagant, lying within the main body of the church enclosed by a parclose screen, but the general trend was more towards a canopied monument with a small altar under. The distance from the high altar was often an indication of the status of the provider. Initially those with means were the only ones able to afford this, but over time the guilds and the fraternities (religious brotherhoods) also established them. This provision enabled even the poorest members of society to benefit from masses and to have their names entered on the Bede Roll so that commemorative prayers were said for them in perpetuity.

Following the Dissolution of the Monasteries all chantries were dissolved by decree in 1548, their altars were destroyed and their endowments confiscated, and much of the money was used to found church schools. In cases where the chapel formed an independent addition to the church the ownership remained with the founders, notwithstanding the fact some could not cover the running costs after the seizure of the endowment. As a result, many chantries were made over to the church, but a few families retained the space for use as a private pew, some being given pierced screens for privacy and occasionally a private access, such as the one at the Church of St Mary at Langley Marish in Slough. A few chantries survived the purge, including four celebrated examples at Winchester Cathedral – one being to the dedication of Bishop William of Wykeham.

The vestry is the part of the church where vestments and items relevant to the running of the church are kept and where the priest enrobes before worship. It is usually an adjunct to one side of the choir but occasionally can be at the end of the east wall just behind the altar. Members of the choir normally have a separate room in which to enrobe, known as the choir vestry. The sacristry (*secretarium*) is also a depository for the holding of vestments, church plate and important documents, and is where the priest enrobes but differs from the vestry in location, in that it is always adjoining the presbytery or chancel and is usually only entered by way of a priest's door. Nevertheless the exact distinction between this and the vestry is sometimes difficult to determine.

In the year AD 806 it became possible under church law for anyone to be buried within the confines of a church building. In reality this was only available to those with power, wealth or influence – the likely exceptions being a much-revered local cleric or someone in society who had acquired saint-like status. The earliest known intra-church burials have been traced back to the early part of the twelfth century, where interred remains have been found in the flooring covered by a coffin-shaped ledger slab. A grave of this type becomes a lairstal and the stone covering a lairstone. Small cast-lead crosses known as mortuary crosses have been found in some and were used in the belief they dispelled any influence the devil could have on the afterlife.

In the cathedrals and major churches people of exceptional eminence were sometimes laid to rest in a prominently positioned tomb within the main body of the church, usually extravagantly worked and decorated in stone with a life-sized effigy. Few were interred in this way, though, the main exception being those in some chantry chapels. In the upper eschelons of society people often built a vault beneath the church long before their demise. These were small and generally had limewashed walls and a curved ceiling, and were accessed by stone steps going down to the entrance, as distinct from a burial chamber, which is sealed. In the seventeenth and eighteenth centuries a number of family vaults were constructed in a similar style, the only difference being that they had a range of loculi (shelves or recesses in which coffins or urns could be housed).

New churches built between the eighteenth and nineteenth centuries were at times given raised floor levels to provide for burial vaulting underneath. It also remained possible for those with means and social standing to be granted an intramural burial – interment in a grave or chamber beneath the floor of the church. As towns developed and expanded, burial space often became a problem and new or extended churches sometimes built communal vaults under the aisles and the chancel, with the whole or part of the chancel often being declared a vestry vault for the incumbent and those who followed him.

The practical difference between a burial vault and a crypt is usually in the size and the quality of the finishing. Crypts (*crypta*) are regularly much larger and are fully vaulted, with a finish generally plainer and similar in style to the upper parts of the church. They were originally built as places for the remains and relics of saints, and in the cathedrals and major churches many had altars to enable pilgrims to pay full homage. Rochester Cathedral has one of the finest and best preserved crypts in England, which also has some early groining of the highest standard.

Heart burials are rare features; they have a small casket sunk into a niche covered by a commemorative stone with a head-and-shoulders carving clutching a heart. The practice originated during the time of the crusades when the body of a fallen soldier could not be returned to his relatives. Sometimes his heart was removed and transported back for burial in his home church. A well-preserved example survives in the local church at Mappowder in Dorset.

Many churches do, however, contain elaborate memorials known as tomb chests (see Monuments and Memorials, page 231). In the Gothic Revival phase the desire to return to the past even extended for a short period to the re-creation of these memorials

Church Fixtures and Fittings

The early cathedrals and the larger monastic churches had a substantial and decoratively carved stone screen known as the pulpitum, which divided the choir from the nave. In location and function it was similar to a rood screen (see over) but was heavier and constructed more substantially. Many had a gallery over, which was sometimes elaborated with a substantial canopy above. The pulpitum usually featured extravagantly carved statutes of saints and apostles and spanned the piers of the crossing. Most had a central doorway with one bay on the western side supporting a rood under which was a reredos and a nave altar for the laity – sometimes called a Jesus altar. Before the Reformation laity were always kept separate from the clergy; in the smaller Saxon churches this was achieved by a narrow chancel arch. In the fullness of time this changed to a wider arched opening marked by either a rood screen or a beam with a rood over (*rood* was the Anglo-Saxon name for a cross). In the cathedrals and major churches the screen was more usually closed (solid) throughout the whole height; this might also have been the case in some churches at parish level, but the top part was generally open pierced work. In the major churches the rood (crucifix) became a central feature of the interior, carved and painted in considerable detail (Fig. 120).

Also prominent was the rood loft or jube (a raised platform over the rood screen) which was accessed by a small vice (stairway) from which the clergy could preach. Occasionally this was used by instrumentalists and the choir, and later sometimes became the location for the organ keyboard. Protected front and back with balustrades, most have an infilling of decorative carved panelling (*lambruscare*). Many had a gilded canopy immediately overhead, and above this some had a series of intricately worked and richly decorated panels set into the ceiling known as the rood celure (Fig. 120). In a few isolated cases the rood loft can be found cantilevered out from the chancel wall without a screen underneath, as at the church in the village of St Margaret's, Herefordshire. Medieval rood lofts have survived in the cathedrals at Lincoln, Exeter, Rochester, Southwell and Norwich, and exceptionally fine examples at parish level can be seen at Flamborough, near Bridlington, and Attleborough in Norfolk. Most roods and those parts associated with them were removed during the Reformation, but some of the original screens were spared and have survived to the present day. During the Gothic Revival period of the nineteenth century a few replacements were installed.

In Ripon Cathedral the stone great choir screen remains a superb piece of craftsmanship from the Perpendicular phase (Fig. 121). Canterbury Cathedral has a magnificent fourteenth-century stone screen installed by Prior Henry d'Estria, and the early fourteenth-century pulpitum at St David's Cathedral is one of the best examples of an original medieval screen in Britain. There can be no doubt that the original heavy stone screens muffled the sound between the chancel and the nave, which is almost certainly why most were replaced with wood during the fifteenth century. Closed screens also isolated the clergy from the laity, so the provision of

120. Restored interior of Holy Rood Church, Watford – *from top:* restored rood and sanctuary ceiling; the original painting of the celure (the monogram IHC corresponds – as does IHS – to an abbreviation of Christ in the Greek uncial script which was used between the fourth and eighth centuries); restored north gallery ceiling (*photos by kind permission of Howell and Bellion, Specialist Church Restorers, Saffron Walden*).

121. Stone screen in Ripon Cathedral

open screens helped to establish an improved unity between them – albeit in a somewhat detached fashion.

After the Reformation the disappearance of the rood resulted in the dividing partition between the chancel and the nave changing to the chancel screen, which altered to be more open and interlaced in style (the word chancel comes from *cancelli*, which is Latin for lattices), and by the eighteenth century was much lower in height. A parclose screen is one which separates a chapel or shrine from the main body of the church. Typical forms rest on a plinth divided by vertical posts, between which are open lights with pierced carvings and other forms of decoration. An ornamented screen known as a tower screen is occasionally found dividing any access from the nave to the western tower by an intervening area termed the tower space. Many chancel screens were removed during the Victorian restoration phase, but most of those screens used to protect tombs and other items were left untouched.

The term altar (sometimes *awter* in old manuscripts) is from the Latin *altarium*, meaning an elevated place, reflecting how the high altar stands on a predella. A predella is a raised platform, but at times the word is also used to describe a small shelf supporting a reredos or a triptych (described later). Most of the very early Celtic and Anglo-Saxon churches had free-standing altars in wood, but in 1076 the Council of Winchester ordered all altars to be in stone. They usually took the form of a rectangular or square stone or marble slab marked or incised with five crosses – one on each corner and the fifth in the centre. The heavy slab was supported in different ways: many were fixed on solid masonry, others rested on piers, and a few on a robust and centrally placed pedestal. The early ones sometimes had a cavity for the reception of sacred relics, which was called a confessio or a *sepulchrum attares* (later termed a loculus). If the cavity was concealed with a stone lid it became a *sigillum*. A stone altar or an altar with a stone top is often referred to as a mensa (from the Latin for table); an early example is in the Church of St Lawrence, Bradford-on-Avon, Wiltshire.

Many altars in the later stages had either a richly painted front panel or an altar frontal cloth known as an antependium. Some also had riddel curtains which screened the altar at the back and sides and were supported by riddel posts at the four corners (Fig. 122). In addition to embellishment and decoration the curtains had the practical purpose of

122. Mensa with riddel curtains and posts

protecting the altar candles from draught. In medieval times a veil was always hung over the altar during Lent and every church had a tabernacle (*tabernaculum*) on or near the high altar. This held the sacrament and took the form of a small and often highly decorated receptacle on or in a small niche immediately behind the altar. In some churches it was suspended over the altar by means of a pulley system; in a few cases the pulley wheels are still in place.

In the Norman period they were generally placed in shallow square recesses which occasionally had carved figure decoration. By the Early English stage tabernacles had become more enriched and more deeply recessed, with carved figure work around and sometimes a canopy over. Various designs emerged during the Decorated phase – a notable feature was the depth of the niches in the semi-octagonal or semi-hexagonal shape. By the Perpendicular stage some forms had become highly elaborate and intricate with panelling, canopies, pinnacles and numerous carved figures and designs. Following the break with Rome all tabernacles were removed, although they are still a regular feature in Roman Catholic churches.

Another feature seen during this period was the celure (also ceilure, Fig. 120), a painted or specially panelled section of a roof or ceiling immediately over an altar or rood. Sometimes known as the 'canopy of honour', a good surviving example is open to view at St Mary's Church at Hennock in Devon. A large wood or stone canopy cantilevered over an altar or bishop's throne is termed a ciborium and was a regular feature in medieval times. It eventually went out of fashion but was occasionally reintroduced during the Victorian revival. A cloth canopy above an altar or a bishop's throne is called a baldacchino (also called a baldaquin or baldachin). Always richly embroidered, this is either suspended from the ceiling or rests on pillars just above head height. It is a feature which enjoyed a limited revival during the twentieth century.

The altar at the most eastern part of the sanctuary was always described during medieval times as the high altar, but until the Reformation the presence of the rood screen made it difficult for most of the congregation to see it. For this reason some churches had a small altar at the junction between the presbytery and the nave to enable a priest to officiate and coordinate activities with those at the high altar. A hagioscope or squint was often formed in the wall between the chancel and the nave for this purpose and was cut as a rectangular opening, but in an oblique direction so as to give the priest a direct line of sight to the high altar. Sometimes this would taper through the thickness of the wall, the narrower opening always being on the chancel side to make it less conspicuous. Two original squints which give a clear view of the altar can be seen in an early Norman arch at the Church of St Mary, Great Washbourne, Gloucestershire.

Following the Reformation stone altars were removed and replaced with wooden ones or with communion tables of wood. This enabled them to be moved to the centre of the chancel after changes to the communion service. A strong Puritan movement then developed and pressed for the altar to be in the nave, which was powerfully resisted by William Laud, the Archbishop of Canterbury from 1633 to 1645. His firm stand resulted in the altar being moved back to the original position and in the introduction of cancelli, a form of latticed railing with a broad top rail. From this point, railings in front of the altar became a regular feature and were especially popular throughout the remainder of the seventeenth century. The communion tables made during Elizabethan times have large, richly decorated bulbous legs and much ornamentation to the rails, but those from the Jacobean period are less so and have more subdued decoration. In the Church of England the altar arrangement has hardly changed since the time of Archbishop Laud, but during the 1960s substantial alterations were introduced in the Roman Catholic churches and the altar was often relocated nearer to the chancel steps.

A fixed screen known as a reredos is generally found at the back of the altar to enhance the visual impact; in parish churches they usually rise to just below window-sill level. Most are of wood, freestone, marble or alabaster and with the exception of those made from wood it was sometimes the practice to use animal bones for fixing in lieu of iron. This overcame the risk of damage from rust which was a particular problem with alabaster as it is very vulnerable to iron oxide staining. In earlier times the point of focus was often achieved through brightly painted murals, though as an alternative the back of the altar was adorned with an embroidered tapestry termed a dossal (or dorsal). In the cathedrals and great churches the reredos became a major feature worked in heavily carved masonry or wood and sometimes extended to the full width and height of the east wall (Fig. 123). Most with such expansive proportions date from the second half of the fourteenth century and many were painted in brilliant colours. Apart from a few exceptions, they were all enriched with a profusion of niches, figures in high relief, pinnacles, canopies and delicately worked carvings.

On occasions the visual emphasis towards the east wall was made with a triptych (Fig. 123), which is an altarpiece of three freestanding panels that have been hinged together and depicts religious text and presentations in gold leaf and richly coloured paints. A diptych is the same but has only two panels. In some cases the panels have subsequently been fixed

123. A triptych (*above*) and a reredos (*below*)– both ways of focusing attention on the east wall

permanently to the east wall. The triptych and diptych are features which enjoyed considerable popularity in the Georgian period.

Some churches have a low shelf between the altar top and the sill of the east wall window called a retable, upon which either the triptych or reredos sometimes rests. When the ledge or shelf is elevated well above the altar it becomes a gradine. In cathedrals the high altar always has free open space around all sides, whereas in parish churches it is normal practice for the altar to be set against the east wall of the chancel.

Sedilia (from *sedile*, a seat) are stone seats (predominately a group of three, but occasionally two or four) which have been recessed into the south wall of the chancel close to the altar, for use by the clergy (Fig. 124). Most from the fourteenth century onwards have been graduated in height and represent the order of rank between the priest, deacon and sub-deacon; the earlier forms are more likely to be found built at the same level. In some churches they can now be seen in absurdly low positions if the chancel floor has been raised during later alterations. They always have individual piers and arches between each seat and canopies over. Delicate stone carving is a particular feature, and many have a piscina, although this is often omitted. The piscina is a stone bowl either projecting from, or recessed into, the south wall near the altar. It is used for the washing of

124 Sedilia with adjoining piscina

hands and the cleaning of vessels and must drain into consecrated ground forming part of the church. In some cases there are two piscinas – one for the washing of hands and the other for cleaning the vessels (Fig. 124). If a piscina is found in any other part of a church in isolation it is a certain indication an altar was previously positioned at that point. Sedilia of exceptional quality can be seen at St John's Church, North Luffenham, Cambridgeshire, while others of particular note are at the churches of St Giles at Sandiacre, and St Lawrence at Whitwell in Derbyshire and in the church at Ottery St Mary, Devon. A rare instance of sedilia made from carved wood is in St David's Cathedral.

An aumbry (*almariolum*) is a cupboard in which the altar plate and the chalice is stored, usually set into the north wall near the altar (Fig. 125), or it might be in the south wall, forming part of a fenestella, a canopied indent which sometimes houses in group form the aumbry, a credence, the piscina and the sedilia. A similar but smaller recess is the locker, which also has cupboard doors and sometimes provided storage space for church plate and other valuables. It is mostly found in the north wall and a few still have doors, but most are now open recesses. They can often be identified by the marks left from the original hinges. The locker may be distinguished from the aumbry in being much smaller and less conspicuous and is usually in a northern location.

125. Aumbry

The aumbry should not be confused with the dole cupboard, which is similar in appearance but is pierced with holes to admit air. It was used to contain bread and other foods for distribution to the poor, and many are still in existence. The regular method of distribution was from a table in the porch, and a rare example survives in the Church of St Peter and St Paul, Eye, Suffolk. Before the Reformation the monasteries attended to the needy but after the Dissolution it became necessary for the parish churches to help fulfil this function. Dole cupboards were always placed near the church entrance.

The credence (*credenz* – literally a sideboard) is the place where the bread and wine are placed before being consecrated. It can be a table at the side of the altar or a recess or a shelf next to the piscina. Sometimes curious tall, narrow recesses can be found cut into a wall. These were originally used as stave cupboards and had doors, and are the places where the staves for the banners were kept. They are features more regularly found in Suffolk and Norfolk.

In a number of churches evidence remains of an original Easter sepulchre (Fig. 126), which was always located on the north side of the chancel and within close proximity of the altar. Also called the tomb of Christ, it symbolises Christ in his tomb and is usually a recess. It is believed to have developed as a fixture during the thirteenth century, although before this it was erected as a temporary structure immediately before Easter and then dismantled afterwards. It functioned as a place to take the host, and was first consecrated on Maundy Thursday and then placed in the Easter sepulchre on Good Friday. Early on Easter Sunday it was taken out and returned to the altar. The shape and style can range from a simple niche to an elaborate and canopied recess with rich carvings more often intricately worked with representations of the sleeping soldiers. During the reign of Elizabeth I many were destroyed or their use abandoned, but originals of exceptional quality have survived at St Peter's, Navenby, and the parish church at Heckington (Fig. 126), both in Lincolnshire. Other fine examples are in the churches at Hawton, Nottinghamshire, and Patrington in the East Riding of Yorkshire.

The baptistery is the part of the church reserved for the font and the administration of baptism; the area is normally located close to the entrance of either the west or south door (the word font is derived from the Latin *fons* – a natural spring). The enlargement of many churches during the nineteenth century resulted in some building a separate baptistery as an addition, projecting from the side wall of the nave. The shape and style of a font can be a helpful indicator as to the likely age of a church, but

126. Easter sepulchre at Heckington Church, Lincolnshire

evidence of this type needs to be treated with caution as the font may have been retrieved from another source. In the thirteenth century ecclesiastical law required that all fonts were given lockable covers – a situation which remained unchanged until the Reformation, when a large number were forcibly removed. Many were crudely prised away and broken off, with the tell-tale signs still visible. Later font covers reappeared and many are large and canopied, with some being operated by pulleys or counterbalances.

Most of the early fonts were stone or marble, with some being lead lined. A few were made of cast lead, followed later by a large number carved from alabaster. There are also some exceptionally rare examples in bronze or copper. Saxon fonts, often described as drum or tub fonts, usually taper slightly down towards a stepped base. Some have spirals, arcading or cable-moulding decoration. The Normans gave their fonts massive proportions and they are usually found ornamented with monsters and motifs, many of which appear to have Celtic or Scandinavian origins. A very old Norman font can be seen in the Church of St John the Baptist, Morwenstow, Cornwall. In common with the Saxon fonts, the dimensions and shape were chosen for total or part immersion. A roughly hewn and very early Saxon stone font can be seen in the Church of St Andrew, Didling, West Sussex (Fig. 98). The design of the church is of particular interest as it defies a tradition in having no break or demarcation between the nave and the sanctuary, which at the time was observed strictly and without question.

Most of the Early English fonts are hexagonal or octagonal, supported by a central circular shaft with smaller additional shafts at the corners. In the Decorated period the bowls became much smaller, and the use of marble went out of favour. Continuing the octagonal or hexagonal shape, the fonts of this period also have deeply incised outer carvings, often in the form of blind tracery or heraldry, and occasionally have crockets and miniature finials. Fonts made during the Perpendicular period are exceptionally elaborate and often feature panels of the four evangelists (Mathew, Mark, Luke and John) and various religious symbols. Niches were also regularly cut into the pedestals.

Interpreting and placing the various styles can be difficult as they are often the outcome of a transitional phase between the old and the new. Figure sculpture is fairly common, and in the later stages bowls were either round, square or chalice shaped. A surviving lead font from the Norman times is at the Church of St Mary in Childrey and another at the Abbey of St Peter and St Paul in Dorchester, which are both in Oxfordshire. A very rare black marble font is in All Saints' Church, East Meon, Hampshire. Known as a Tournai font, this style is essentially Norman, and each one has a distinctive and unique design; another is in Lincoln Cathedral.

Many early medieval churches featured an ambo (the Latin word for both), a raised platform which was used for conducting the liturgy and the reading of the scriptures. During the fourteenth century travelling friars began to influence a new direction in the way church services were conducted by placing a much greater emphasis on the sermon. This eventually established the need for an improved rostrum from which more effective delivery could be made. The outcome was the gradual introduction of the pulpit which replaced the ambo.

The early designs for pulpits were taken from the reading desk (or reading pew), an important item of church furniture at the time. The desk was usually placed at the east end of the nave, from which the priest conducted much of the service. At this stage the reading desk always had two steps – the epistle was read from the lower step and the gospel from the upper. The medieval pulpits developed to become taller and more slender than those now in use. Resting on a central pillar, most had carvings representing the four evangelists; the majority were in wood, and those carved from stone usually had monastic connections.

Many remaining stone pulpits date from the Decorated Gothic period, but the greater numbers are from the Perpendicular phase. They can be attached to a pier or wall for additional support, with a few bracketed out from a niche in the wall. During the fifteenth century pulpits became a growing feature and following the Reformation were installed in all churches. A few are square, but they typically developed into hexagonal, octagonal and other shapes, often beautifully worked with rich carvings and tracery. A number have a sounding board or tester (*teste*) – a horizontal board immediately above the pulpit that is used to deflect speech in the direction of the congregation – most of them six or eight sided.

The liturgical changes after the Reformation resulted in increased direct communication between the priest and the congregation, which gave the pulpit a more prominent function. During the seventeenth and eighteenth centuries two- or three-decker pulpits appeared and combined the pulpit and reading desk into one unit (Fig. 127). Each stall had a different level, with some accessed by individual stairs. The highest level was reserved for the priest, the next for the reading desk and the lowest for the clerk's desk. Although he was a layman, the parish clerk took the lead in all the singing and assisted the priest in the administration of the church. Two-decker pulpits provided for the priest and reading desk only.

In the nineteenth century changes in presentation caused the pulpit to be less of a fixed point, which resulted in a large number of the two- and three-decker pulpits being removed. By this time the pulpit in some churches had advanced well into the nave and all were required to be repositioned close to the chancel arch. The reading desk also became less important and the parish clerk lost many important duties, a change which greatly reduced the social prestige and standing of that office. Three-decker pulpits can be seen at the Church of St James at Stanstead Abbots

127. Three-decker pulpit

in Hertfordshire, Old Braddan Church on the Isle of Man and St Mary's at Whitby in North Yorkshire, which is complete with tester and candle holder. Among the churches with two-decker pulpits are St Mary's, Great Wasbourne, Gloucestershire and St Andrew's, Hannah, Lincolnshire.

Church Lighting and Heating

In medieval times most of the congregation could not read or write and learnt the responses by rote. As a result minimal lighting was needed, and by modern standards was totally inadequate. Candles were the main source of artificial light and were fixed in candlesticks and candelabra of wrought iron or brass, most of which were highly decorative and intricately worked. In the smaller churches, where the cost of candles could be difficult to meet, cresset stones were regularly used, which were flat stones with a series of hollows into which wicks were floated in oil. The principle source of light often came from a *corona lucis*, which was a type of chandelier similar in design and appearance to a coronet. These had a series of candles set into a ring with a drip tray immediately underneath for the melted wax. They were often elaborately worked and were hung from the ceiling or a beam with chains; some also had a mechanism for raising and lowering the corona. During the eighteenth century the cost of candles steadily fell as a result of the development of the whaling industry. Spermaceti, which is a white waxy substance obtained from the head of the whale, gradually replaced tallow as the base material for candle making, and resulted in the increased provision of candle lighting in churches.

The other source of artificial light was the oil lamp, which was often a cheap and suitable alternative in the small parish churches. In addition to other oils, many of the coastal parishes were able to use fish oil at minimal cost. If candles were unaffordable another option was to use rushes soaked in melted fat. These were used in clusters set in rushlight holders with a reservoir for either oil or melted fat, and the heat marks they made on walls is sometimes still traceable.

With the expansion of gas lighting during Victorian times some churches installed gas chandeliers, but the main disadvantage of this was the large quantities of vitiated air they produced. This was overcome by inserting a series of ventilation pipes in the ceilings, connecting directly to the external air thereby encouraging perflation and improved air quality. The pipes were connected to ceiling roses and bosses in order to make them inconspicuous.

It is easy to assume the apparent lack of heating in medieval churches meant congregations were obliged to endure most uncomfortable conditions during times of severe weather. In fact this was not always the case and there is evidence to show how a number were heated by braziers. Strategically placed around the church, these took a different form to those seen on building sites years ago. A round bowl made from wrought iron rested on a tripod and was covered by a perforated lid with handles. A few have survived and remain preserved, notably those at the Church of St Mary, Barking, Suffolk, and All Saints' Church, Hilborough, Norfolk. By Victorian times some churches had low-pressure hot-water installations which relied on gravity circulation for the dispersal of heat. Others had gilled Gurney stoves, designed to ensure the efficient dispersal of the heat produced. These were patented by Sir Goldsworth Gurney in 1856 and were installed in a large number of cathedrals and larger churches, including York Minster and Salisbury Cathedral.

Church Monuments and Memorials

Memorials developed from a practice in early medieval times of carving designs on stone coffin lids and lairstones. By the beginning of the thirteenth century this had progressed to inscriptions and imagery being worked on tomb chests, a feature which grew to be highly elaborate and intricate from then on. The term tomb chest is misleading as these are memorials and not places of interment. Moreover, they should not be confused with table tombs (also described as altar or chest tombs), which are box-like tombstones in graveyards. Most tomb chests are freestanding but they can be found projecting from, or recessed and arched within the substance of a church wall, a feature often created during the fourteenth, fifteenth and sixteenth centuries.

In the late sixteenth century tester tombs appeared, with effigies of the deceased placed under an overhead tester (canopy) resting on columns. At this stage effigies placed on top of a tomb chest were a regular characteristic, with many being made long before the death of a person. Another variation around the same time was the dresser tomb, in which the sides were heightened above the tomb lid and made into an arch to form a recess.

Between the fifteenth and sixteenth centuries tomb chests always displayed small figures carved on the sides called 'weepers', changing later more towards the depiction of angels. In the late sixteenth century a further alteration put images of people in a kneeling position, and in the seventeenth century they appeared as despairing mourners in lolling or prostrate positions – many of these were a form of artistic licence that came to be seen as irreverent and tasteless. In the sixteenth and seventeenth centuries heraldry was also incorporated into various depictions, especially if a family had military connections. Alabaster was a favoured material for tomb work along with Purbeck marble, but occasionally other stones are found used in this way.

From the mid-seventeenth century tomb chests were mainly superseded by wall monuments, many of them elaborately carved and canopied, with some extending down to the floor. More modest versions are usually termed wall tablets or memorial tablets (Fig. 128). In the late seventeenth century and into the eighteenth century canopied wall monuments went out of fashion and the cartouche became popular. Usually made from marble the cartouche has the appearance of a sheet of paper curled at the sides and rolled. Monuments and memorials made during the Renaissance are often in the Classical style or have features which accord with elements of Classicism.

Most wall monuments are found fixed with metal dowelling; wrought iron was often used in the past. In the sometimes damp environment of a church, however, this can result in the iron rusting and causing staining and cracking, especially to marble. In an effort to overcome this problem, dowels are occasionally found sheathed in lead. Copper and bronze have also been used, although stainless steel has been in regular use in more recent times. It was sometimes the practice to coat the back of a marble tablet with two coats of shellac as a prevention against damp, or an outline of the monument was occasionally skimmed onto the wall using gypsum plaster, to overcome any undulations on the wall face. Larger monuments are often found seated on cantilevers together with dowelling, as shown in Figure 128.

The use of brass plates engraved with figures and memorial inscriptions originated in the early part of the thirteenth century and remained in fashion until the later stages of the sixteenth century. Many do not mark the place of interment and are mostly found set into large flagstones in the floor of the church, but they also occur fixed to walls and on the top of tomb chests. The earlier types were made from more than one piece of brass fixed to a coating of pitch, and the receiving slabs were recessed to ensure a flat surface. Later the plates were made from a single sheet held in position by brass rivets driven into lead plugs. In the earlier examples inscriptions are more likely to be found picked out in a mixture of soot and natural resin (often described as lampblack), but later the practice was to use coloured enamels made from pigmented varnish. People are generally depicted in a life-size or near life-size form and are presented in a way which conveys much about them through a range of heraldic symbols, especially for the clergy, judges, academics, merchants and those in the military. Women are usually dressed in heraldic kirtles (gowns) and mantles or the widow's veil. After the Reformation many brasses were stolen and the metal used for other purposes. Palimpsests (from the Greek word *palin*, meaning again) are often an interesting item and are original brass plates which have been removed and reused. The plates were re-engraved on the back and reset with the new face outermost. Brass plates went out of fashion towards the end of the sixteenth century but enjoyed a short return during the Gothic Revival phase in Victorian times. At one time they were essentially a privilege for the gentry, but from the Industrial Revolution onwards they started to become affordable by many in the middle classes. After the art of making brasses declined, commemorative stone floor slabs returned to favour, most being large flags termed ledger stones, which were either incised or carved in low relief.

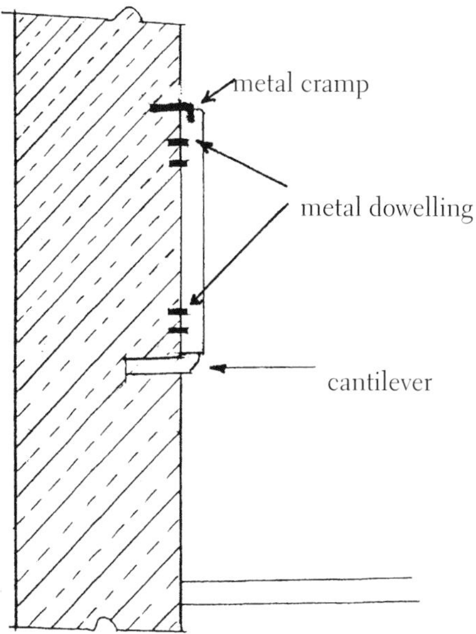

128. Wall monuments and method of fixing.

4 Miscellaneous Features

Writing and Numbers

In the hands of an expert, lettering on an old document can provide important clues of its date. In general terms many of the early church writings are in the Lombardic style, although a number are also found in uncial, which was in more regular use until the end of the eighth century. Much later work is in textur, which is a form sometimes called black letter. A number of variations have developed from this, including Gothic cursive and Tudor black letter. At one time it was regular practice to date brasses, memorials and similar items with Roman numerals. When one of these symbols is followed by one of equal or lesser value, the number indicated is equivalent to the sum of the values of the individual symbols. As an example, 8 in Roman numerals is VIII = 5+1+1+1 = 8. When a symbol is preceded by one of lesser value the number indicated is equal to the difference of the values of the symbols which in the case of say number 4 is expressed as IV = 5-1 = 4 (see below).

~

Roman Numerals

1	I	11	XI	25	XX	75	LXXV	700	DCC
2	II	12	XII	30	XXX	80	LXXX	800	DCCC
3	III	13	XIII	35	XXXV	85	LXXXV	900	CM
4	IV	14	XIV	40	XL	90	XC	1000	M
5	V	15	XV	45	XLV	100	C	1500	MD
6	VI	16	XVI	50	L	200	CC	1900	MCM
7	VII	17	XVII	55	LV	300	CCC	2000	MM
8	VIII	18	XVIII	60	LX	400	CD		
9	IX	19	XIX	65	LXV	500	D		
10	X	20	XX	70	LXX	600	DC		

~

Hatchments

Presentations still seen in the interiors of some churches are diamond-shaped wood panels known as hatchments (Fig. 129). They are a relic from a practice which originated in either the seventeenth or eighteenth century and in some regions continued into the first part of the nineteenth century. They gave public notice of a recent bereavement and were exhibited outside the home of the deceased before being placed in the church. They also featured in the funeral procession and it was usual for them to be returned to the house for an interim period before being fixed permanently in the church. They more usually relate to a member of the local gentry or someone of high standing. They are painted in heraldic form and always display the armorial bearings of those entitled to them, together with any motto or crest of the deceased. Heraldry and symbolism were also used in a way which enabled the marital status of the deceased to be readily identified. A widower, for example, was given a black background with his armorial bearings and those of his wife impaled (the heraldic term for dividing the two armorial bearings vertically and placing the two halves side by side). A woman who had died before her husband was given a

129. Hatchment

half-black and half-white background, the white on the left side and the black on the right. If the husband had died first the background was reversed. A shield with one half of an armorial bearing and the other side blank indicated the husband of the deceased was not armigerous (not entitled to a coat of arms), while a widower whose wife was not armigerous was given a black background with his armorial bearings displayed in full.

Consecration Crosses

In medieval times it was regular practice to put a series of consecration crosses on both the inside and outside faces of church walls; to avoid wear from people brushing past they were placed about 8 feet (2.5 m) above ground. Always totalling twenty-four, three were fixed on each internal wall face, followed by a further twelve around the outside walls. The rare remaining examples can be found in different forms, with some in red paint, others incised into the stone surface, and still others as metal casts affixed to the wall face. They all follow the same form and depict a broad circle within which is a cross (Fig. 133k). Above or below each internal cross was a candle bracket and, although few remain some original fixings are often still visible. The consecration ceremony was very protracted and involved each cross being anointed with oil by the bishop. In West Sussex two painted consecration crosses can still be seen in the nave of St Andrew's Church at Ford. Other examples can be found in the parish churches at Uffington in Oxfordshire and Ottery St Mary in Devon.

Royal Coat of Arms

After the Reformation, parish churches were expected to display the Royal Arms in a position where the congregation could readily see it. Henry VIII regarded this as an important expression of loyalty and change, but the succession of Mary I resulted in them being removed by order, a decision subsequently reversed by Elizabeth I following the reinstatement of the new order. After the Commonwealth it became compulsory for every parish church to display the Royal Arms above the chancel arch (Fig. 130). A limited number have survived, but most have subsequently been removed to a less conspicuous position. Apart from certain exceptions they took the form of a painted square wood board, with a few painted on stretched canvas. Some surviving examples have been wood carved while others are plaster or metal casts. In the early part of the twentieth century the practice was revived but soon faded.

130. Royal coat of arms from 1660

Pigeon Lofts

From the time of the Normans until well into the medieval period the consumption of pigeon meat was greatly restricted. The building of a pigeon loft or dovecote (*columbarium*) was a feudal privilege granted only to the nobility, abbots and lords of the manor, but the concession was extended later to parish priests. Heavy penalties were meted out to anyone caught stealing or killing pigeons. In churches they are more likely to be found in a part of the tower or in the chancel loft. Entry to the loft is usually by way of a small high-level external doorway accessed from a movable ladder, although a few have an entry from within the church. They are a feature that can be mostly identified by the presence of a small elevated opening together with a protruding ledge upon which the pigeons could alight, or from clear signs of this having existed in the past. A rare surviving example is in the chancel roof at the Church of St John, Elkstone in Gloucestershire, which dates back to 1160.

Sundials

Until the middle of the nineteenth century few churches were without a sundial to mark the hours of the day in local time (Fig. 131), but these quickly became obsolete following the introduction of railway timetables and the adoption of Greenwich Mean Time. Sundials first appeared on the southern walls of churches in Saxon times, their original purpose being to ensure the bell was rung at the correct stage for the canonical hours – the services which had to be held in accordance with the breviary (a liturgical book governing the routine of worship for those in holy orders). They were also used for calling people to mass and for everyday social and trading activities within communities.

Tide dials are of Saxon origin and divide the hours of daylight into three-hour time spans known as 'tides'. The dial is calibrated to begin at 6 am and end at sunset (Fig. 131). Any remaining traces of a tide dial are more often found as engraved stone slabs into which was set an iron gnomon (the projection which casts the shadow). Scratch dials are another surviving relic from the past, but most have weathered and eroded away to a point where they can be easily missed. They take the form of roughly inscribed circles within which are radiating lines emanating from a central hole that once held the gnomon. The lines are always spaced 15 degrees apart. Mass dials

131. *Left*: sundial; *right*: Saxon tide dial

are found close to a priest door and helped priests perform chantry masses at the correct time. An early mass dial can be seen at St Mary's Church at Bibury in Gloucestershire, and an original tide dial at the Saxon chapel in Coolhampton, Hampshire. At the porch of the Church of St Peter and St Paul in Pickering, North Yorkshire is a later eighteenth-century sundial.

Developments in Presentation

During the early part of the Reformation churches were stripped of many items and much imagery, but this left the interiors bare and uninteresting. As a remedy and to help edify the people Queen Elizabeth I ordered panels be fixed containing the Ten Commandments, the Lord's Prayer and the Creed. They were originally fixed under the chancel arch but most have since been removed; and a number have been relocated elsewhere within the church.

Some medieval churches still have the rings from which were hung aumbry lamps. At one time it was the practice to hang a lamp with a red light before the altar, and to change this to white in the presence of the reserved sacrament. A lamp with a blue light was hung before the images of the mother and child. In most cases the light source was a slow-burning candle with a drip tray under. Occasionally, odd recesses can be found high in the wall of a chancel which more often turn out to have been provided for acoustic jars. They were used in the belief they resonated and improved the sound from the choir; good examples of these are at St Andrew's Church at Lyddington, Cambridgeshire, Fountains Abbey in Yorkshire and St Gregory's Priory in Canterbury.

A few medieval churches with monastic origins still have a stone building, or the remains of one, within the curtilage of the site; this is likely to have been used as an almonry for the storage and distribution of alms to the poor.

Signs and Symbols

In medieval times symbolism was used regularly to convey messages, and art and design had an important role in this – the inferences were often subtle, poignant or controversial. It also gave artists a rare opportunity for self-expression, where they could work in double meanings and innuendo. The early Christians realised the potential this had, particularly as it was considered irreverent to put sacred names into print, making artistic or symbolic images a suitable alternative. Church art and symbolism steadily developed from this and expanded to become a major element in medieval art. The visual and psychological effects of this also had profound implications on social thinking and behaviour. Most of the symbols found in churches belong to the Christian tradition, but some nevertheless pre-date Christianity but have gradually become part of Christian iconography. One such example is the ankh (Fig. 132), which was used in Egyptian times as a hieroglyph for 'life' but can now be seen in most churches. The Christian symbol has long been the cross, but it has became widely used in many other different forms and ways, including in heraldry (Fig. 133).

Mention has already been made of how church architecture in the medieval Gothic period was determined through a complex series of geometric shapes, ratios and proportions. This not only had a critical influence on design; it also penetrated into the shapes of symbols and in the use of numbers. The eight sides of a baptismal font, for example, represent new life, and even the number of points on a symbol such as a star has a particular purpose and meaning. This ranges from five points for the star of Epiphany to twelve points representing the twelve tribes of Israel.

The number seven also has a special significance and not only refers to the seven days of creation but also the seven virtues and the seven deadly sins, among other things. Various symbols were also given to individual martyrs, and the status of clerics in minor orders can sometimes be associated with a particular symbol. The illustrations in Figure 134 are a selection of the symbols and signs more commonly found in a church. The Agnus Dei (Lamb of God) in Figure 134j represents sacrifice, while the tributary in Figure 134g refers to the Trinity, as does the shield in Figure 134i. The labarum in Figure 134a is derived from the first two letters of the Greek word CHRISTOS; the symbol in Figure 134b has the same meaning but with the inclusion of the first and last letters of the Greek alphabet – alpha and omega (the beginning and the end). Again

132. Ankh

133. Different forms of the cross – (a) Latin; (b) Greek; (c) patriarchal; (d) suffering; (e) tau; (f) Celtic; (g) papal; (h) St Peter's; (i) Easter; (j) crucifix; (k) consecration; (l) Iona; (m) flory; (n) Saxon; (o) moline; (p) trefly; (q) bottony; (r) recercely; (s) patonce; (t) Malese; (u) fleuree

134. Signs and symbols

Figure 134c is similar but has the letter N, which is an abbreviation of the Latin word *noster* and in this context is a reference to Jesus as friend and saviour. The monogram IHS (or IHC in 134d) is frequently found on pulpits, altar cloths and other items (see also Fig. 120) and is generally accepted as a shortening of IHCOYC – the Greek word for Jesus. In the course of time the Greek C was replaced by the sigma, or S in Latin (Fig. 134e). The three interwoven fishes in Figure 134k are a sign of the Trinity, and the cross anchor in Figure 134f is the message of hope. The Sacred Heart in Figure 134h is more common in Roman Catholic churches but also occurs in some Anglican ones.

Occasionally features in a church can be completely outside the Christian tradition. One such example is the central window in Andreas' parish church on the Isle of Man, where there are twelve panels in stained glass portraying the signs of the Zodiac together with the sun and the moon. They are signs which pre-date Christianity and are regarded as pagan. Why they have been included remains something of a mystery, although there are a few older cathedrals on the continent where this has occurred. Another surprising inclusion is the stained-glass east window in the Chapel of St Paul at Stansted Park, West Sussex. This window has been worked wholly in Jewish symbolism and must be unique as it occurs in a consecrated Christian church without any firm explanation for how it came about.

The early Christian missionaries recognised the important role that pagan shrines and symbols could play in the promotion of Christianity, and took great care not to alienate the pagan communities through force or undue pressure. In this they deliberately avoided presenting their message as a replacement for an existing ideology and began by either adapting or incorporating pagan icons into the practices of the early Church. This is why so many pagan symbols continued to appear on items such as gargoyles, corbels, brackets, misericords, capitals and bosses until the time of the Tudors. The subtle and successful way they pursued this induction resulted in a range of pagan signs taking on a different meaning in the Christian sphere of influence. A good example is the Green Man, which originated as a representation of the power of nature and the seasons and is now a sign of Easter and the Resurrection (Fig. 134m). Depicted as a male head wreathed in foliage it appears as a decorative feature in many churches. The eagle is another well-known sign where the meaning has changed from a sign of strength to one of spiritual strength over the temptations of sin. The eagle is now most likely to be seen on lecterns, but was originally used as the symbol of St John the Evangelist and his gospel (Fig. 134l). The pelican was especially popular between the twelfth and thirteenth centuries and signifies redemption, sacrifice and atonement (Fig. 134n). The dragon has been used in many ways and by many different cultures but in the Christian world it is associated with destruction and evil (Fig. 134o).

The deeply mysterious wodewose (Fig. 134p) was adopted as a sign of wholesomeness and strength. The origins are unclear, but the symbol has always been presented as a hairy-bodied creature or wildman usually depicted holding a club and fighting lions, serpents or dragons. The unicorn began as a sign of purity which the early Christians linked to purity and chastity, particularly in connection with the Virgin Mary (Fig. 134q). The griffin (Fig. 134r) is a mythical beast which has a lion's body, wings and an eagle's beak and claws. Mostly found in church heraldry, it symbolises watchfulness and courage and was originally used by pagans as the guardian of treasure. The wyvern (Fig. 134s) is similar to the dragon and breathes fire, but has a reptile's body and only two legs. It usually has a serpent's tail and is interpreted as a sign of pestilence and plague. The familiar phoenix stems from the pagan tradition, and it was believed to rise again from the ashes after being consumed by fire (Fig. 134t). It is now used as a symbol of immortality and resurrection. To entrench their teaching and to create a lasting impression the early Christians used bestiaries as visual aids. These were books which illustrated real and imaginary animals, many of which became part of the heraldic tradition. A number of these depictions can often be discovered in the decoration on ancient tombs and memorials.

Church Bells

Church bells became an important element in many aspects of everyday life, especially in rural communities. They first featured in the Celtic church sometime in the sixth century, and by the eighth century had come into general use throughout the British Isles. They also had a central function in the workings and routine of the monastic orders and were used at such regular intervals that some establishments operated ringing times by a mechanised clock device. At parish level they marked the time of day and, in addition to calling people to worship, rang out the Angelus in the early morning and at noon and in the evening. At one time they sounded the curfew – a reminder at bedtime to douse out the open fire in the interests of safety. They were always rung at times of celebration, including weddings, baptisms and feast days. When a death occurred the bell was tolled slowly three times and after a pause it gave another three rings; this was done twice more for a man and once more for a woman, and was immediately followed by a series of slow rings recording the age of the deceased person.

In the early stages of the church some deprived communities were reduced to using a hagiosideron, which is a shaped piece of metal struck in a similar way to a bell. Communities with insufficient funds to finance the cost of a tower usually opted for a bellcote. This took the form of an upward projection to the western gable which had either one or two open spaces for bell fixing to which was attached a rope going down to the ground (Fig. 51). Alternatively, an aperture was made in the western gable end for the bell housing. A bellcote at the eastern termination of the church or above the chancel arch would have originated as a sanctus bell, which at one time only rang at the saying of the sanctus or at the more solemn parts of the mass. A surviving example from the fifteenth century is the sanctus bell at the Church of St Mary Magdalen, Newark, Nottinghamshire.

Up to about 1300 bells were normally hung from a spindle, but after that point they were mounted on a headstock attached to a wheel. The spindle then served as an axle and was operated by a rope attached to the rim of the wheel. At one time it was the custom to dedicate the bell to a saint with a suitable inscription being scored into the metal. Many bells were either removed or rendered unusable at the time of the Reformation but most were reinstated and sometimes upgraded in the post-Elizabethan era. Change-ringing started in the mid-seventeenth century and is essentially a unique feature of British life which involves an assembly of bells being rung in a series of different orders. Some churches can ring five, six, eight, ten and even twelve peals.

At one time bells were made by itinerant craftsmen who did the casting close to the church, which can often explain local names such as bell lane, bell corner and bell field. The casts were tuned by chipping the inside to flatten the tone and by chipping the edge to sharpen it. For a long time bells were hung on a carefully balanced robust timber frame known as a cage but modern forms are now more often made of either iron or steel. Constructed from green oak with pegged mortice and tenon joints, many surviving examples are around 300 years or more in age. The gradual drying-out of the timber and the effect of vibration from the ringing action often caused jointing to loosen, a problem which was usually overcome by tightening the connections with timber wedges. The early medieval cages are found to have large oversized timbers and are generally much taller than those constructed later, while those built from the late eighteenth century onwards generally have timbers that are much reduced in height and size. Large cross-timbers which bear onto the surrounding walls take the weight of the cage, which is bolted onto them.

The belfry is always found close to or at the top of the tower, with louvred openings (*abat-vent*) on each wall face, and the ringing chamber is located on a platform below or at the foot of the tower. Access to the belfry is normally by way of a stee (an open ladder) or a vise (a spiral stairway), the latter often being built into a turret attached to the side of the tower.

5 Investigating the Development of a Church

Many of the first churches were founded on the ruins of dolmen and stone circles or are linked with sites which had previously been used for pagan ritual. The primary aim at the time of the Christian missionaries was to provide shelter for the altar and the priest celebrating mass. Later these basic structures were either replaced or rebuilt, but in a few cases parts of the original walling remain traceable; in others much of the original stone was reclaimed and reused in the building of a new church elsewhere. By the twelfth century most parish churches had become two cell and some were cruciform. Every church is different, but subsequent changes usually follow a familiar pattern, and many major alterations seem to have been made at around the same period of time. Later changes and alterations can obscure much of the original, and for this reason it is usually better to begin from the middle core of the building and work outwards, taking particular note of the ratio between wall height and breadth as this can alter in any subsequent work. In the thirteenth century increased ceremonial often necessitated the removal of the apse and the lengthening of the chancel.

Close scrutiny of the walling will invariably reveal a distinct divide between the original and the new. If more accommodation was needed it was generally answered by the provision of a north aisle; the south aisle was usually built at a later date. Where this has occurred there are likely to be clear differences between features of the two aisles. During the fourteenth century the demand for more space continued and mostly resulted in the widening of the north aisle. This period also saw the addition or enlargement of porches and the more general installation of a sacristy next to the chancel. It was also the time when many twelfth-century chancel arches were replaced by wider ones and the building of a south aisle also became more of a regular feature.

By the fifteenth century the country had started to recover from the devastating effects of the Black Death and prosperity returned through the wool trade. As people became richer or more financially stable they turned their attention towards church improvements. Many of the original towers were removed and replaced with much larger towers, and aisles were often further extended and enlarged. In the sixteenth century the quest for improvements continued, much of it seen in the provision of additional side chapels and in the further rebuilding of porches, with a large number financed by the various guilds. Later this stage also saw church towers further raised in height and in some churches the replacement of the single bell with a peal of bells.

Location can be a useful indicator of the original function, as many existing parish churches were first built for monastic or collegiate purposes. If a church is placed in the heart of a village or town it is likely to have been constructed to serve that community, whereas if it is in an unexpected or unsuitable position there is probably a good reason, which church records may be able to disclose. There could also be many other possibilities, including an express grant of land and even the whim or intransigence of the local lord of the manor.

When tracing the development of a church the process needs to be carried out through an orderly and sequential routine. Notes taken at random can cause an analysis of the findings to be unnecessarily more complicated and for future references to be made more difficult and even wrongly interpreted. Start by making a general inspection and become familiar with the overall layout. Then draw a sketch plan (preferably using graph paper) and start by putting in the north point and from then on operate from a constant level, with sill height sometimes being the more convenient. After taking a series of measurements, always add them together and check the result with a running measurement along the same length. Also check the accuracy of the process through diagonal measurements, taking them from corner to corner, but never assume the quoins are at a true 90-degree angle. When drafting a drawing or sketch plan allocate each feature a reference number, which should also be used with any notes appropriate to that item. By working in this or a similar way the whole exercise can then be drawn together in a coordinated and precise form. It is also well worth taking and dating a series of photographs to supplement the notes and sketches.

Fully recording a church or preparing a measured drawing often involves different priorities and needs. The exact purpose of the undertaking needs clarity: for example the format for an archival record will differ in many ways from plans for an alteration or extension. To ensure all this can be successfully achieved the use of non-invasive technology may be necessary to reveal features that would otherwise not be apparent. This can include equipment that transmits either ultrasonic or acoustic wavelengths, which make very accurate identification. Advances in the use of x-ray and gamma-ray applications can be of particular value, but the equipment may only be used by trained technicians. Infra-red equipment is another extremely useful aid for tracing inconsistencies and defects. A heat-sensing camera measures the level of thermal radiation, which can then be interpreted into crucial information such as the presence of dampness, concealed forms of construction, bonding failures and such like. This is particularly important in rubble-filled flint walling where the correct slenderness ratio (the relationship between the effective height and the effective thickness) may have become depleted. With this type of construction the hearting is rather prone to deterioration and unequal consolidation, which can cause the formation of voids, resulting in the stability of the wall being weakened.

With suitable electronic equipment the information gleaned from an inspection can be transferred to computer or videotape. External elevations and other features, including interiors, can be expeditiously recorded by photogrammetry. With the aid of highly sensitive equipment the system compiles with remarkable accuracy two- or three-dimensional images. Advanced analytical photogrammetry is operated through three-dimensional coordinates that feed into a CAD system from which scale plans and other drawings are produced as prints. A much cheaper but more limited alternative is the use of rectified photography, which enables reliable photographs to be taken and used to scale. A rectified camera lens accommodates the distortions caused by the effects of perspective and camera tilt by means of a rectifying enlarger. The resultant prints are equated to scale by taking hand measurements of all key dimensions and inserting a scale rule into the finished images. The technique does, however, have the disadvantage of being unsuitable where the subject matter has excessive depth or penetrating recesses.

One of the main difficulties in making a correct analysis is in dating some of the architectural features. Unless established records can provide a clear and reliable answer an element of uncertainty is often likely to arise. The various building styles changed gradually, and there were prolonged phases of overlap during the transition from one period to the other. This resulted in mixed architectural features, especially in parts of the country where the response to new ideas was much slower.

Similar care needs to be applied to historic timberwork such as old porches and roofs. Marks, scores or indentations can be helpful indicators in identifying age but need to be understood fully. It was the practice of carpenters to score preformed timbers when ready for assembly with a system of marks resembling Roman numerals. Similar marks were made for setting out, compass arcs and suchlike. Hewing marks were used for the conversion of logs into timber baulks, and plumb and level marks follow a similar theme. Timber imported from the Baltic was similarly marked by the merchants and is a practice which continued until well into the twentieth century (Fig. 60). Saw marks can also provide helpful information. The techniques of circular sawing, band sawing and pit sawing all leave distinctive patterns on the sawn face. The rounded marks made by the circular saw are unmistakable and pit saws produce a rather rough and irregular finish, while band saws cut clear vertical lines. Axe and adze marks are clearly distinguishable from them.

Caution and an allowance of sufficient time in the examination of a church will invariably reveal evidence which would otherwise not be immediately apparent, especially in cases where the external fabric has become heavily soiled or weathered. Differences in texture and minor variations between materials can so easily be missed, which may nevertheless be critical in the sometimes fine margin between an accurate or inaccurate conclusion. The composition of the mortar can often provide important analytical evidence. The chapel in Figure 135 is a good example of this: the badly soiled facework gave an initial impression that the whole structure had been built at the same time, but a careful examination disclosed slight differences in the wall texture between the dotted lines as shown. It then became apparent that part B was a later addition, which led to the finding that a buttress had been removed from part A and along

135. Development of a chapel

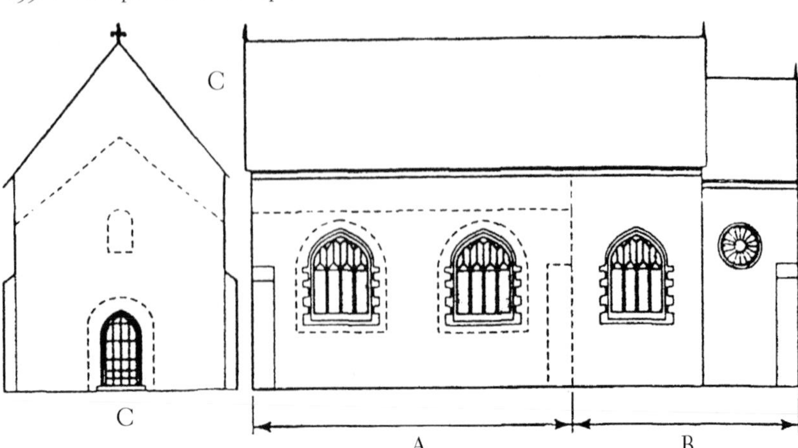

the side elevations larger windows had replaced earlier ones. It was then apparent that the roof height had been increased, and further examination found a blocked-up window at C, and signs of the insertion of a larger entrance door. Much of this evidence could have been missed or have taken longer to discover but for a close scrutiny of the mortar at the outset. Chance digging into the mortar joints revealed differences in the aggregate and in the lime, which put the investigators on alert from the onset.

The sands used in many of the earlier mortars often tend to be coarser, but clearer variations are more likely to be found in the lime. Lime was originally produced in clamp-fired kilns, which resulted in fragments of fuel and kiln slag getting into the lime and then into the mortar. It was these differences which proved so helpful in the early stages of the case quoted. Nevertheless, no firm conclusions should be made until any possibility of newer mortar having been used in repair work or repointing can be excluded. The flush joint was the traditional method of wall jointing. As methods of lime making gradually improved, the differences in age and quality are more difficult to determine and may need laboratory analysis, whereas clear variations in the aggregate content can still be a likely pointer towards certain works having been carried out at different times. Black mortars are essentially a feature of the nineteenth century; the ingredients are a mixture of lime, ashes or ground clinker and blackened sand obtained from an iron foundry or a blacksmith.

Up to the middle ages many parish churches were built in random rubble stone either coursed or brought to course, with ashlar mostly being used around door and window openings and in other important features. Uncoursed random rubble was rarely used in church work throughout this period, although in the later Victorian and the Edwardian phases it can be found in alterations and extensions, and is usually distinguishable from any original work by the nature and style of the pointing and occasionally some brittleness in the mortar. Moreover, the tooling and laying of the stone is likely to be different from older masonry, which at parish level was often coarser and less exact.

The main difference in much later work is invariably in the way the stone has been cut, and it may not even be from a local quarry. At this stage competitive pricing and cheaper transport became the determining factors, with the stone from another location often having slight but subtle variations in texture, colour and workability. Vertical mortar jointing and toothed work are both reliable signs of an extension, and crudely laid masonry may have been plaster faced originally, which is a finding that does not necessarily indicate poor workmanship. Floor levels that are lower than the surrounding ground are another indication of antiquity. String courses, cornices, plinths and similar features that have been interrupted are a clear sign of later alteration works.

Differences in the weathering of stone can be an indicator of older and newer work, but not necessarily so. If parts are more exposed to the elements than others the scouring effect of severe weather can erode away the surface and prevent the accumulation of a matured face. This can convey a misleading impression of age, and any doubts or concerns over origin are more reliably determined through an examination of the way the stone has been cut and worked.

The mortar to most medieval stonework was left flush with the face, but in some areas a technique known as galleting was occasionally used in later periods. It is more often seen in districts where the irregular nature and roughness of the stone made finer jointing difficult or impracticable. It frequently served the dual function of wedging in the seating of some larger stones and reducing the sometimes stark appearance of thick mortar jointing. Masons took the opportunity to turn the technique into an art form and many individual craftsmen became known for their own decorative styles. The practice was also applied to flintwork using small slivers of flint from the knapping process, but it is less likely to be found in early flint walling and became more of a feature in the nineteenth century.

Disturbance to the masonry around window openings is a sure indication that the original windows have been replaced by larger ones. Squints (or hagioscopes) set between the nave and the chancel are a pre-Reformation feature and, although many have long been blocked up at both ends, some evidence often remains, such as arching over the original opening. Most squints were set at about sill height and were around 2 feet (60 cm) in width. Close attention should also be given to any buttressing and whether it differs from the original work.

Additions made to churches during Victorian times often imitated the original style, but differences in the application of the stone and in the overall finish to the building work usually provide sufficient evidence to differentiate between the nineteenth-century work and the original.

A church which has clearly not been altered or extended in any way is likely to be Victorian. Moreover, churches built from the sixteenth century onwards have been less prone to extensive change as increasing prosperity enabled many communities to cater for the present and the future. Any subsequent need for extra seating capacity was more often met through the provision of galleries. As part of a desire to update the appearance of a parish church in the Gothic style, buttresses can occasionally be found to have been added as an architectural rather than a functional item. Apart from differences in the stonework, some have not been properly toothed into the structure and may even display signs of rotating away from the main part of the church.

At around the late medieval period a number of steeply angled roofs were taken down and rebuilt to a much lower pitch, which created opportunities for the work to include the construction of a clerestory to both sides of the nave. It involved the raising of the walls over the arches in the nave and upon this was seated the new roof. Up to this stage only a limited number of parish churches had a clerestory as an original feature. They are still seen much less frequently in the parish churches around the flint building regions in southern England, which is likely to be due to the generally weaker nature of the wall construction.

Before the Reformation various side chapels were housed within the main body of the church, each having an altar and a piscina. While the original side chapels may no longer exist, some of the piscinas have survived to the present day and are a clear sign of pre-Reformation beginnings. Any small unexplained recess in the north of a chancel is likely to have been an Easter sepulchre. If sedilia are below normal seating height it is confirmation the floor level of the chancel has been raised at a later date, which probably occurred sometime during the nineteenth century. It is also well to keep in mind that some parish churches began life as part of a monastic foundation and in order to lower maintenance and running costs have since been reduced in size. Demolition often went as far as the open arcading, which was filled to form the external walling, and the foundations to the original areas are often still detectable. If a church has a stone vaulted ceiling this is a strong signal it had either monastic or collegiate beginnings – few parishes had the means to cope with the heavy cost of such work.

It is worth giving some attention to the carvings on corbels and corbel tables and to the individuality of the craftsmanship. These features were worked in a variety of ways and, although they were in the fashion of the time, they nevertheless gave opportunities for self-expression to the masons who carved them. Some of the more interesting styles are from the Norman period and include elaborate carvings of grotesque demons and monsters, a feature which perpetuated well into the late Perpendicular phase.

When looking at a church that dates from early medieval times, the original purpose of a blocked-up opening or scars to the masonry can sometimes be mystifying and perplexing. If no rational solution is apparent consider whether or not it was the location for an anchorite cell. Few have survived to the present day but evidence of them having existed is still being discovered.

A series of hooks fixed around the front of the sanctuary are likely to have been used to hang the Lenten veil; it was the practice in medieval times to veil this area throughout Lent. The pulleys which worked the original *corona lucis* have also often survived and are a clear sign of antiquity.

In the years before the nineteenth-century Gothic Revival and the refurbishment policies which followed, a large number of old churches had been allowed to deteriorate, causing considerable damage to the structures. As a result much important evidence from the past has been lost, and some later insensitive improvement schemes have also resulted in valuable historic features being harmed or obliterated.

Until more recently accurate dating mainly depended on documentary evidence and the examination of physical elements, but the application of modern science has enabled substantial advances to be made in the analytical process. One such example is carbon-14 dating, which is determined from three naturally occurring isotopes designated as 12C, 13C and 14C. They do not happen equally and when, for example, a tree dies, it ceases to be part of the carbon exchange with the biosphere and no longer takes in carbon 14. From this point the level of the carbon content falls at a rate which can be determined by the law of radioactive decay and is the factor through which the age of timber can be calculated.

An alternative method for the dating of timber is dendrochronology, which is based on the examination of tree rings (the term is derived from the Greek *dendros* – a tree – and *chronos* – time). The rate of growth of a tree varies from year to year according to the nature of the climate, which is something that can be seen in clear differences between the growth periods. By comparing the number of growth rings with weather patterns from the past, the age of old timbers can be determined with reasonable accuracy. Information of this nature can be of particular value when used in conjunction with the differences in carpentry styles that have occurred at various stages from the early medieval period onwards.

A more recent development is a system of identification known as luminescence dating. It is based on the emission of reflected light from crystalline minerals and can be applied to date fired-clay materials such as brick, pottery and terracotta. While it does have certain limitations it is yet another example of how modern technology is playing an increasing part in the enhancement of our knowledge of the past.

When undertaking an investigation, the fabric of a church must not be interfered with or altered in any way without the grant of a faculty, which is a licence issued by either the diocesan chancellor or the archdeacon on behalf of the bishop.

Index